THE
WONDERFUL
WORLD OF
WOMEN'S WEAR
DAILY

THE
WONDERFUL
WORLD OF
WOMEN'S WEAR
DAILY

Katie Kelly

Saturday Review Press

NEW YORK

Published simultaneously in Canada by

Doubleday Canada Ltd., Toronto

Library of Congress Catalog Card Number: 71-154275

ISBN 0-8415-0126-2

Second Printing

Saturday Review Press

230 Park Avenue, New York, New York 10017

Printed in the United States of America

Design by Tere LoPrete

To Jack Lough, Mrs. Flotree, and Mrs. Kelly

THE WONDERFUL WORLD OF WOMEN'S WEAR DAILY

1

Remember the Good Old Days? When Mom could pack the kids off to a John Wayne movie and the boy would come back wanting to win the Second World War and the girl would return wanting to be the girl he left behind? When Jack Armstrong could get the guys to eat Wheaties and Corliss Archer bespoke Truth about a world of saddle shoes and bobby sox and page-boy hairdos? When it was easy to tell the Good Guys from the Bad Guys (the Good Guys rode horses with names and sang songs into the sunset)? When the burning issue of the day was whether Roy Rogers kissed Dale Evans after they got into that sunset? Ah, yes, the Good Old Days. When life was just a simple Saturday matinee and all the world's influences were right there in plain sight: John Wayne, Apple Pie, and red-white-and-blue. Simple Truths. Simple *Vérités*.

But times change—and nothing has changed more in the past few decades than those things which influence American Life. John Wayne has given way to a cross between the Marlboro Man and Mick Jagger while Corliss Archer is somewhere between an activist marching right out of *Ramparts* and the chairman of the local environment group.

Thanks to the Pill, musical chairs has given way to musical beds. Television has indeed put us smack dab in the middle of a Global Village, where Corliss Archer is no longer the Girl Next Door. Most likely she's Grace Slick. Neighborhoods do change. Our median age is edging ever closer to twenty-five while medicine makes it possible for 10 percent of our citizens to become Senior with a lifespan of seventy plus years. Result: the Generation Gap. The computer makes life one big numbers game where the individual is reduced to somebody who bends, folds, and mutilates just out of sheer spite—or is it perhaps to pathetically prove to someone, somewhere, that he does indeed really exist? A live, full-blown American human being who might still weep at movies, bite his fingernails, have indigestion, experience joy and pain, and go through life much like the surfer in search of the perfect wave as he, too, searches for some small ounce of perfection be it in soufflés, speed reading, gourmet cookery, or orgasms.

Thus: a world of ever-increasing and ever-complicated influences. A topsy-turvy world ajumble with color TV, chattering computers, Pill-popping promiscuity, and a world that Grandma would not only fail to recognize but would probably drop dead in. Given all those high-octane influences competing for our attention, it is strange indeed to stumble upon a newspaper with a highly selective nation-wide circulation of only 85,000 that packs any sort of wallop other than when it hits the bottom of the trash bin wrapped snugly around the day's garbage. *Women's Wear Daily* is no general release movie, no prime-time television program, no household word. Yet it is, to many, as sexy as the Pill and just as necessary. To others it is not so much the paper around the garbage—as the garbage itself. But to be fair, even those detractors admit they cannot do without their daily dose of WWD, for to most, WWD is like a dangerous drug: mild at first, but steadily more demanding. (Who could believe a newspaper that forces readers to wade through a forest of zipper ads, personnel changes in Texas department stores, and death notices for upstanding but obscure Jewish garment manufacturers could be anything, especially addictive?) Once hooked, a daily fix is necessary. It becomes a ritual rivaling the Salute to the Flag and bedtime prayers.

When *Women's Wear Daily*—"WWD" as it is chummily called—was started in 1910, it was strictly a trade paper whose mission was to cover the wholesale and retail garment industry. Hardly an impossible one, hardly an interesting one, at least for outsiders. To its credit, WWD has remained steadfast and true to that original commitment. Like a Boy Scout who grits his teeth and helps Old Ladies across the street, no matter how much it may turn out he (1) hates Old Ladies; (2) hates helping anyone but especially Old Ladies. Well, if a Boy Scout is anything he is honorable. And there is a lot of the B.S. in us all, even WWD. So there it was and there it remains: a trade paper, running red-hot stories about chain stores, company mergers, shoplifting, and shrinkage. A rend in the fabric market. Plans to put hosiery in vending machines. How the kiddie apparel market is doing. Montgomery Ward defends its credit policies. Rainwear market sees spring shower of business. Established fabric mill plans to shut down. To the virgin reader—the first-timer who wonders how he got in that position in the first place—WWD's jazziest piece would seem to be one on a Chicago boutique. Or a fashion show in Atlanta. Important to the garment industry—but . . . yawn. A newspaper gently geared to killing an outsider with boredom. *Ennui.* Indifference.

But wait—WWD may look like every newspaper's grandmother, but looks can be deceiving. In reality, WWD is like a new nun shedding the veil only to reveal a pair of HotPants.

WWD is the little old lady who one day, not so long ago, kicked off her high-heeled sneakers, unwrapped her braids, threw back her head, and cut loose with a yell of pure ecstasy. The Shameless Old Lady of the Fourth Estate. A clothes closet swinger. Hotcha!

All those hundreds and thousands of people directly connected with the U.S. garment industry—designers, manufacturers, store owners, buyers, salesmen—may gobble up WWD with their morning coffee and donuts. But so do hundreds and thousands of others who have not the slightest interest in or connection with the garment industry, other than they know it is somehow vaguely responsible for the clothes that are hanging in their closets and on their backs. Very interesting, all those outsiders scrambling for their copies of WWD.

What's the attraction? Nude girlies in the bra and girdle ads? Free money? Kinky notices in the classified section, tucked between the "Lingerie Salesman Wanted" and the "Ruffling-Shirring Box Pleating, Crochet Stitching, Hemming, Smocking, Multitucking—Work Wanted" ads? Not a bit of it. These outsiders—socialites, publicists, media types, status seekers, and just plain grass-roots gossipmongers—are scrambling to read about a very special world of people, places, and things put together in a very special way by WWD. For WWD has become a High Campground of a very specialized kind of trivia: fashion gossip. Beyond the very hard news about the industry it serves, WWD is very much its own newspaper. It is gossipy, bitchy, dogmatic, autocratic, hip, and, above all, terribly, terribly interesting, full of intrigue, innuendo, hints, and rumors. Who's doing what with whom? And while wearing which designer's creation? What are the parties? Where is the action? Which nightclub is it this week? Which restaurant is the one to be seen in? Where is the hemline? The waistline? What is the latest Onassis rumor? Who is Callas having lunch with? What is the *latest* Onassis rumor? Who was overheard saying what between the artichokes and the white wine at Restaurant X? What girl was dancing crotch-to-crotch with what other girl at what Paris party? Hmm-m-m.

Jackie Kennedy Onassis is a subscriber and when asked if she reads it, has been known to snap back without an ounce of charm, "Not if I can help it." Some Beautiful People (called "BPs" by WWD) even have their subscriptions forwarded to them as they jet around the world in search of whatever it is they are currently in search of—sun, snow, sand, money, male bodies, female bodies. All of these. None of these. Although no one has yet killed for his issue of WWD, great is the interest generated in WWD. So what about its influence?

The mass media of America is notoriously incestuous. The television networks are cumbersome creatures with vast staffs, bulky equipment, and incredibly complex chains of command. For the most part they stick to the obvious stories, straight off the AP ticker, with little time left over for investigative reporting. (Additionally, they are intensely paranoid and fearful of dropping big-business advertising sponsorship. "The Selling of the Pentagon" notwithstanding, the networks are rarely seen walking around with their necks stuck out. They are only too easily convinced someone will walk up and chop them off.) The dailies, with rare exception, do likewise. Only periodically will a *New York Times* or a *Washington Post* or a Chicago *Daily News* dig down under the fluff and the flak to come up with hard-hitting stories on police corruption or dope traffic or misuse of city funds. The news magazines are in there, nibbling off the newspapers. It is a complicated process of feeding off one another.

But out there, standing just beyond the media feed bag, is *Women's Wear Daily*. In a world where imitation is indeed the sincerest form of flattery, WWD tends to be a bit fussy about what it eats. It would rather instigate than emulate, and it is in a powerful position to do so. It is a daily clothing industry/fashion newspaper rather than a general news daily or a monthly fashion magazine. It has the edge on the fashion news and therefore the influence. And having been a family-owned enterprise for so long, it was just that much easier to do exactly what it wanted to do with both the newspaper and the news. For if the editor and the chairman of the board are also the owners—are they not free to cover just about anything they want, even if it has the most tenuous ties (or even none at all) with the garment industry? Of course. Why not? As long as the revenue keeps coming in. (The new owners, Capital Cities Broadcasting, are so far refusing to tamper with success.) No general news daily or weekly news magazine or monthly fashion magazine could ever have hoped to mount such a crusade as the Midi Skirt Battle as *Women's Wear* did, for example. That it made such an impact and had even the amount of success it did is testimony enough to its influence.

Believe it or not, this funny little newspaper—published out of grimy offices on East Twelfth Street, in part leased from Yeshiva University—is perhaps one of the single most influential newspapers in the United States. This is partly because it is a monopoly; there is absolutely no competition for WWD. The fashion magazines that come out only once a month, and therefore must operate with a lead-time of up to three months, cannot touch WWD. The regular daily press cannot—nor does it want to—begin to give the in-depth coverage to the garment industry that WWD does. So here is a newspaper covering what is the fourth largest manufacturing industry in the United States. The industry that determines what designers design, what store buyers select, and what women buy when they wander into a specialty shop or a department store. It's money, honey, big money. The garment industry is a $24 billion business. And WWD has it in the palm of its little hand. WWD can, without a doubt, help determine what a designer puts on his sketch pad, what stores hang on their racks, and, therefore, what women put on their bodies from one season to the next.

Beyond fashion, the whole style of American life is at stake here. Thanks in no small part to *Women's Wear* and its near-daily chronicling of who ate what at New York's top French restaurants, there are those in the world who feel that starvation is surely staring them in the face if a decent French restaurant is not within limo distance. French food. Not pizza or take-out Chinese or black beans at a Cuban eatery. French food. (Oh, maybe a campy hamburger every now and then at P.J. Clark's or Daly's Dandelion or The Ginger Man—but that's just for kicks. For fun. But for pleasure and profit—it's the French luncheon.) *Women's Wear* wades in with shopping hints (small *très cher* boutiques on Upper Madison Avenue) and travel hints (ski at Aspen, sun in Palm Beach). Through its dwelling on such things, *Women's Wear* encourages a life full of charity luncheons and shopping sprees in a world peopled with socialites and fashion designers.

Among its faithful readership, then, develops a whole incestuous code of behavior. Of action and reaction. And these readers are no slouches. They themselves are influential. Designers, socialites, businessmen, authors, show biz types, trendsetters. And so they work on each other—*Women's Wear* and its readers—in an ever-widening gyre. Eventually some of that activity is bound to spin off and hit the rest of the RealWorld that is hovering on the outside of *Women's Wear* and its own tight little sphere of influence. Thus, in its very own special way, *Women's Wear* has both the power and the glory: the power to promulgate—the glory of reporting it happen.

Grown men are known to tremble if *Women's Wear Daily* frowns upon them. For in the tight little world that is the American fashion world—a world that includes socialites as well as designers—a bitchy barb from *Women's Wear* is like being stabbed by a gladiator wielding a well-honed trident. It hurts.

The world WWD covers must wake up with an Alka-Seltzer stomach every morning, agonizing over what WWD might or might not say. Trends are made and unmade by

WWD with all the ease of freezing water into ice cubes and then boiling them to make hot tea. And often they are just as pointless. Designers quiver to see whether they are In or Out. Manufacturers approach their copy of WWD with one hand over their eyes, the other over their ulcers as they pray they have interpreted a WWD trend correctly. Is is knickers or HotPants? Midi skirts or maxi skirts? Belts or no? Cloche hats or cowboy hats? Or no hats? Socialites agonize until they are reassured that WWD still loves them and speaks glowingly of them at the latest charity bash. WWD watchers, therefore, are as numerous as Kremlin watchers or China watchers, eagerly scanning its pages to glean the latest gossip and trends along with the very hard news of the industry.

This is not to say that WWD is strictly a New York phenomenon, an inside newsletter to the East Coast Establishment. That blouse buyer at Brandeis in Omaha is just as avid a reader of WWD as the coat buyer at Bloomingdale's in New York or the better-dress buyer at Bullock's in Los Angeles. Specialty shops in Atlanta, boutiques in San Francisco, department stores in Detroit. They are all on WWD's subscription list. And although that list is small—82,766 is nothing to set the Hot Line ringing—it is mighty, for therein is the power structure of the entire garment industry, one of the mightiest industries in the United States, albeit without the monied glamour of, say, Wall Street or the sheer stud appeal of the steel and oil industries.

There they are, devouring their daily dose of WWD. Shooting up on WWD and getting stoned out of their minds. The designers—Oscar, Bill, Geoffrey, Valentino, Giorgio, and Halston. All the guys. My God!—belts are back. Blazers. Civilized Clothes for the Civilized Woman. Hats. They riffle through the pages, the sketches skimming off the pages like shots in the dark. HotPants. Civilized shoes. Civilized blouses. Around them are stacked bolts of fabric, racks of dresses. Chiffon, silks, satins. All the tools of their trade. Tricks of their trade. Seamstresses shuffle in and out, machines whir off in a distant back room. A model glides in, is examined, glides out. Sketches are pinned, tacked, stuck, stacked everywhere. Colors and patterns spill out over the room. Down on the street, the buses and trucks push their way through the pushcarts and pedestrians on Seventh Avenue, heart of the nation's garment industry.

Buried farther back in the bowels of Seventh Avenue, a manufacturer lights another cigar. It's his third of the morning and he hasn't even gotten past the "Buyers in Town" section of WWD. Christ! We just got the skirts up and now WWD's shouting about Midi skirts. Longuettes. Longuettes, my ass! I cut thousands of minis and now this sheet's pushing long skirts. What's this—knickers? HotPants? Bootlegs? Gauchos? Knickers, knockers. Business isn't bad enough—I should worry about the Name Game!

Up on the East Side, where the pushcarts have given way to prams pushed by polite nannies wearing white uniforms and sensible shoes and where the pedestrians have unlisted telephone numbers and maids who speak with Portuguese or German or South American accents, the pretty lady with the perfect hair expertly skips the front few pages, zeroing in on the Eye and Eye View pages. These are the gossip pages that are the Walter Winchell of WWD, chronicling the comings and goings of the various socialites, designers, and celebrities who skim across the brittle surface that now passes for New York Society. Hmm-m-m-m. Female sportswear designer lunching at Orsini's with WWD fashion editor. Hmm-m-m. Nureyev's back in town. Jackie O caught nibbling a hamburger at Daly's Dandelion with ex-footballer Rosey Grier. On and on it chatters, like a monkey in a zoo. An interview with Sly of the Family Stone. A squib on Mrs. Fred Harris and her Indians. Hmm-m-m. The item about the charity got in. That should sell a few more tickets. What's-her-name had lunch at Restaurant X yesterday. Somebody bought ten turtlenecks at that Italian boutique on Madison Avenue. An order for blue jeans for Prince Andrew at another little shop. Pictures of The Ladies coming out of a luncheon at the Plaza.

Out in the RealWorld—call it Omaha or Dallas or Denver

or Seattle—the buyers settle down in their offices, coffee mugs leaving rings on the newsprint. Denim is the big fabric news, eh? Followed by bleeding madras. Lots of smocking for spring. HotPants, indeed. We called 'em short shorts. Belts at the waist. Red stockings! God! OK, if that's what they're pushing, that's what the manufacturers will churn out—and that's what we'll buy. And that's what the ladies will wear. What's next? The Peasant Look is dead. Too bad for accessories—there was a fortune to be sold in all that glop. WWD predicts a return to dresses. Voile, chiffon, jersey. Fine. And wrappy coats. All the ladies will have to toss out those tiny armholes and nipped-in waists. OK. Next . . .

My God! *Women's Wear Daily.* WOMEN'S WEAR DAILY? It sounds like—like—like a trade paper. WOMEN'S WEAR DAILY? Interesting? Interesting. Ver-r-ry interesting. And therein lies the tale . . .

Turn-of-the-century Chicago was a lusty prairie city as full of life as a stein of well-aged malt liquor and just as feisty: political bosses, corrupt ward-heelers, a far-out and wide-open tenderloin, the very rich and the very poor, where Jane Addams found ripe and ready ground for Hull House. The Chicago school of journalism, where the corner bar had not only Irishmen but reporters bending their elbows and telling their tales. Chicago was where young men went West from—and where young men came West to.

It was into this bruising city that the sixth son of a Dutch Reform minister from Flushing, New York, came to find his fortune. What he found was the foundation for today's Fairchild Publishing Company. Young Edmund Fairchild, youngest son of the Rev. Elijah, actually did not intend to break into the publishing field. What young Edmund was looking for was something more stable, more secure. More—more respectable. A business, perhaps. Among his first ventures was selling soap and yeast from a pushcart, which he trundled through that swirling tapestry that was Chicago in the late 1800s. The soap and yeast were homemade, of good quality. The buyers that were found were loyal to the earnest young man from Flushing.

In 1890, Fairchild made the acquaintance of a fellow boarder in the Chicago rooming house where he was staying. John Wald was a printer, up to his letterpress in printer's ink, turning out everything from Firemen's Ball tickets to programs for the Loyal Order of Hibernian's annual St. Patrick's Day blast. In his printing enterprise, Wald owned a grocery store trade paper and the two men decided Edmund could be of service gathering bits of information and getting it down to the printshop before deadline. Done. Additionally, Wald owned the Chicago *Herald Gazette*, a trade paper for the men's wear industry dealing in such reportage as the latest in fly-front trouser buttons, what was new in union suits, and the latest in detachable starched collars. Hardly stop-the-press, but a form of the Fourth Estate nonetheless. The *Herald Gazette* was not the most successful of papers. In fact, it was not even solvent. Nonetheless, when Wald offered Fairchild an interest in it, Edmund, after much soul-searching about involving himself in something as cloudy as journalism, finally made the big decision and bought a piece of the action at the *Herald Gazette*. At first, his major contribution was packing his pushcart—in between bars of soap and cakes of yeast—with copies of the *Herald Gazette*, which he would then peddle along his route. Life and sales must have been at least good, for Edmund was soon joined by another expatriate from Flushing, his brother Louis.

By the time the Chicago World's Fair rolled around in 1892, the Fairchild brothers were hooked. Printing presses rumbled and roared for the Fairchild *frères*. Oh, not that they were looking for a more glamorous kind of journalism. No, brothers Edmund and Louis were still too tied to that polite parsonage back in Flushing for that. But hooked they were. During the Fair the brothers put out a hand-mimeographed sheet full of Fair news for the clothing industry people attending. When the Fair was over, the two bought out Wald's interest in the *Herald Gazette* and continued to expand the mimeographed sheet.

By 1900 the brothers were ready and eager to return to New York for an assault on the Big Town. Chicago might have been a brawling prairie town, fit for blushing boys whose collars itched and whose new shoes squeaked. But like so many since then, the brothers figured out that no matter what Chicago was, it wasn't New York. So off the two packed themselves for the return journey to New York City and the founding of a publishing empire that, while boring enough in name and pursuit, ultimately turned out to be one of the most switched-on publishing ventures ever.

The *Herald Gazette* eventually evolved into *Men's Wear*, a bi-weekly magazine devoted to that industry. The mimeographed World's Fair sheet, also transplanted to New York, was twisted and turned until it finally emerged as the *Daily News Record*, which now reports the business aspects of the men's and boys' garment industry. Both enterprises were full of facts and industry statistics. In 1910 the Saturday edition of *Daily News Record* started a little feature that the two men were interested in, but hardly willing to take a major chance on. At least not at that time. Each Saturday a single page was devoted to the business happenings in the women's garment industry. More talk about fabrics, tucking and pleating and garment closures. Maybe even a sentence or two on hemlines and waistlines and accessories. A humble beginning, but a beginning nonetheless, for what eventually became *Women's Wear Daily*.

The progress of *Women's Wear Daily* is very much like the plain lady who stands on the sidelines in basic black serge. Around her swirls the competition, awash in a sea of chiffon and lace. Then, when her moment arrives, our heroine quietly walks to the middle of the crowd, introduces herself, and takes over while her competition never even notices. At least, not for a while anyway. Now *that's* razzmatazz. Perhaps not class, but razzmatazz nonetheless. For who would have thought a dowdy-looking little lady from New York's garment center would carry enough clout to eventually knock out such fashion pushers as *Vogue* and *Harper's Bazaar?* Be mentioned with heady reverence by top designers who trip over their lisps in an attempt to say a good word about someone who, until recently, could not be guaranteed to go out in public with her stockings straight and her underwear straps tucked in? Ah, yes—you've come a long way, baby.

But back to those humble beginnings. When *Women's Wear* first broke loose from the back pages of *Daily News Record* it was truly all-American. Humble, unpretentious, somewhat dowdy and if not downright scorned by her more continental cousins in the publishing field—*Scribner's Magazine* and *Harper's Monthly* and Frank Leslie's *Illustrated*—at least politely but pointedly ignored. After all, who could classify as competition something that came out every day on newsprint with nary a Gibson Girl to its name. But come out it did, until it finally became the strong point of the Fairchild publishing empire.

Empire? Fairchild publishing empire? What's this? Publishing princes? With such publications as *Men's Wear* and *Daily News Record* and *Women's Wear?* Oh, yawn indeed. Oh, *yes* indeed. By 1917 the Fairchild enterprises had moved into premises on East Thirteenth Street, then the center of the New York garment industry. The business had expanded through a sea of serge and suitings so it could take on Edmund's son, Louis W. In 1924, Louis W. joined the firm upon his graduation from Princeton. First he was in the research department, then he worked in circulation, and finally, about 1926, he made it to the newsroom of *Women's Wear Daily*. The family empire was taking shape. Shaping up.

And lo—a publishing empire was in the making. From then on, the publications came tumbling out. In 1931 what was to become *Home Furnishings Daily* was started to serve that particular industry. Everything made it through the Depression intact, and nobody from the Fairchild family had to sell apples—or soap—from pushcarts or stand in soup lines to make it through those grim days. Boom time came at the close of World War II. In 1945, *Footwear News*, a weekly aimed at the shoe business, was begun. In 1952 *Supermarket News* was launched followed by *Electronic News* in 1956. *Metalworking News* was started in 1960. In 1961 came *Drug News Weekly*, which folded in 1968, but not after some agonizing and painful death throes. It was the first and, to date, only mistake ever made by the publishing Fairchilds. *Women's Wear Daily*, *Home Furnishings Daily*, *Daily News Record*, *Footwear News*, *Supermarket News*, *Electronic News*, *Metalworking News*, the late *Drug News Weekly*. An empire so real as to be unreal.

Women's Wear and the rest of them constitute no empire of class publications. These are no heavy, four-color fashion publications printed on slick thick paper with artsy photographs by Avedon and Lord Snowdon. The kind women buy for their coffee tables at a dollar-plus a throw. These are no tuned-in political publications with heavy articles by former-secretaries of state putting the political ills of the country at the feet of the other party or by deep-think political reporters who solve the country's problems while getting bored and bombed on presidential jets.

For one thing, *Women's Wear* is in its own special way all of these. On page one Negro Representative Julian Bond accuses J. Edgar Hoover and Attorney General John Mitchell of "cooperating and conspiring to systematically kill members of the Black Panthers." Nearby is a headline heralding: "Christmas Sales Jolly for Stores." On the same page a WWD survey indicates that the extra selling day at Christmas proved a holiday bonus for the nation's retailers. Democratic candidate-to-be George McGovern rates a two-page spread in an issue that simultaneously predicts that red stockings are getting a leg up in the fashion scene and ladies will be rushing out to buy dresses now that pants purchasing has peaked. A two-page spread on Norman Mailer is accompanied by a photo of him picking his nose. Pulitzer Prize-winning author Russell B. Nye (*The Unembarrassed Muse*) is interviewed in East Lansing where, under a photo of John Wayne in a white hat, he proclaims that "It's the bad man who is really a good man—the Zane Grey formula." Meanwhile, it's "Holiday Sales Off to Sluggish Start" and "Retailers See Tough 1st Half" and "Saks Aming for Exclusive European rtw" and "Abraham Silks Has Silver Lining in Home Sewing" and "Huge Demand Sends Madras Price Soaring" and "Margolis Joins Sheffield Watch" while "Stern Is Named President, Ochs V-P by Zsa, Zsa, Ltd." *Lterati, politicali, fashionali. O, tempora, O Mores!* Oh, boy! But wait—there's a story on Halston twitting the guys for playing bridge with old ladies, announcing that "no self-respecting homosexual has had to do that for years." Look at those headlines on the Royal Visit: "Prince Charming and the Petulant Princess." A piece tsk-tsking Jackie for having fresh bibb lettuce flown to her aboard the yacht Christina. Well . . . that does snap things up a bit, right? Provide some glitter in the gloom of sales figures and corporate mergers. It may not be slick paper, but one must admit it is a highly slick style. Language is even becoming controversial in WWD as they periodically throw in words that are bound to be a blow at the midsection of some of their more middle-brow readers. Sly of the Family Stone saying, "I'm happy as a mothafucker," is not guaranteed to make the day of the neighborhood corset salesman. Commenting on the new Andy Griffith series, WWD said he "rushed in at midseason with downhome shitkicking in a new CBS series." Folks were probably so stunned at the "shitkicking" reference that they failed to notice WWD didn't even mention the name of Griffith's new show. Ah, well.

For the flesh fiends lurking on their subscription list, *Women's Wear* offers some of the most tantalizing sketches in the fashion press, or anywhere for that matter. Nipples poke through to the world in sketches of skinny-rib sweaters. Bottoms protrude tantalizingly through pants and skirts and nighties. When WWD wanted to show where the various designers stood regarding skirt lengths, they sent a sketch around to each of their favorites indicating they were to draw in hemlines for daytime, hemlines for evening wear. WWD then reprinted each designer's hemline indication. The sketch was that of an unclad female, complete with a patch of pubic hair. It might not be *Screw*, Virginia, but it's not *The New York Times* either.

Today *Women's Wear Daily* stands at the top of its class. No matter that it is a ver-r-ry private school and WWD is operating as the single member in that class. Who's fault is that? Certainly not WWD's. It is merely carrying out the highest dictum of our proud land: practicing free speech under the free-enterprise system.

Heading up that corporate class of one, is John Fairchild, the son of Louis W. and grandson of Edmund, the original founder of the empire. John is chairman of the board of Fairchild Publications and credited by *Time* as being the "man Behind the Midi Mania." Not quite 1970's Man of the Year, but then who wants to be Willy Brandt anyway? That kind of kudo would make anyone head of his class, even in a class of one. Sharing the honors of running WWD was James Brady, publisher of WWD for six years until the Hearst Corporation spirited him away from the Fairchild family in mid-1971. "I'm going because it's a better opportunity and more money," said Brady in one of the few statements he made on the subject of his leave-taking. Well, that was one story. One disgruntled former employee, who was among the bodies that fell when a belt-tightening move cut a swath through the ranks and forty people were axed, tells a somewhat different story. According to her, Brady was miffed because he had been passed over for the job of president of the company. Capital Cities Broadcasting, which bought the Fairchild business in 1968, saw fit to give the job to one of its own rather than a Fairchild staffer, namely Brady. Then there was the rumor that Jim Brady was eased out by the Capital Cities powers because WWD's ad linage was down (down from a 1969 count of 8,244,791 to a 1970 count of 6,410,604). Nonsense, said Brady. "Everyone's linage is down." True enough. Even Fairchild himself sniped at that one. "Absolute baloney," he snapped. "Jim's done a superb job. He wants to be on his own, do something different. If he ever wants to come back, he can. He's so terrific." According to a Hearst spokesman, Brady was hired to "strengthen and give greater depth to our publishing and broadcasting activities."

Actually Brady's departure was a pinch of this and a dash of that, all adding up to a better offer from Hearst. If WWD is the nitty-gritty of the fashion world, the Hearst empire—eight newspapers, eleven magazines, a paperback book company, four radio and three television stations—represented The Big Time. Especially when one considers that one of those eleven magazines is the prestigious *Harper's Bazaar*.

So be it. May he rest in peace at Hearst.

In a way, Brady's departure was an end of an era down at WWD. If John Fairchild had put some bounce into the paper, Brady came along and put some snap into the bounce. If Fairchild was devoted to the Beautiful People, so was Brady. Additionally, however, Brady was a newsman devoted to the hot story and hard news. If Fairchild was the Flash of their particular brand of journalism, Brady was most assuredly Scoop.

Rounding out the triumvirate was June Weir, fashion editor and vice president of *Women's Wear Daily*. These three turned out one of the best-read and best-heeded newspapers in America today. And if that seems strange, considering its circulation and considering its seemingly limited audience with their very specialized interest—stop a moment. Granted, a few people snatch up WWD to see what

Jackie O wore where in Paris or Athens or New York or London or wherever her plane or yacht or limousine touched down. Granted, a few more read it to figure out what kind of clothes to hang in their closets. But many read it because not only are WWD reporters good eavesdroppers, but WWD has a remarkable tendency to print those eavesdroppings. And though the *Times* or *Time* or *Newsweek* might publicly turn up their news noses at such a means to an end, they are quick enough to pick up on those WWDroppings. Any given *Time*'s "People" section can be counted on for at least one item straight from WWD. *Newsweek*'s "Newsmaker" section admits it could hardly function without WWD. When Kandy Stroud caught Attorney General John Mitchell at a cocktail party, in a loquaciously quotable mood after warming up with a couple of scotch-and-waters, it was picked up by the wire services, the *Times*, and pretty soon everybody was in on the story. (According to *Time*, according to WWD, according to Stroud, Mitchell called Henry Kissinger "an egocentric maniac," who loves "to appear in the newspapers with Jill St. John." He railed out at the "stupid kids" who don't know the issues and accused former Arkansas Governor Winthrop Rockefeller, then in the throes of running for re-election, of assuring his win by "buying the votes of the far left or the hard right or the black vote.")

Often the lifting is done without permission even though there is something called the Fairchild News Service, which sells its features to paying subscribers around the country. Now neither *Time* nor *Newsweek*, the major grabbers of WWDroppings, is a paid subscriber to FNS and, like as not, they run the item *sans* credit. Periodically, however, conscience pangs or good taste prevail and, in the case of *Time*'s pickup of the Mitchell piece, not only was WWD given credit but so was Reporter Stroud—something *Time* only recently started doing for its own staff reporters. The Fairchild folk shrug their shoulders and let sly smiles flit across their faces. Who cares? It's a measure of their success and they know it. No measly subscription fee to FNS could begin to make up—either in prestige or money—for the pure professional satisfaction of having the newsmagazines and other media snitch copy from a trade publication the likes of WWD.

In addition to being ripped off by the competition (imitation may indeed be the sincerest form of flattery) WWD finds itself in the peculiar position of being talent broker for its journalistic competitors. Because it is so widely read and circulated among editors, publicists, and show business types, there is a continual brain drain at WWD. It was during his stint as movie and television critic on WWD that Rex Reed became popular. Kept getting his name up on billboards. "Best show of the season!" Rex Reed, *Women's Wear Daily*. "Award material!" Rex Reed, *Women's Wear Daily*. "One of the year's best!" Rex Reed, *Women's Wear Daily*. It was when Rex began getting so much exposure in the drama section of the Sunday *New York Times* that *Women's Wear* sacked him, on the grounds that by having an interview run in the Sunday *Times* he tended to undercut himself, or perhaps even scoop himself, in *Women's Wear* the following week. (Not that Rex minded. He went on the talk shows and made as much hay, and moola, from that event as he did bad-mouthing *Myra Breckenridge*, the movie destined to keep him from stardom forever.)

Eugenia Sheppard, today the reigning *doyenne* of the fashion world, began her career at WWD covering the millinery beat. Among her first interviews: Sally Victor. (Remember her?) Bernardine Morris of *The New York Times*—yes! of *The New York Times*!—began her fashion life on WWD. Dede Moore, who now writes heavy-breathing pieces for *Cosmopolitan*, is ditto a WWD dropout. Isadore Barmash, another *Times* staffer, is a WWD product.

Julie Baumgold, who now writes hot-shot pieces for *New York* magazine, was once a reporter for *Home Furnishings Daily*, the publication dealing in such subjects as bathroom fixtures and bed linens. Miss Baumgold now does articles on what it's like to shoot a movie in 1970 starring Orson Welles from the 1940s. Heavy stuff like that. Certainly a step upward from toilet bowls and towel racks, right?

And Chauncey Howell, WWD's ace reporter who once got himself smuggled into the House of Detention (Chancey Howell, he was called after that), found himself in the awkward position of having to get an unlisted telephone number because people kept calling him up day and night wanting to discuss his various articles.

Beyond the has-beens, WWD even has a string of would-have-beens malingering out in the New York journalistic jungle. Daphne Davis, now a contributing editor on *Rags*, the underground's fashion magazine, remembers bombarding WWD with letters of application. "I would have gotten down on my knees," she says, "if only they would have let me in the door." Instead, she ended up working for Nancy White at *Harper's Bazaar*.

In 1968 Fairchild Publications merged with the Capital Cities Broadcasting Corporation, a company which owned five television stations and six radio stations. It was an unexpected move—one not rumored in the Eye pages as a conversational snatch overheard at a secret meeting at "21" or The Ground Floor. Daniel W. Burke, vice president of publications at Capital Cities, says both sides were out sniffing for just such a deal. Quite frankly, Capital Cities was bumping headlong into some pretty stiff FCC regulations governing ownership and licensing and figured they'd better diversify or else. "We looked at various franchise operations," said Burke. Soft-drink bottling. Like that. Safe. Comfortable. All-American. Some of them they tossed out pronto. Distilleries. Legalized gambling. But the idea of a newspaper (in Capitalese "an allied form of advertising-supported media") was tempting. Tantalizing. Radio. Television. Newspapers! Yeah.

Capital Cities' stations run the gamut from WPAT in New York to KPOL in Los Angeles. WPAT serenades New Yorkers with enough strings and saxophones to lull even a talkative taxi driver into a soporific stupor. WPAT often devotes great chunks of time to the same song—recorded by everyone but the original artist: the Beatles as done by Hollywood Strings, Mantovani, Kay Kyser, the King Family (humming). KPOL, on the other end of the dial, is primarily a news station, devoted to presenting varying political opinions on its news commentaries. Burke, a public-spirited sort from upstate New York, got to New York by way of Detroit, where he ran Capital's WJR radio. He sighs when comparing the differences of the audio and the visual in the Capital household. "There is one dimension of newspapering that is lacking that is of great concern to me and that is the public service aspect of broadcasting." (Oh, Fairchild Publications, can you satisfy this company's do-good yearnings? Can WWD find happiness among the public services announcements? Can a girl from the garment industry find happiness in the corporate family? Stay tuned. . . .)

Meanwhile, down at the Fairchild empire things were—well, not a mess, but then not as neat as Grandma's dresser drawers either. The two older members of the empire, L.W. and Edgar, were retiring. John Fairchild, who had the Battle of the Midi staring him in the face, would be left alone at the command post. According to Capital Cities, Fairchild just felt he was not up to such a responsibility. My God, man, determining hemlines is a full-time job. Coining words, organizing pictures. It is no simple matter to get the ladies of the country to drop their hems. From Capital's side, Burke explained that Fairchild "really felt deficient and inexperienced and ignorant of certain business functions and was practical enough to realize he never wanted to remedy those deficiencies." In other words, again in Capitalese, "these were not areas of high personal interest and Fairchild felt if he could find friendly people who had some experience in those areas" he could concentrate on the more earthshaking questions of hemlines, waistlines, belts, and buckles.

The two sides met and—ZAP. It was love. Stars and moons and the Hollywood Strings. The deal was signed May 15, 1968, and then things really started moving. Capital Cities was no slouch when it came to this $10.5 million transaction. No sluggards for those 10,047 preferred shares or 175,136 shares of common stock.

Not that things were financially fuzzy down at Fairchild. In fact, business was at its best when Capital Cities bought the old family firm. Fairchild himself was Big Daddy to the whole shebang, overseeing all those trade papers plus trying to keep up with the whole Fairchild operation as it had expanded over the years. There were then thirty domestic bureaus handling news and reporting for all the papers around the country, plus eleven foreign bureaus. There was Fairchild News Service, a subscription device to provide an outlet for Fairchild features along with, hopefully, increasing the scope of Fairchild influence and prestige.

John Fairchild was, and still is, toying with the idea of a weekly woman's newspaper, called simply W. A dummy issue was printed (dated April 3, 1970). It is, interestingly enough, the same size as the *Times*. The economic recession temporarily shelved W—For the WOMAN Who Is First. Whenever "money loosens up a bit, we'll be ready," says Burke. The front-page index for that dummy issue listed such feature departments as Beauty/Health, The Dollar, Environment, Faces/Places, Fashion, Sporting Life, and Going. It was a typically fashion/Fairchild/feature approach to all of these subjects. Environment had nothing to do with murky waters or heavily burdened air. Instead, it dealt with lizard tables from Tiffany's (Environment—what surrounds you. In the home. Get it?). The layout of W is bright and brisk. Large pictures. Big blocks of copy with capital letters leaping out like lizards. Headlines boxed in bright blue. Interviews with Actress Glenda Jackson, Henri Bendel President Geraldine

Stutz. WWD's drama critic Martin Gottfried reviewing Elvis Presley's Vegas opening. A front-page story on Women's Lib, Swedish sex pills for men, and Mary Lindsay's view of politics. It is a larger-than-life *Women's Wear*, having gleaned all the pizzazz out of WWD—leaving out the nuts-and-bolts reporting—and concentrating it in one place.

When Capital Cities moved in there was a total reorganization. Fairchild became a director and an executive vice president of Capital Cities. On December 1, 1970, upon the retirement of his cousin, Edgar, Fairchild became chairman of the board and chief executive officer of Fairchild Publications, Inc. At the time of the merger, both Fairchild and Brady were pulled off the other publications to concentrate on WWD. Brady became senior vice president and publisher of WWD. Publicly, both were happy with the new arrangement. "Jim warmly embraced the concept of having full authority and responsibility for only one publication rather than a weak, watered-down, confusing set of responsibilities for all of them," Burke said of the shifts. Additionally, Fairchild News Service was pared back from thirty domestic bureaus to twenty-five; from eleven foreign offices to eight. Beyond that, each other publication has its own editor and publisher.

Capital Cities also modestly allows that although it had a money-maker, it taught Fairchild about budgeting and how "to do the kind of things that very few family businesses ever do. Things they were suffering terribly from lacking." The eight publications—all at one time headed by Fairchild as publisher, while Brady had over-all editorial responsibility for each of them—were broken down into four publishing groups. John and Jim were kept intact as a team, their power and influence being restricted solely to *Women's Wear*. Capital Cities thinks this is a Capital idea. They are pretty shrewd: with John and Jim involved in all the publications, that "often produced a tendency for people who were mad at us with regard to one of the publications to just damn them all with the same sweep of the hand," said Burke.

Today the Fairchild domain, while not awe-inspiring when compared to such sprawling publishing empires as *The New York Times* or *Time/Life*, is formidable in its own way. Each of the eight publications constitutes a kind of monopoly in its own field. (Face it—can a country, even the richest in the world, support two *Supermarket News*papers?) The total circulation of the eight is more than 400,000—up from 372,211 shortly before the Capital Cities merger. Of that total, *Women's Wear* is 82,766—which is up from 73,000 just before the Capital Cities action. (Estimates indicate that WWD's total circulation breaks down like this: 30,500 are retailers, 20,000 are manufacturers, 4,800 are wholesalers, and a full 23,000-plus have absolutely nothing whatsoever to do with the women's garment business. Those 23,000 include society jet-setters, restaurateurs, gallery owners, and hairdressers, with a full 2,600 being mass media types.)

And money? They seem to be doing all right. At the time of the agreement with Capital Cities the total revenue for all Fairchild publications was $27 million with WWD being responsible for some 30 percent of that total. And since? Revenues are up beyond $33 million with a $5.5 million profit. Not bad for a recession. Now whether the upswing was because of the merger or in spite of it is anybody's guess at this time. The point remains: Neither party was hurt by the merger.

As for the direction *Women's Wear* will take, Burke wants to give the impression at least, that they are operating under a free and democratic theory of hands off. The Home Team and the Visitors. Uptown and Downtown. Just how long that theory is operable remains to be seen, for Capital Cities hardly sat through the hemline crisis covered with calm and cool. As they see it, even "if every woman in the United States drops her skirts, thereby vindicating John's observations and judgment, in some ways John is still a pariah to many people in the business because he was associated with a radical, violent change which many people feel hurt their industries for anywhere from eighteen months to two years." This is a charge that has been leveled time and time again at John Fairchild: he dropped the hems and the bottom dropped out of the business. Capital Cities tries desperately to be charitable. But it is chary charity. "In some cases the industry is shooting the messenger who brought the bad news. John reflected the opinions of the most important people in that particular activity—but he also had a great deal to do with having influenced and produced those opinions in the first place." Well said, Capital Cities. Who needs friends when your foster father is so understanding?

Ah, but fathers, even foster fathers, do tend to worry about their children. Especially such fresh youngsters as those publishing prodigies down at Fairchild. Yes, they are a worry. But what's a father to do? "The fact is it's worrisome. Antagonisms are bound to build up about anybody with as much visibility and around whom so much controversy swirls. And those antagonisms can sometimes be translated into business difficulties." The father leans back in his chair. What sort of look is that, flitting across his face? Smug pride? Well-controlled terror? "But that's often what happens with enthusiastic, outspoken people. That's just part of the warp and woof of living with John." Now that's a frown coming up. Starting up there near the eyebrows, running up the forehead, furrow by furrow. "We're obviously troubled if John turns out to have egg all over his face." The furrows dig in tighter for a minute. Then—the furrows recede, dropping away one by one like footprints being washed out with the tide. Ah, smooth again. "Regardless of what happens—he's our guy." Oh, God— let's all root for the home team! Go John! Go Jim!

But no matter what happens, barring the Empire toppling altogether or being overrun by outside hordes, John Fairchild is in pretty fair shape. He may have come out of the Midi crisis with a discernible layer of egg on his face but then, when egg dries it can always be scraped off easily, right? He is firmly fixed financially: his annual salary, as negotiated through the Capital Cities merger, is a neat $90,000 per year based on a ten-year contract. After that, John's contract will be renewed on an annual basis. If by some chance, the egg remains on his face six years from now and he is sacked, it will not be the worst way to go to the bank: he would leave with a guarantee of half-pay for fifteen years. Plus retirement benefits which come to $22,297 per year. All of which just goes to show that John Fairchild does not have all his eggs in one basket. Much less on his face.

3

To think of power is often to think in terms of symbols. Cecil B. deMille whose authority was backed up by his riding boots and a cast of thousands. Lawrence of Arabia with Peter O'Toole's sparkling blue eyes. Patton with his pearl-handled revolvers. Raquel Welch and her double-breasted sexuality. Ike with his golf cart. Jackie Onassis with her checkbook. Like that.

But, power with a cleft in his chin? Power with a giggle? Power with lopsided grin? With LBJ ears? And a bemused expression on his face? Where are our heroes of yesteryear with their power and their glory? And their pearl-handled revolvers? Gone, alas, like that sunset Roy and Dale were constantly riding off into. Power now rests in the hands of everyday people, people who giggle and grin and scratch their heads. People like John Fairchild, chairman of the board of Fairchild Publications.

Sitting there in his offices down in the Fairchild Building, John Fairchild looks so—so ordinary. He could be mistaken for your friend at Chase Manhattan. Or your banker at Bankers Trust. Conservative right down to his three-piece suit (when was the last time you saw a three-piece suit?) and neat black side-buckled slip-ons. Cuff links. Pocket handkerchief. Dark suits. Safely-patterned suits. White shirts. He looks like the man from whom you could borrow the money for the family room. He would understand. He even looks as if he would understand if you called it a Rumpus Room. He also looks so vulnerable, perched right out there in plain sight at his messy metal desk. Why, any irate fashion designer could just walk in and—hurl an invective at him.

Around him *Women's Wear Daily* throbs and teems and turns about. John Fairchild sits there, cool and conservative. He won't wear down as the day wears on.

There was probably not a day in the life of John Fairchild when he did not know he was destined to go into the family business. It was a foregone conclusion. Like dogs named Rover. Being the grandson of the founder and son of the owner is a little like earning the second million dollars. There is nothing new in it. "My father always wanted it, you know." A wry little grimace sneaks up from that cleft in his chin. Like Old Joseph P. Kennedy always wanted a president. Like Old Money wants to marry Old Money.

(But what would John Fairchild have done if he had not gone into the family business? Been a banker? Clerked in a bookstore? Been a—gasp—bum and squandered the family fortune on mad things? Hardly. "Oh, Lord—can I confess this?" He winds his fingers in his hair, leans back in his chair. Good heavens, man—what is it? "I'd *love* to be a ski instructor.")

So much for that.

To repeat: There was never a day in John Fairchild's life that he did not know he was destined to enter the family business. He was born in Newark, New Jersey, on March 6, 1927. His grandfather Edmund already had three thriving publications in the empire—*Daily News Record, Men's Wear*, and *Women's Wear*. John's father Louis was heading up *Women's Wear*. It would be the dominant publication in John's life.

Despite the divorce of Fairchild's parents and his subsequent move to St. Louis with his mother, he never lost touch either with his father's side of the family or with their business. He was educated at Kent School, a preparatory school in Connecticut. Summers were spent hustling coffee and copy at *Women's Wear*. By the time Princeton rolled around he had toyed with the idea of medicine or science, but since he was admittedly "absolutely gross with numbers" both were struck from his list of possible pursuits.

During his Princeton tenure, he dropped out and enlisted in the Army, serving eighteen months and rising ingloriously to the rank of staff sergeant. Caught between wars—WWII and Korean—he ended up in the Pentagon, doing public relations work and writing speeches. He even posed for recruiting posters. Uncle Sam wants you. Join the Action Army.

Fairchild returned to Princeton to finish up a degree in humanities and began working summers in the Paris bureau of *Women's Wear*. Part of his duties at this time included acting as waiter when Burt Perkins, the then Paris bureau chief of WWD, and his wife, would throw dinner parties. There was Fairchild, scion of the family fortune, hovering around empty soup plates and dirty forks and wine glasses and cigarette butts. Standing behind chairs waiting for the fish course to go. Waiting for the meat course to go. Waiting for the dessert to go. Picking up the dirty plates. Discreetly removing a pea that fell off a plate. Filling the wine glasses. Meanwhile, the fashion greats were passing beneath his serving fork. It's Dior. It's Balenciaga. It's Givenchy. Finally young Fairchild could stand it no longer. Soup plates and dirty forks forgotten, one night the boss's son put aside his humble disguise and—sat right down at the table! With CHRISTIAN DIOR! "Hello, I'm John Fairchild." It was so—so—MGM. The Hardy Boy makes good. And he swung into a conversation on high fashion. Needless to say Perkins was horrified, but then you don't sack the boss's son and strip him of his basic black uniform and his napkin. Send him from the back door, threatening to blackball him around town. You'll never lift another soup plate in this town, Fairchild! Hardly. Help of any kind was always hard to find.

He found he really liked journalism. Maybe not fashion. Maybe not retailing. Maybe not the subject matter—but he really dug journalism. Reporting. Writing. Sharp pencils. Notebooks. Collaring store executives. Scooping the *Times* and the *Trib*. Racing back to the battered Royal to rap out a hot piece on Macy's before the copy deadline ran out on him. Well, maybe it wasn't quite *Front Page*, replete with rapes, robberies, storms, sodomy, death, and destruction—but it was a hell of a lot better than writing speeches at the Pentagon. Or rescuing stray peas at Parisian dinner parties. Besides— his math *was* terrible.

Moving right along, Fairchild found himself smack dab back in Paris in 1955 heading up WWD's bureau there. Paris was just about right for the John Fairchild of the 1950s—it was full of challenges. Pitfalls. Not the least of which was the house he and his wife, Jill, ended up with. As Fairchild described it in *The Fashionable Savages*, his book about those early fashionable days, the Villa Loli was a magnificent-looking house. A grand salon with a gold leaf ceiling three stories high. A red velvet banquette squatted on a priceless Aubusson rug. Grand salon. Petit salon. Delicate Louis XVI chairs. A pair of eighteenth-century silver peacocks standing on a Hepplewhite table. Two five-candle Baccarat crystal candelabra. Shimmering chandeliers. Wow. To two innocents abroad—plus their two-year-old son—how do you do the dusting? What if the candles drip? Tinker Toys on the Aubusson? Tricycle banging into the Hepplewhite? Ah, but the house was to get its revenge. The furnace smoked furiously as it gobbled up two and one-half tons of coal

purchased on the French black market. At night Jill looked as
if she were going to an ice hockey match wearing a ski bonnet,
a pair of John's wool socks plus a sweater to bed.

Up to this point Fairchild had been tolerated as the boss's
son. The punk kid from Princeton. The guy who thought
scooping the *Trib* on later retail closings was right next to
winning the Pulitzer Prize. Big deal. But Paris—ah, Paris.
Here is where John Fairchild really cut loose, burning up the
wires between Paris and New York with his HotCopy.
Nothing was up beyond Fairchild's and WWD's reach. Nothing was beneath them. They would rise to any heights, stoop
to any depths to get a story.

Fairchild remembers those first few collections, when
WWD was always hustled to the back of the salons. Rejected,
but not outright. Thought of in condescending terms. Much
like having *Dogs News* cover a presidential press conference.
Much bowing and scraping for *Vogue* and *Harper's* and *Elle*
and all those big, slick fashion mags. There were those editors,
tottering under the weight of their hats and gloves and
prestige, on those little gilt chairs in the couture salons. Front
row material. Fairchild fairly fumed to himself back there in
the salons' Siberia. After all, you *can* see better in the front
rows. But all the while, devious plots were racing through his
head. Horatio Alger was about to force his way to the front of
the bus.

One imagines him in the finest RKO tradition—staring
fiercely out at a Paris skyline that contains *everything*—the
Eiffel Tower, Sacre Coeur, l'Opéra, Montmartre—shaking his
fist at a rosy red Parisian dawn. "Paris—I'll get you yet!" the
American youth vows.

John Fairchild set to work. Among his more unlikely ways
of achieving distinction was hanging around the Ritz bar.
Drinking up the gossip. The Ritz bar is like New York's
Times Square or Rome's Via Veneto or just plain old Main
Street: sooner or later everyone worth seeing, and overhearing,
passes through it. John Fairchild sat and drank it all in and

talked and eavesdropped and picked up on things. Snippets. Gossip. Rumors. Have-you-heards. All of which were duly recorded and transmitted back to East Twelfth Street. Then he hit the collections with a fury. From his disadvantage point in the back of the salon, Fairchild started doing what no other fashion editor in history had dared do: pan a collection. There he was, the Clive Barnes of the fashion world, wielding a pen that was indeed mightier than the scissors. He turned the *tableaux*, taking the pins right out of the designer's mouth—and sticking them into his backside. Fairchild flailed away, making sure he just took bits and pieces of flesh, but never went in for the kill.

Additionally, Fairchild cultivated a network of tipsters and stool pigeons. There are those who say he must have known every baster and ripper in Paris, ready to spill his guts out.

Meanwhile, back in New York, John's father worried. Slow down, you move too fast. L.W. had visions of John's wild schemes backfiring. Of John taking pratfalls into pitfalls of his own making. Ending up with—egg on his face, perhaps? Memos flew back and forth. Some say the old man even had a network of spies spying on John, all of which must have made the streets of Paris awfully crowded. John's spies running into John's spies. Whose side are you on? Who's on first? An old Abbott and Costello movie.

Bit by bit he did indeed make Paris "sit up and take notice" of *Women's Wear Daily* and its brash young man. He cultivated friendships first with the staffs of the couture houses. Finally, John Fairchild was in the In-est Crowd of all—the couturiers themselves. It was a heady life, all right, for this all-American boy from Newark via St. Louis via Princeton. WWD was making it! Parties at Pierre Balmain's elegant country house outside Paris—with its own Siamese teahouse and running stream. There was WWD's Man in Paris, surrounded by the likes of Balmain himself, Princess Mia Pia of Italy, Prince Alexander of Yugoslavia, and "some Danish prince and princess" or other. No matter that it was the 1950s and most of those titles were *sans* substance, flattened under a tank or two during World War II. Prince. Princess. BALMAIN! One party soared on until dawn (protocol and royalty, y'know) with Fairchild gleefully playing Balmain's favorite game: "balancing with one foot on a bottle of Dom Perignon 1947." Gone were all those dirty soup plates. Gone was the back row. This was the Big Time. Gotcha, Paris! Drinks with Chanel, sitting on a Louis XVI chair sipping scotch while she squatted on the floor—at his feet. Dinner with St. Laurent. American boy makes good. WWD moves up from the back of the bus. Banquets, parties, and balls.

In fact, so beautiful were the circles that John and his wife were moving in that the ultimate rumor began circulating about John himself: the rumor that he was having an affair with a noted French designer. "I've only been propositioned once in my life by a male designer," Fairchild says candidly, "so I must not be very attractive to them." There were even rumors in Paris he was having orgies. Omigod. Ugh. Utter nonsense, he sighs. "I guess I am really just an old, tired square." The rumors still persist today, partly perhaps because that is just a fringe danger of working anywhere near the fashion industry. (If WWD were still a stodgy nuts-and-bolts paper, Fairchild would probably be accused of stomping his wife with his bowling shoes. Which might even be worse.)

While John Fairchild was doing his number in Paris, he met a chic chick named Carol Bjorkman. Now Carol was really something. Small, brunette, a product of Pittsburgh (she magnificently overcame that handicap in a hurry). With a short stopover in Hollywood (one forgettable movie in 1948, *Letter from an Unknown Woman*), Carol then jumped into the fashion foray. Dress buyer for Saks Fifth Avenue. Contacts. On to Paris. Carol went to work for a new house that was having its ups and downs but would eventually overcome. More contacts. It was while she was doing duty for Yves St. Laurent that she met one John Fairchild. He talked her into writing a column for WWD. Done. It was Carol Bjorkman's column—called simply "Carol Says"—which gave the tone and direction to fashion coverage that Fairchild was looking for. It took Eugenia Sheppard's fashion coverage for the New York *Herald Tribune* and improved upon it. If Eugenia Sheppard successfully mixed up batches of fashion coverage, society gossip, and personal pieces about both worlds, Carol Bjorkman threw it in the blender and came out with the perfect mix: fashion gossip.

At first, bits and pieces of Carol were used to illustrate her column. An eye. An ear. Lips. Carol blossoming—VOOM!—out of *a décolletage.* Hinting. Tantalizing. At first no one knew for sure who Carol was, but it was interesting to speculate. All over Paris, people sat down and tried to guess who had been circulating at That Party, at That Dinner, at That Do, at That Soirée. Who was nearby when that *bon mot* dropped out with such a dainty thud, only to be picked up and printed in the next day's WWD. Carol knew her way around—celebrities, movie stars, fashion people. Few circles were closed to her. And her ears were always open. John Fairchild knew a good thing when he saw it—or when he overheard it. And a Brenda Starr was born. She attended parties (sometimes with her poodle Sheba), swept through Paris and New York on the arms of various escorts. She was seen—and she was read. She was sharp, often prickly. In 1967, at the height of her career, she died of leukemia.

By the time Fairchild was ready to leave Paris, he had gone through enough changes to make a head swim. From the back rows, to the front rows. From condescension to recognition. From the smart-ass guy from that trade rag, to Mr. Fairchild from *Women's Wear Daily.* From the boss's son to Mr. Fairchild. It was not an easy task and if his pen sometimes dripped bright-red human blood, some of it was bound to come off on Fairchild's vest. In fact, so bloody were the battles in those early days that the Paris fashion community dubbed him *le blouson noir*—the Black Shirt. And for a country scarcely a decade out of World War II and the Nazi occupation, that was no mean tag name. And, indeed, Fairchild rolled roughshod over the Paris fashion world like an entire Panzer division coming in for the kill. And if, to the casual observer, this seems a bit of an overreaction on the part of Paris, it is important to note that fashion always has been—and still is, although in diminished quantity—a major economic force in France. (The French fashion industry is one of the oldest and largest businesses in France, protected both by law and tradition.) To fault the French fashion industry at that time was a little like kicking old ladies or cripples. Definitely *not* the thing to do. The industry is so valuable, in fact, that the Chambre Syndicale de la Couture Parisienne was formed to protect French fashions from being pirated by unscrupulous outsiders. (Usually American retailers and manufacturers.) People who would see a collection and then go manufacture cheap knockoffs and thus glut the market with shoddy copies. It was a mark of Fairchild's increased prestige—if not power—that upon his departure from Paris, Daniel Gorin, then the delegate general of the Syndicale, invited Fairchild out for a farewell luncheon. Calling him *le blouson noir*, Gorin admitted he was sorry to see Fairchild go. After all, his successor might be worse.

Once back home from Paris the fascination and the interest continued. Fairchild's book, about those early years, *The Fashionable Savages*, clearly showed his thinking, which was, of course, reflected in the pages of *Women's Wear*. He had his favorites—The Impeccables: Gloria Guinness, the Duchess of Windsor, Mrs. Gilbert Miller, Mrs. Paul Mellon, Jacqueline de Ribes. (And as if being one of The Impeccables were not enough, Fairchild chose two and elevated them even further. Mrs. William S. Paley [Babe] and Mrs. Loel Guinness [Gloria] became two Fashion Goddesses. But wait—there was even a further breakdown. Fairchild and WWD dubbed Gloria Guinness—The Ultimate. Whew! It was like putting a cupola on the pedestal.)

For the younger set, Fairchild coined the title The Lo-comotives. They included Isabel Eberstat (wife of photographer Frederick Eberstat, who was a classmate chum of Fairchild's at Princeton), Gloria Vanderbilt Cooper, Amanda Burden (daughter of Babe Paley).

He was endlessly fascinated by these women. WWD reporters huddled in corners at their dinner parties and their charity balls, meticulously documenting every detail of dress and design to be faithfully reported in WWD the next day.

"Both Paley and Guinness have beauty, fine bones, grace and charm," Fairchild wrote in *The Fashionable Savages*. "They stand out from the Best Dressed Crowd because they lead. They have their own style. They dare to be different. Their taste is not regimented. Babe Paley gives the impression she doesn't care about fashions. She always looks right. She looks better than right." And on and on. It is a lot of hokum, and no one knows it better than Fairchild today. Even a Goddess can slip off her pedestal. And when a Goddess slips, she makes the same kind of splat! that any ordinary lady makes when she hits the dirt. When Fairchild did a Sensuous Woman list in 1970, he not only omitted Gloria Guinness, but took her to task in public. "If only she would leave those strict little Balenciagas in the closet and let that Latin blood run wild," WWD suggested of the Former Fashion God-dess—the Goddess La Guinness, as Fairchild once enthused, who "was ahead of Paris. She always has been." When she spoke, "her words were music." Well, so much for La Guinness.

But in the 1950s and 1960s, John Fairchild was enamored with it all. So much so he could speak of the fashion world as "the Fashion Forest." He could describe being in fashion as being "a little savage." Those creators of the Fashion Forest he dubbed The Fashionable Savages. "The creators live in a rarefied part of the forest. Some design in Paris—The Exotic. And others on Seventh Avenue—The Primeval." Fairchild was touched with the romance of it all. Some would say he was just plain touched. Or out of touch, as the case may be. Well, he was in Paris and Paris does strange things to us all. And The Ladies? They were "Fashion Goddesses, a small group of very special ladies who stand savagely apart from other women." And John Fairchild dug it all. But back home in the 1960s, John Fairchild changed. It took a while, but he changed. Perhaps it was just the onslaught of America, for America in the 1960s was an America of change. Even in the midst of the destruction raging around us we felt that this was, indeed, a far better world than that 1950s world we had so sleepily emerged from. That 1950s trip that had us all snoozing in our seats, only to awake and find ourselves in the midst of something very real and very vital. That was no bad dream—that was reality confronting us.

From his 1950s trip to Paris—a trip that lasted well into the 1960s—John Fairchild changed. And if Fairchild changed, so indeed did WWD.

It was subtle. During the late 1950s and early 1960s, WWD was slowly but surely turning away from being strictly a trade paper. It became a bright, snappy chronicle of everything from the garment industry to high fashion. It was preoccupied, in those early days of the Fairchild rule anyway, with the flash and the glitter. The banquets, parties, and balls. The reading public could depend on WWD to tell who wore what to which party and what was served for dinner.

Then came another injection. WWD started getting political. Artsy. Literary. Interviews with Ramsey Clark and Walter Cronkite and John Gardner. An assessment of Harlem three years after Martin Luther King's death. A page devoted to book reviews and movie reviews and theater reviews, all of which they had had over the years but which now—what with all the notoriety now being attached to the jazzy new WWD—were being noticed. And noted. And, unlike many editors of trade papers, John Fairchild makes no attempt to draw a thin, tenuous line between, say, an article on Norman Mailer and the garment industry. It can't be done. It would be silly and sophomoric to try. And if there is one thing John Fairchild knows, it is not to be silly.

WWD has been criticized—from the garment industry to the Beautiful People—for being pretentious. "Who needs an article on Ramsey Clark," sniffed one garment industry executive. "We deal in fabric, labor, the market. What is this drek?" Pooh, says John Fairchild. He doesn't look like a concerned citizen, sitting there at his desk down on East Twelfth Street. Joking with the girls when they scurry by. Talking about shirtwaists and skirt lengths and fabrics. For one day, little John Fairchild emerged from that Forest and lo! discovered there was a whole RealWorld out there, full of Real People who fought and died and polluted the air and went on strike and got clobbered by the cops and beat up on students. Looking back over his shoulder, it must have been a shock to discover that Forest was really some sort of unreal Oz. So why not have articles on Ramsey Clark and George McGovern and John Gardner? Besides, if you own the paper, you can do anything you want can't you? Within reason, that is. As long as the advertisers don't take it out on ad linage. And since they didn't—and don't—why not?

Where John Fairchild was once thoroughly intrigued with the Fashion Impeccables and the Best Dressed Ladies and those marvelous, divine, super, smashing, fun little Savages scampering around the Fashion Forest Primeval—now John Fairchild professes to see an altogether different Light in the Forest. "Fashion. Pooh. It comes from the streets. Who's best dressed? Those girls in the subway. I don't know their names." Well—rest assured those girls riding the subway, hanging on all those endless straps in the IRT and the BMT and the IND are *not* your basic Babe Paley or Gloria Guinness or the Duchess of Windsor. Those girls clutching frayed paperback novels and containers of coffee from Chock Full O'Nuts are not drinking that coffee in a Dior dress. Or reading those paperbacks in a Chanel suit. Or hanging from those subway straps in a Balenciaga coat.

No, John Fairchild professes to be much more concerned with other things these days. "Those people are a joke," he now insists of the BPs. "Wasteful and unimportant. To be living like that in this day and age is unforgivable. They are boring, vacuous, dull. Irrelevant. There is a pack of idle ladies who supposedly set the standards for Society today. They are collectors of people and places which are 'In' for a minute or two. One day it's Truman Capote. Then it's Leonard Bernstein. Awful way to live. Terrible." Ugh. Yuk. Ick. A person can fairly see the goose pimples of disgust rising on John Fairchild's forearms.

Fairchild himself even wrote a novel about these people he despises so, *The Moonflower Couple*. A perfectly penny-dreadful novel which most WWD readers automatically assumed to be about Carter and Amanda Burden. "Well-l-l-l, not necessarily," Fairchild said. "I had Jackie Kennedy more in mind." No matter. It is a deadly put-down of the very people WWD talks so lovingly and lavishly about. A young rich boy who can't figure out what to do with his life so he goes into politics. For all the wrong reasons. A lovely young bit of fluff who revels in her needlepoint and her yummy new apartment and maybe—just maybe—her marriage to that young rich boy. The book, explained Fairchild, "is a story about how a woman is destroyed by her husband's ambition and the Beautiful People scene around her. It shows the vacuousness of the Beautiful People." Fairchild shrugs his shoulders when asked what he thought of his first venture into nonfiction. "Of course I liked it," he said. "It made $14,000 for me." (Now he's planning another book. Nonfiction. Or *more* nonfiction, if you prefer. "About all the people I know." Can you wait?)

Actually, "I'm very concerned about the future of this country," Fairchild says. "We are teetering on the brink of something awful here. Europe is still much more carefree but we're always in some sort of state of Future Shock. This is an incredible period of shock. Garbage piles up; we don't have decent transportation. We can't go out on the streets at night. We wonder if there is justice in America. We see our environment being needlessly polluted."

Good heavens, man—you are not a frivolous thing after all, are you? Yours is not a *peau de soie* world bounded all about by The Ladies, The Impeccables, The Locomotives, and the RealGirls all decked out in their Longuettes, HotPants, and BootLeggers. Lordy, no—you really do live in the RealWorld, don't you, John Fairchild? John Fairchild—this is YourWorld!

Not that John Fairchild is not a truly pragmatic man, one who fully realizes that if you are indeed in charge of your own destiny, you can indeed mold a world of your own making. Especially if you own the newspaper. "When I came to *Women's Wear* with any sort of power, I found myself working with a bunch of old women who kept coming up and telling me how bored they were. How boring all this was." He waved his hand around that vast, endless room stretching on for yards and yards and yards. Filled with men, women, desks, coffee cups, paper. All the tricks of the trade known as journalism. Well, now, what Fairchild and WWD did was "simply react to the times we were living in. This is a constantly changing world, you know. And I think people who read our papers are some of the most intelligent people in the country. They are living, breathing human beings who live in the world around them." Well said. After all, "not everyone can read *The New York Times.*"

Hence, John Fairchild sees himself as a sort of massive void-filler. For all those people in his constituency who cannot or do not read *The New York Times,* fear not. There is John Fairchild, scooping away into that endless pit that is the public mind for not having read the *Times.* John Fairchild, super-snooper-scooper. John Fairchild, shoveling away. And, really, "the paper was so dull. In the beginning we were very much like college sophomores running around trying to change things. Full of ideas and enthusiasm." There are still those who think the end result of all those college sophomores is something rather sophomoric. Ah, well. It took Christianity a while to catch on, too. And look—there are those who consider WWD the Bible of the Industry. And somebody has to play God to that Bible, right? (It all fits, don't you see? WWD is the Bible of the Industry. Tiffeau says Fairchild has "the power of the devil." *Time* calls him cherubic. Tiffeau likens June Weir to "a nun with a knife in both pockets." Heavens, maybe there is something going on here!)

One thing that John Fairchild still does, despite his philosophical change of mind, is deal in Capital Letters. In that respect, he is the Christopher Robin of journalism. A woman is not just sensuous, she goes into some secret list in John Fairchild's head—a head that contains many secrets and many lists—and comes out a Sensuous Woman. When Jackie Kennedy blossomed into shorter skirts, bikinis, and shifts during the summer of 1966, WWD quickly called her a RealGirl. Anyone who is on Fairchild's list of worthies is lumped in with The Ladies—The Ladies who lunch, shop, plan charity balls, chatter, gossip. Last year there was the Savage Woman who was slowly replaced by the Civilized Woman.

Actually, John Fairchild's brand of journalism—a brash, get-it-first-and-then-run-with-it kind of journalism—is just part of the family tradition. John's father, Louis W., was the sort of man who lived for hard work. Up and at it, he was into the Fairchild office by seven-thirty every morning, usually coming in on Saturdays and Sundays, too. Constantly armed with a clipboard, a one-inch stack of newsprint, and a stubby pencil, L.W. would start dashing off notes and would continue to do so during the day. His scrawl was nearly illegible and all day long, editors and writers would be seen wandering around with scraps of newsprint in their hands and bewildered expressions on their faces as they tried to puzzle their way through L.W.'s handwriting and meaning. By the end of the day, L.W. would have worked his way through the entire inch of paper on his clipboard.

One thing L.W. hated and that was being scooped. Scooped by anybody—but especially the *Times* and *The Wall Street Journal*. "Why didn't we get this????" he would scratch out on his newsprint, then whip off to the appropriate editor.

He did not want to come out the same day with the same news—he wanted to come out the day before with more and better news. That attitude is more than prevalent at WWD today—it is pervasive.

To see John Fairchild sitting so calmly in those offices on East Twelfth Street, it is hard to picture Fairchild, Boy Reporter. Damning the consequences while rushing full speed ahead to full recognition and final vindication for all those back seats in the back row. The Fairchild who won and then moved through that heady world that was the Paris fashion world of the 1950s. That all-powerful world that dictated what the women of the world would wear—and pay exorbitant prices for. The world that saw a single Balenciaga blouse go for a cool $1,000—and the woman who had it made in duplicate—is gone. And so, for that matter, is the John Fairchild of the 1950s. The Scoop Fairchild who would do anything—well, practically anything—for a HotStory. The surface flash, at any rate. Indeed, Fairchild would have one believe he is a "tired, old square." A fuddy-duddy who sits home with a good book, his wife, Jill, and their four strong children, exuding all the quiet virtues of the American upper class. Secure in their class. Not scrambling for the front of the bus. Not scrambling to be first for the most. Indeed, the fight is over. John Fairchild seems to have settled down, happy to play out his Life-with-Father role over in his East Side co-op. To hear him tell it, life is little more than getting up in the morning, getting into one of those conservative suits, riding the subway to the office, and sitting around all day playing the calm executive. He sits at a cluttered desk, piled high with periodicals; drinks coffee ordered in from the kind of coffee shop that puts the coffee in a styrofoam cup, encloses a little cellophane sheet containing sugar, plastic stirrer, and a stiff paper napkin upon which Chapter One of the Great American Novel could be written. No china teacups or Porthault guest napkins for John Fairchild, chronicler of the Beautiful People.

Lunch might be somewhere snappy—La Grenouille, Orsini's, La Côte Basque, La Seine, Lafayette—but it's a business lunch, often with a designer. And John Fairchild works on those business lunches, make no mistake about it. It was he who spotted Jackie Onassis at Lafayette wearing what was—to her and at that time—a mini. John relayed the message to a photographer who hustled over to Lafayette in time to catch an up shot of Jackie O emerging from the restaurant with her kneecaps bared. The upshot was the shot seen round the world. A good personal friend of his is Douglas Auchincloss, an editor at *Time* magazine. Fairchild will pick up an Eye piece just from seeing Douglas wheel up to La Grenouille— (certainly one of New York's most chic restaurants, due in no small part to the constant shilling done for it in the Eye column of WWD)—on his bicycle, then later offer fashion columnist Eugenia Sheppard a ride home on it.

After work, his nights are ho-humdrum enough to bore even a Senior Citizen. Back onto the subway, dinner at home with the family, read a good book while the stereo set pumps out Mahler or Shostakovich, then off to bed. On his rare nights out, he goes to a movie (not much call for that, though, since he is known to sneak out of the office at any hour of the day to catch a film in Greenwich Village, which is just a skip from the Fairchild Building). Maybe a small private dinner party given by designer Oscar de la Renta and his wife, Françoise de Langlade, former editor of Paris *Vogue*. The simple life. No charity balls, no black-tie benefits. No wild nights at New York's super chic little spots: Nepenthe or Elaine's or Le Club. No offbeat slumming in Chinatown or Harlem or the East Village or the Bowery. All those fun things to do while ensconced in the safe security of a limousine and a sable coat. John Fairchild is as dull personally as WWD is not.

His one seeming extravagance is a $200,000 cottage in Bermuda. Ah, there's a bit of the High Life bubbling through. There's something ordinary mortals can clutch at and crow about and marvel at the differences between the very rich and the rest of us. Finally. Mrs. Fairchild and the kids pack off to this retreat—a three-bedroom bungalow furnished mostly in wicker furniture and bright colors—in the summer. Jill does her own cooking. John wings over every weekend to lend a hand barbecuing steaks. Otherwise it's a nap in the hammock, sunbathing, and skindiving in the soft surf. Ho hum; pass the Sea 'n' Ski.

Two desks to the west of John Fairchild used to sit James Winston Brady. James Bond Brady, as Fairchild sometimes called him. Jim Brady is very deceptive; for one thing, he is very easy on the eyes standing somewhere between a Tyrone Power (handsome) and a David Steinberg (cute). Few journalists have ever worked under newsmen who could come close to filling that description. Like Fairchild, Brady also wandered around in a three-piece suit, usually navy blue or black. Unlike Fairchild, however, Brady preferred to take the jacket off and work in his shirtsleeves. This tended to give him a more casual air; the air of reaching down to the common man. A man in shirtsleeves, it seems to say, gets hot. Might even sweat. Look, boys—I'm one of you. While the man who sits over there forever mired in his three-piece has just a touch of the untouchable.

Brady is the true New York boy. While Fairchild grew up in relative comfort and ease on the outskirts of the City, with prep school and Princeton always visible on his horizon—(not to mention WWD itself—it was always *something* to fall back on), Brady was growing up in the middle-class confines of the Sheepshead Bay section of Brooklyn, the older of two sons. His brother is a diocesan priest whom Brady characterizes as being "a liberal, but one who works within the Establishment. I mean—he's not married or anything. At least, I don't think he is." Jim Brady is a product of the New York parochial school system. Nuns, priests, catechism, confessions. Years of sandlot baseball and cold showers—the good old days of Roman Catholicism. Lace curtains and Sunday roast beef dinners. Stick ball and stoop ball.

Jim Brady headed uptown to Manhattan College, a small Catholic men's school in the Bronx. He majored in English, served with the Marines in Korea, and "when I got out I couldn't get a newspaper job" so he ended up back in school, this time going to N.Y.U. at night "working toward a master's in English." He never got it. "Too busy working during the day and drinking beer and chasing girls at night." (He caught one of them. Remember little Florence Kelly from Brooklyn? That's the one. Two daughters now.) Brady was by this time working in the advertising department of Macy's, turning out copy for The World's Largest Department Store. A more propitious occurrence there could never be. For who should be sent up to Herald Square to do a story on Macy's, but—you guessed it . . .

Fairchild, back in his reporting days, was sent up to Thirty-fourth and Broadway, Herald Square, to do a piece on Macy's. During the course of his intrepid reporting, who should he interview but Jim Brady. Well, now—hearty handshakes and camaraderie—the boys hit it off just fine. Before you could say "remember me to Herald Square," Fairchild had spirited Brady away from Macy's.

From there on it was merely a matter of putting his feet down where Fairchild feet had trod before. His first assignment for WWD was as a reporter covering the retail beat. Then in 1956 he shipped off to Washington to cover the Senate. After three years, he went to London as bureau chief. In 1960 when John left Paris to return to New York to become publisher of WWD, who should grab the Paris beat but—you guessed it—Jim Brady, going in as European director. By 1964 both were home, and who was there waiting to take the giant step into John's publishing shoes but—right on—Jim Brady, Publisher of WWD. To some this was merely following in the boss's footsteps. To others it was gentle nipping at the heels of the kennel's Top Dog. No matter. The two men professed to be great friends, and nobody has spoken out to deny it. Indeed, it was debatable as to who held the most power at WWD—the giggle or the grunt. Most staffers, however, voted for Brady while Brady was still there. "John is an idea man," one editor said. "He sits around and thinks things up—lists of Fashion Victims and names of things. Brady did all the nitty-gritty involved in putting a product out every day."

There was an affinity between the two men. They were each other's alter ego. Or, perhaps, alternate ego. Although one could hardly picture them racing up to one another and laying on a Brother-ly hand slap, they were, indeed, like Soul Brothers. The Dynamic Duo of WWD. Together they constituted an unbeatable and—considering the Battle of the Midi—an unbreakable and unbowable team. If John Fairchild seemed to pick his way through the pieces of flesh that daily constitute *Women's Wear Daily*, Jim Brady—shirtsleeves flapping—was in there wading. He is tough, crisp, and can be immeasurably hard when the need arises. "I have seen him pick at a person until they fell apart," says one WWD writer. "They deserved it, though," she added. According to most he was fair, but tough. Sometimes cruel. But, according to some, "They deserve it." On the other hand, when a staffer was truly on the team—one of the Brady Bunch—life could not be more beautiful there at 7 East Twelfth Street. (There is the story of the young reporter—now gone to glory at a small but powerful weekly magazine—who, while having a professional discussion with Brady, dissolved in tears. Please, he cautioned her, "If you must weep, do it on your own time." She pulled herself together enough to comment later on the situation: "He's so *cute!*")

From time to time rumors flew around the Fairchild Building, linking Brady to one sweet young thing or another. Mostly, however, the gang figured it was all for show. Or, chauvinism. (However, when Steffie Fields, a leggy young lady reporter, hit the Fairchild offices tucked into her HotPants, Brady wandered past her desk to check the scene out. "Well—she rings my bell," he reported back. Jim Brady, RealGuy.)

June Weir, fashion editor and vice president. First of all,

she does not—repeat *not*—look like Ethel Merman with short hair. Nor is June Weir a tyrant who rides roughshod over the emotions of her fashion staff. No, June Weir looks more like—oh, a high school home economics teacher, maybe. Her hair is unfashionably short. She wore lipstick and nail polish long before Valentino told us we should. There is not one chi-chi bone in June Weir's body. Other fashion editors might walk around mentally wearing hats and gloves and speaking in high-pitched tones of hysteria. Not June Weir. June Weir smiles a lot.

She was born in Youngstown, Ohio, and majored in journalism at Ohio Wesleyan University. And then? "Why, New York, of course. Where else?" She parts her lipstick and laughs. "Why, when I grew up there was no question about where to go. New York. So, I just packed my bags and took the first train." She spent her first year in New York studying at Tobé-Coburn School for Fashion Careers, then ended up in the merchandising department of Macy's. Although she didn't run into Jim Brady there, they were working in The World's Largest Department Store simultaneously. In 1954 she moved to WWD. "I was a summer replacement," she recalls, "covering every beat there was. Whenever someone would go on vacation, I'd have to become an instant expert on accessories or lingerie or shoes." It was touch and go all summer, and into the fall, whether June would remain with WWD. But with luck and pluck and a few resignations, a slot was found for her and she has been there ever since.

In 1966 she was made fashion editor and then—over some strenuous objections from the solidly male power structure at Fairchild—she was named a vice president of Fairchild Publications in 1969, shortly after the Fairchild merger with Capital Cities Broadcasting.

June Weir is truly a holdover from the 1950s, when people did indeed grow up and want to come to New York. Where New York was both the beginning and the end of the road, and a yellow brick road at that. It was Oz and the Emerald

City. The glittering end of a magical rainbow of the mind where glamour struggled with power and both gave way to mystery.

June Weir is married to William K. Baron, a ship's officer for the United States Line. They have no children. "But I wish we did," she says. She takes a somewhat maternal attitude toward some of her staffers, dispensing advice like a doctor armed with placebos. One young staffer who was becoming more and more discontented with New York finally told June Weir she'd had it. "She was all set to head down to Palm Beach for the winter, then take off for the West Coast in the spring. I told her she was crazy—go West right away." Figuring the girl was a journalist at heart, one who would pine away on the beaches of Florida, June would have none of her crazy scheme. "You'll be miserable," she told the sweet young thing, meanwhile scurrying around to find a bureau slot for her. When last heard from, Palm Beach had faded from her mind and she was living happily ever after in a Fairchild bureau out West.

Another discontent came roaring up to June one day saying she and her husband had had it with New York. The coughing, the crowds, the pollution, the high rents, the Bad Guys. They'd had it. June inquired after their plans, was told they were heading off to the Southwest. Maybe Phoenix. Do things with their hands. Hubby would do auto repair work or construction or cabinet-making. She would get into leather or teaching or something. "I just said—do it. Do it right now. If you wait around you'll settle down into a rut and never try anything different."

There she is, administering advice and consent on everything from skirt lengths to a do-it-yourself life in Phoenix. But as for herself, June Weir is fiercely loyal to her adopted city.

And fashion is her passion, make no mistake about it. "Clothes are the one thing people all across the country have in common," she says logically. We might not all see the same movies or read the same books or go to the same shows—but we all wear clothes. That is the tie that binds, blest or not. June Weir couldn't be happier anywhere else than she is in her job down at WWD. "I've seen WWD change a lot," she admits. "It was rather straight and stiff when I started there. Then John Fairchild came in and things began to loosen up a bit."

WWD moved right along with the 1960s, that flamboyant era of banquets, parties, and balls. "That was the time when fashion designers became celebrities in their own right. One of the things WWD did was make designers come alive. Up until that time, designers were just labels on their wonderful dresses; WWD made those labels come alive. We helped humanize them and the women who wore their clothes. It was a wonderful period for the newspaper." And now? "But we've all changed now. WWD is merely a reflection of the times. Everything has slowed down from the flamboyant high-living period of the 1960s."

June travels a great deal, covering the major European collections every year, flying around the country for various functions and collections and to keep up with what is going on across the country. Even she, confirmed New Yorker that she is, admits there is a whole world out there West of the Hudson. "People actually want to go to places like Atlanta and Chicago to live," she says, at once marveling at the fact while agreeing that there may be something to it. "Today you can go from New York to Los Angeles and everywhere in-between find little shops that you might have found only on Madison Avenue or down in the Village a few years ago. And there are very creative young designers springing up in Chicago and Houston and San Francisco." Sigh. Not that she sees a creative New York crumbling around her, headed for the dust heap in a cloud of pollution overlaid with some choice rapes and muggings. Not at all. There might be a lot of action Out There, but to June Weir it is merely a twitch on The Body.

Jim and John and June put together a good, professional

staff which they are constantly in danger of losing as outside forces keep reaching in and snatching them away. *New York* magazine. Radio stations. Free lancing. *The New York Times.* One would expect the staffers, working as they do for such a contradictory newspaper, to be either as deadly dull as yesterday's dress design, or as slick and chi-chi as the Beautiful People they chronicle so minutely. The fact is, they are both. Or neither. Most have no connection or interest with either the industry world they cover or with the glittery glossy world of the BPs. Jim Brady himself comes as close as anybody to living in that world, frequently frequenting such watering holes as Elaine's and parties at Valentino's.

The rest are, for the most part, just simple down-home folks, who do their own shopping, clean their own apartments and their own vegetables, and relish the free movies that come their way via WWD's abiding interest in movies as fashion pacesetters.

When Gail Rock came to New York, lanky and low-key from Valley, Nebraska, she wound up as a production assistant on the *Today* show. Four years later she found herself scurrying through the Fairchild empire as a reporter for *Home Furnishings Daily*. Her beat was linens and domestics. Nebraska would be better than this. Fortunately for Gail, Fairchild and Brady were tinkering around with an idea that involved some sort of arts page. Some sort of artsy page. Some sort of, well—where they could review movies and television shows and books and restaurants and make more meaningful comments on—well, arts and pleasures. Aha! ARTS AND PLEASURES. In August, 1970, Gail was dragged hardly kicking and screaming out of bed sheets and bath towels to edit the Arts and Pleasure page. Now it's Gail Rock's name instead of Rex Reed's.

Martin Gottfried is WWD's theater critic and is considered by some to be the best young critic in town. His reviews are thoughtful, incisive, and terribly educational, and fun to read. Gottfried comes in about once a week to pick up his mail, trying to do this chore after six o'clock when he figures most people have gone home. The rest of the time he shuttles his copy back and forth by messenger. On those rare days he descends on WWD, he barrels his way through the bull pen, the long fringe on his brown suede vest flailing out like some sort of medieval weapons. "God—it's so fucking awful out there," he cries, gesturing broadly to the RealWorld outside the third floor windows. "If I stood and pissed in the street nobody would notice. Nobody would care. IT WOULDN'T MAKE ANY DIFFERENCE!" He mumbles on, charging through desks and midi skirts and shag haircuts, tripping on the corner of the Xerox machine, finally fading out of sight down the hall. But—a theater critic. For WWD. Wow! That implies a lot. So Clive Barnes doesn't wear fringed suede. So what?

Gottfried, who worked his way up through the ranks, was once a reporter on *Home Furnishings Daily*. When Tom Dash retired as WWD's critic after many years, John was casting about for a new critic. He sent big Martin and some others out to see *La Dolce Vita* and Martin won the contest. He's been reviewing ever since. He sees everything and usually has something to say. Not that WWD, and especially Brady, always agree. Brady recalled the time Gottfried once reviewed a play where right up there in plain sight IN THE LEAD he likened Charles Manson to Jesus Christ. "Well, journalistically it worked," said Brady. "And I didn't change it." But when the review appeared, Brady whipped a memo off to Gottfried. "I just told Marty that was a crock of shit," said Brady. As a gesture of the paper's respect for Gottfried, they are once again shipping him off for his yearly jaunt to Europe. "We're in the middle of a recession, like everyone else," explained Brady one rainy afternoon in February. "But the recession be damned—Martin's got to get to Europe and see what's going on."

One of WWD's best-known reporters is Chauncey Howell. Chauncey Howell wears a crewcut and old sweaters with fuzzballs on them. He looks to be one step from white socks and bowling shirts. "I was on television once and here were all these old guys with their long hair and bell bottoms and tinted shades and wide ties—and they looked so silly."

Chauncey is the one who did the front-page piece called "Radical Chic at the Big House," a report on the New York Women's House of Detention, while Angela Davis was imprisoned there before being extradited to California. "First a girl is stripped naked, then given a shower and a DDT spraying and, finally, laid out on a steel examining table and 'given a good old gynie!' by one of the prison's lady doctors," Chauncey wrote. He also informed WWD's readership that the smocks at the House are long because, in the words of the warden, "they got a lot of bending over to do." There are signs that admonish "No Slow Dancing." As Chauncey summed up, "Herbert Marcuse never told Angela Davis about the tragic absurdity of places like the Women's House of Detention. That she might be able to 'radicalize' the ladies there, as her supporters hope and her enemies fear, is as silly an idea as feeding chicken soup to a corpse." He has told of Norman Mailer "taking a leak" and characterized some as "everybody's favorite male chauvinist pig, wife-stabber, and ear-biter."

Every once in a while, WWD feels compelled to crank up a party. Usually it is a Christmas party geared up by the Art Department, which takes up a collection of ten dollars a head. One year, for reasons unknown, the party was a Hallowe'en party held in a private home around the corner from the Fairchild Building. It was a mad, gay evening. Brady arrived in high spirits and wearing a false mustache. Two of the more liberated ladies on the staff—figuring it's Hallowe'en so this must be a costume party—wore their karate suits. According to one participant, the generation lines were firmly drawn. "You were either bombed or stoned" by the end of the evening.

On the whole, WWD's staff is not all that different from every other staff around town. They bitch and moan and complain and weep into their typewriters, but they get their job done.

As far as the editorial staff goes, unions do not have a chance. "Everybody is so terrified of the Guild down there," said one young lady who, along with a few militant others, went so far as to work union talk into casual conversations. "My God—the paranoia. There are older guys working there who were burned by strikes on other newspapers—they don't want anything to do with it. Little girls who don't need the job let alone the money—they don't want anything to do with it. People who are scared to death of losing their jobs—they don't want anything to do with it." As a result, it is a scramble to squeeze every dime possible out of WWD and Fairchild Publications. "Beginning salaries? It's whatever you can beat out of them." One female reporter relates how she had to threaten to quit before they would give her a raise. "I actually wrote a letter of resignation and handed it in. Then the sweet-talking started, and finally they came through with some dough. But unless you have the guts to stand up to them and call their bluff—and hope they won't call yours—you don't stand a chance."

"The pressures are terrific on the paper," admits one of June Weir's girls. "You are never just working on one story or one project. You're working on many, many—and it's incredible. I've often wished I could have a nervous breakdown just so I could get out from under some of that pressure." One girl almost did. Whether or not it was all due to WWD is debatable, but certainly the idea of WWD contributing to her unsteadiness cannot be denied. A person is merely the sum total of her separate parts, and if WWD is one of those parts, it must share in the blame.

On the first big Moratorium to End the War Day, a contingent of staffers approached Brady and spoke of their intention to take the day off to participate in activities. Fine. When Women's Lib Day rolled around, a group of The Ladies informed Brady they would be taking off to participate in those activities. Whereupon Brady graciously offered to sit down and discuss their grievances, which he did. Salaries (too low), discrimination (a man with no experience and a woman with years of experience are treated differently: he is hired as an editor at a higher salary), expense accounts (men get them; women are encouraged to let industry males "take them to lunch"), overtime (men balk and/or get paid for it; girls are told "how lucky they are" to be covering snazzy parties or going to free movies looking for fashion ideas). It was a heart-to-heart. The Brady Bunch rapping it all out. Brady, intense and sympathetic. The Bunch, intense in their liberation. Came the August 26 aftermath and Brady nearly had a Palace Revolution on his hands: The Ladies took one look at WWD's nation-wide roundup story on strike activities and reacted. Taking a copy of WWD they sliced into the story with marginal notes, the gist of which was: "WWD is unfair to women." Brady was presented with this one-of-a kind copy and "was furious," recalled one of The Ladies. "Absolutely livid. He came storming over to my desk in a rage." He hauled up all the old arguments. What do you have to complain about? Didn't we sit down and talk? Blah, blah, blah. Talk such as this, at WWD and elsewhere, is endless. A few changes are made. A few inroards cut into the problem. Then it lies dormant, or so it seems.

Some say it is merely a case of know your enemy, sisters. John Fairchild still clings to the idea that women can get what they want simply by being cute. "I think the whole Women's Lib thing is silly. A woman can get anything she wants by being charming." There are those who insist, however, that charm won't pay the rent. Fairchild stands back and points proudly to June Weir. "She's our only female vice president." To him the key words are "female vice president." To others, the key word is "only." "Oh, there were a few old fuddy-duddies who objected when June was made a VP, but we did it anyway. I love working with women."

At a general staff meeting one of the girls asked, "Is it true that we are going to have a girls' softball team and we're all going to wear HotPants and play Carter Burden's girls from

The Village Voice?" Nonsense, reassured Jim Brady. "We're going to have a male softball team and you girls are going to be cheerleaders." No! No! cried John Fairchild, perhaps writhing under the vision of irate lady staffers picketing that softball game. Picketing the game with signs screaming publicly *Women's Wear Daily* UNFAIR TO GIRLS and NO HOTPANTS FOR BRADY and LET US PLAY BALL. Omigod. "No," insisted John Fairchild at that staff meeting. "We're going to have an *integrated* team!"

The one thing Jim Brady absolutely could not cotton to was the idea of abortion. "During the whole Women's Lib thing of last summer we rapped a lot with Brady about what women were unhappy about and what they wanted out of life," said one female reporter. "The one thing he could not accept was our philosophy on abortion. I guess it's his whole Irish Catholic hangup. He is really still a middle-class Irish boy from Brooklyn."

Actually, Jim Brady should be much more complex than that. And probably is. Irish Catholic, yes. Middle-class boy from Brooklyn, yes. But add to that the fact that he is a self-confessed "editorial animal" and you add a dash of hard-nosed newsman. Determined, dedicated, damn the presses. But then take into consideration the whole ambiance of the world into which Brady was thrust by WWD: the social fashion world, full of BPs and celebrities and banquets and balls. How do you fit in a middle-class Irish boy from Brooklyn who is also a hard-newsed editorial animal. Brooklyn, Paris, the East Side.

"In a way he was a real male chauvinist pig," one of the girls insists of Brady. "But at least his consciousness was raised during the last year or so he was here. He knows what's going on now." How Brady's raised consciousness will serve at Hearst is, of course, anybody's guess.

As for Women's Lib, at WWD or elsewhere, there are those who figure, like the Midi, it had to happen. But then, that's a whole other story. . . .

And then it came, hurtling over the horizon like a super-sized cannon ball marked "Midi Skirt." Oh, America! This is what you have been crying out for. This is your It. Here is your cause. Your chance. Unite. All you have to lose are your legs. Stand up in your mini skirts and be counted. United we stand, divided we fall. The country sprang forward as One, united at last in a common cause: save the Mini. Keep America Beautiful. Don't Litter our Legs. Hard hats moved from heads to legs and the war was on.

And when the walls came tumbling down during battle over the Midi, who was responsible for it? WWD, of course. The Midi became Fairchild's personal battle, one to be carried to every store rack and clothes closet in the country. (Nonsense, retorted Fairchild and Brady—"We just report the news." Nonsense—news is also made, boys.)

WWD's initial involvement with something other than bare kneecaps and vacant thighs came as early as 1966. While most people who queued up to cry through *Dr. Zhivago* couldn't get beyond Omar Sharif's glittering brown eyes and the massed strings sawing away at "Lara's Theme" in the background, John Fairchild (a self-confessed movie maniac) found his own eye zeroing in on those long coats. No more thighs! No more knees! Fairchild was fairly transported with it all. Marc Bohan, designer for the House of Dior in Paris, came to the rescue with a collection featuring mid-calf coats to capitalize on the so-called Russian influence of the Zhivago look. Fairchild was fairly beside himself and "terribly excited by the length," according to June Weir. "He spotted it right then and there as a straw in the wind." By spring of 1967, the longer coat was all over French ready-to-wear and even a few American designers were beginning to let their sketch pens track a longer line. It was then WWD coined the word Midi to cover the length. (Fairchild graciously gives credit to June Weir—for the word at least.) Then, along came *Bonnie & Clyde*, rattling across over the wide screen trailing a flutter of Flatt & Scruggs behind them. It was June Weir who flipped this time. Omigod! Bonanza! If Fairchild got stuck in the snowdrifts of pre-Revolutionary Russia, Weir was riding in the rumble seat of Warren Beatty's roadster. "I saw Faye Dunaway in those clothes, those soft sweaters and long skirts and those cunning little berets, and thought that was one of the greatest things I'd ever seen."

Well, there was a bit of pushing in the pages of WWD, but when push came to shove over the Bonnie & Clyde look, few disagree with the fashion editor who gleefully figured that "WWD fell on its ass" over the B & C look. At least for the time being. But then, even Christ was ahead of his time, folks.

By 1968, however, a few designers—notably Adolfo—were showing long lengths but strictly for evening. This was when Adolfo hopped on the gingham bandwagon and hauled The Ladies up after him. There was Gloria Vanderbilt Cooper trotting off to a Shakespeare Festival benefit in her lavender-and-white checked gingham midi skirt and husband Wyatt in tow wearing his red drum-major jacket. Ethel Scull in her flower-strewn Adolfo midi at Paul Newman's fund raiser for Gene McCarthy at Arthur. Gloria Cooper again, this time in red, white, and black ruffled gingham Adolfo number. Suzy Knickerbocker, New York *Daily News* columnist, said it made her look "ravishing." The race was on.

By this time the Midi was stuck in John Burr Fairchild's mind. Two significant things happened to hasten his hustle to drop the hemlines: in 1968, Yves St. Laurent showed the first "city-pants" designed to put women on the streets in something covering their legs. Said Yves, "This will be the first step towards the acceptance of the long skirt." And in 1969, John Fairchild saw *The Damned.* The plot of it be damned—dig those fashions. 1930s. Slinky. Hitler *haute couture.* How to be nifty while married to a Nazi. Decadence in a slithery satin dress. Fairchild's mind blew into a zillion slinky pieces. Wow! Ingrid Thulin vamping around in a bias-cut dress. Not a kneecap in sight. Fairchild even got so enthusiastic he arranged private screenings for designers, retailers, and manufacturers. "We only report the news," WWD says. Ah, but a little twist to an old story never hurt anything, right? Although Fairchild was not yet ready to moblize his whole army and launch a full-scale Midi attack, he was positioning his big guns.

See how it works, ladies? And you thought you just went to a store, whipped something off the rack, and pulled out your Master Charge. Oh, you innocents. You children. The Church may teach you all about Free Will and Advanced Civics may fill you full of theories about the U.S. of A. being the land of the free and the home of the brave where there is truly Democracy in action. Neither have the least little bit to do with whether or not you make up your own mind about how long you wear your skirts. And the sooner you realize that, the better. Do not waste your time on idle dreams, ladies. Your knees belong not to you but to *Women's Wear Daily!*

Small skirmishes broke out here and there. Rebellious little bands of radicals who took to the streets proclaiming "The Midi Is Dead—Long Live the Mini." Brave little *ad hoc* groups blossomed around the country like the last fragile flowers of summer, protesting the loss of the leg. Construction workers went into a noticeable decline at the prospect of no more noon hours spent chugging Rheingold and ogling chicks. But it was hopeless. The enemy had taken a stand; the citadel of the hemline was about to fall.

Fairchild himself was still touting a "wardrobe of lengths" and the designers were all too willing to go along with him. Hemlines ranged from ankle to bottom with sheer joyous schizophrenia reigning supreme. It was a glorious moment in fashion history, perhaps the one moment afforded a woman whereby she could be totally and completely independent. A few glorious months where she could continue wearing all those micros and minis. Then wear all those skirts she had never gotten around to hemming—the ones left over from 1966 and 1967. If there was an old collegiate plaid or two, they fit right into the below-the-knee range. Oh, bliss. You did not know how good it was, did you ladies—those dear dead days of

1970, when there was indeed freedom of choice reigning supreme in this blessed land of ours. In fact, Valentino was the only designer of note who showed an entire long collection. Even Jackie O was somewhat less than enthusiastic, proving once again she is no pacesetter but is, instead, one hell of a follower. Yves St. Laurent skipped the long length altogether, opting instead for a mixed *mélange* of pants and short skirts.

Ah, but things were happening up there in John Fairchild's mind. One imagines him night after night, pacing up and down his East Side co-op pondering the skirt question. Finally the moment came. *Bonnie & Clyde* be *Damned*—skirts would go down or else. "We made the decision," June Weir recalls. "We jumped right in with both feet."

But starting a fashion trend is not easy. A guy doesn't go around saying, "Hey, let's drop the hems." First there is the decision of how far to go. John Fairchild sat down at his desk—and PROMULGATED. No easy task, rest assured. The result: the ladies of the USA were stuck with—the Longuette.

June Weir, over in Paris covering the collections, first heard the word *longuette* and shuddered. Sounds like lorgnette. Sensible shoes. Supp-hose. Ha-ha laughed some of the wiser Parisiennes, who said it sounded like *plaquette*, the French word for "fly front." Fairchild had, however, made a decision. He had *promulgated*. He even ripped a page out of his personal Cassels French-English dictionary and shipped it *tout de suite* to June Weir and all those scoffers in the Paris bureau, proving for all time that *longuette* meant "long or longish; or too long." And that was exactly what Fairchild wanted. That was, most assuredly, that.

And so it came to pass that *Longuette* dropped down among us. It fell like a lead cannon ball on the populace. The Midi skirt: it pulled the polarized segments of our society together. There was America—marching headstrong and headlong into battle, mini skirts waving on high. But those brave patriots of the first year of the 1970s were doomed to failure. No war is won on the popularity of the issue alone. Vast resources are needed. Time, money, people. The power of the press. Fairchild had the power. And the press. He was waiting only for the glory.

Out came the big guns, aimed right at the Mini. Fairchild blasted away and the mini skirt fell like a virgin before the football team. "Knees Up Mother Brown" teased the headline, on March 19, 1970, while the picture was captioned "Mme. Hervé Alphand and friend." You see, Mme. A. was wearing a midi while her "friend," Jackie Onassis, was still in a mini. "Caught short again," WWD twitted Jackie, photographed striding down the street in May. "Farewell Mini O," crowed WWD, as it announced Jackie's capitulation in September. "Jackie's last stand . . . on the Mini . . . it may be the last time you see those mini knees." Finally. Fashion's leading lady had capitulated at WWD's insistence, they would have one believe. She had seen the light. Been converted. Got religion. The "knees are not getting any better, so The Ladies are planning to take cover for fall," announced a story. The picture was one of Jackie and sister, Princess Radziwill, with blowups of their knees. Can you believe it? Is nothing sacred? God—one would think at least Jackie's *knees* would be free of criticism.

Reaction was swift and merciless. *The Wall Street Journal* wrote a blistering article on the Midi. Brady took to the *David Susskind Show* to respond. "I think *The Wall Street Journal* is just great when it writes about corn futures and hog prices, but when they get into fashion they are not competent to discuss it."

David Susskind took to his television podium like John Wayne taking to his command post. He was in harm's way—tackling the mighty Midi controversy—but damn the consequences. Susskind waded in. "Despite the herculean efforts of WWD—American women simply aren't buying the Midi," he said by way of introduction. Jim Brady smiled a secret smile. (He really perked up when Susskind got to the part about WWD being "the bible of the industry.") A Texas retailer got a few laughs when he said the Midi created a lot of traffic in his store. "Women would take it home and their husbands would make them bring it back." Back and forth. Back and forth. Schlup-schlup goes the revolving door. Out a Midi, in a Midi. "Oh, the whole argument is very old and very tired," Brady would put in periodically, just for the record. It was replacing "We only report the news." On and on the argument raged. Finally David Susskind was ready. He fairly stood in his seat, leonine mane quivering with outrage. The Midi! My God, Susskind cries—"It makes small women look like dwarfs!" And those damned boots that have to be worn with it. Those damned boots—"There's something wrong with a fashion that requires boots!" He was winding up now, getting ready to lay it on. "It makes women look like Toulouse-Lautrec in drag," he snapped. My God—it was Susskind's finest hour, rivaled only by the sarcasm heaped on Women's Lib later in the summer.

"A woman under five feet five wearing a Midi looks like a dwarf walking in a trench," railed *Newsweek*. (Others less charitable figured that the dwarf was wallowing in a slit trench.) "The more rotund resemble a Good Humor bar on two sticks." For a brief moment in time, in lieu of snapping at the heels of a recalcitrant Congress, they took exception with fashion instead. Thus, *Newsweek* figured, is the central question raised: "Is the Midi an idea whose time has come, or is it the first fashion fiasco since the chemise in 1957?"

The New York *Daily News*, in an effort to protect a crumbling American political morality, even did a poll on the Midi. By fall of the Year of the Midi, 1970, *Daily News* pollsters found that a fulsome 82 percent of New York women still had their skirts above their kneecaps. The air had already crisped. The leaves were turning. The stores were getting ready for Christmas—and 82 percent of the ladies were still in kneecaps.

(One large segment of New York's more mobile population did, hesitantly at first, take to the Midi. In pre-Midi days the hookers around Times Square and Rockefeller Center normally wore their skirts somewhere up around their pierced ears. Then they took to pants. But what, many asked—many who consider our nation's whores real barometers of popular taste—would be their reaction to the Midi? Well, it was mixed at first, and then the girls figured out a way to make it work. And that's always half the fun, isn't it—making things work? Sure. They simply bought Midis that buttoned—then left the buttons undone. *Voilà*. The Midi. Not quite what John *et* Jim *et* June *et. al* had in mind, but the Midi nonetheless.)

Pete Hamill, the New York *Post* columnist who has done the most for a kind of pertinent and to-the-point journalism-of-the-emotions in his soul-wracking calls for mercy and justice for all, even took on the Midi. "The next time a girl walks down the street in a Midi you should know what many men feel. Not just that she is uninteresting in an aesthetic sense, but that the purchase of her dress or skirt also reveals something of her character. It tells us that she is frightened of her own judgment. A slave of commercially inspired taste-makers and a woman whose mind must certainly be as dull as the blah years of the 1950s which inspired her clothing." It was a cry from the heart. A mournful lament for the kind of idealism that Hamill is constantly and consistently searching for. God forbid, he cried, we should be finding ourselves in the midst of another 1950s trip.

Brady dismissed Hamill. "Hamill is a professional hand-wringer. An Irishman carried away by his own emotions."

On and on it went. Relentlessly. Strips of pictures would be run daily showing "New York Goes Longuette." "Paris Chooses Longuette." And Rome. And London. Readers were breathlessly waiting for "Nairobi Goes Longuette." Cracow. Cedar Falls. "Red Cloud, Nebraska, Goes Longuette!" (Actually, Red Cloud, Nebraska, and many of the rest of the places have been in longuettes for the last thirty years. They never bothered to raise their hemlines from the Depression.) Close readers of WWD would have caught some repeats of the pictures in those seemingly endless strips of long skirts striding out of the pages of WWD. There was even a "kiddie midi" noted.

Little by little the bastions of resistance fell and by the winter of 1970-71, Fairchild could indeed see himself standing in a sea of longuettes. Provided, of course, he (1) read his own paper; (2) did not go out on the streets. "We only report the news," Fairchild kept repeating over and over during those grim days. Like a reassuring litany. For it was no easy battle. The designers fell first and easiest. They know where it's at, baby. The manufacturers were at first confused, then they too shaped up. It was out in the buying public that the real resistance came. But even that small but brave stand against the giants had nowhere to go but down. For if the designers and manufacturers only design and manufacture longer lengths, what's a department store buyer to do? And what's a lady to do? (Well, at first they bought pants, that's what they did.)

Actually, it was a battle that need not have been fought, for logically speaking fashion had few alternatives. The Mini had gone micro and there was nowhere else it could go and avoid arrest. Down. Down. Done. What irritated most people was the heavy-handed way in which it was done. And since most women do not even know of the existence of *Women's Wear Daily*, much less its incredible influence, they seemed to be once again confronted with a faceless enemy. The Shadow of the fashion world. Once more a citizen was forced to fight Jello-O. A formless, shapeless substance that was wreaking havoc on her life, not to mention on her pocketbook and her closet. What Fairchild did was make the Midi his own personal cause. His own vendetta. Bring those goddamn hems down or else. "It was a game he played," a staffer said of those grim Midi-maniac days, "to see if he could do it. To see if he could pull it off." Well, he did it. But it was not a fair fight. It was like doing a rain dance with the clouds already building, all the while having a hose ready just in case. Only in this case it backfired a bit because the natives got restless when the Midi was all they saw raining down on them from those fashionable storm clouds hovering on their horizons. "I suppose we could have taken a much calmer approach to the Longuette," Fairchild said. But then, "that isn't our style. We approach everything like a tiger, not a cat."

As for the designers, they did not seem to mind. Their creative powers had once again been compromised but fashion being what it is today—a Big Business—they were only too happy to have the decision made by the most powerful man in the business. It saved them one hell of a selling job. After all, some of them had been flirting around with long skirts for many seasons. And it hadn't worked. Partly because the public was not ready for it, partly because the rest of the designers were not ready for it, and partly because John Fairchild and WWD were not ready for it. (Actually, John Fairchild hates both pants and the Mini. He thinks pants are "gross" and "women look like hell in them.")

Back in the privacy of their design rooms, surrounded by their own weapons—scissors, fabric swatches, assistants, color charts—even the designers were willing to take a swat or two at Fairchild, WWD, and the Midi. A gentle swat, honeyed with kind words, but a swat nonetheless. "I decidedly feel the Midi was something Fairchild took as his *cause célèbre*," said Geoffrey Beene (You remember him—he did Lynda Bird's wedding dress. Of course, you remember.) his soft little southern voice coming out like wisps of clouds on a lazy summer day.

"I do not like the Midi," Geoffrey Beene confessed in the middle of the battle. "I think it's too long. I prefer skirts just below the knee or hovering around the ankle. The Midi with boots and all that—" He shook his head, Noo-o-o-o. (After all, said designer John Weitz, "you can't get women to lengthen their skirts while nuns were shortening theirs. *Pax vobiscum* to you John Weitz.)

Up a few flights, designer Bill Blass quite candidly figured that the Midi became "the snob status fashion of all times" worn by a "small handful who want to feel they are really into the scene." Besides, he scoffed, "the vast majority want their skirts longer because they never shortened them to begin with." True. See Red Cloud, Nebraska. He mused, turning his BILL BLASS pencil around and round, reaching absently for the BILL BLASS tie he removed earlier in the morning, tugging at the collar of the BILL BLASS shirt he is wearing with his BILL BLASS suit. Yes, BILL BLASS is a designer. "The surprising thing," he said, "is the influence of a paper like *Women's Wear Daily*." Well, not really—but do go on. "It did tend to intimidate the stores. They were terrified that they would simply not be 'with it.'" Yes, yes, That's it.

Everybody agreed that the time was right for a longer skirt. But the means to this end was a case of foul play. "WWD's role in the new skirt length was that they believed to put over a fashion you have to do it in depth," Blass analyzed. "Actually, any fashion is considered unbecoming until you get used to it. Why, remember the howls of outrage at the first sight of a kneecap a few years back? My God, women were swearing they would never show their knees. But the whole essence of fashion is change. Wait and see. You'll see the leg exposed again."

Across town, John Weitz—perhaps the sexiest of all the designers and a guy who has made it straight to the altar three times—figured likewise. "This was one time *Women's Wear* engaged in tilting. They took a cause and trounced it home." As Weitz, a handsome salt-and-pepper Englishman with shoulders a girl wants to *weep* on, sees it there was never any question about skirt lengths. "Women were destined to start wearing longer skirts, but in the process their believability was sorely dented."

For those worried about Fairchild's credibility, what Weitz had to say was all too true. The Mini madness had peaked. "It's like seduction," said Bill Fine, president of Bonwit's. "Not whether a woman will go for it, but how far she'll go."

Princess Margaret (whom WWD calls "Her Drear") sailed

forth in a midi and did the movement absolutely no good at all. She looked like a leftover warship still fighting the Battle of Britain. There she was, ducks, all snugged into gray flannel, accessorized with a reptile-skin hat and matching boots. "Nothing is going to do more for the Mini," sniffed the London *Daily Mirror*'s fashion writer, Felicity Green. When Perle Mesta rumbled forth for lunch in a New York restaurant decked out in a midi, replete with picture hat and glittry chandelier earrings, Fairchild himself spotted herself and wrote the Eye piece for the next day's paper. He did not call a photographer, however, and wisely so. It would have been another Princess Margaret disaster and who needs bad press like that!

Even the WWD ranks were torn asunder. Confessed one staffer in Chicago, "I bought three—just enough to get me through while John Fairchild was in town."

There were those who took a look around and during the Midi Crisis saw an industry wading in an economic mess the likes of which they had not seen for decades. A crisis they hoped never to see again, once it was finally over. And many who should know place no small amount of the blame on John Fairchild.

Now hear this. The garment industry is no small potatoes. There are 646,000 people directly employed in the manufacture of women's clothing alone making it one of the major employers in the country. Only such behemoths as the construction trades, the steel industry, and the manufacturers of communications equipment employ more. As for manufacturing, the apparel industry is the fourth largest manufacturer in the United States.

Production figures alone are enough to send a lady to her knees in the middle of a shopping spree. Americans spend a total of $25.4 billion dollars on women's and children's apparel each and every single year. That is a lot of flashes for the old credit card. A total of 173,484,000 blouses are made each year. More than 162,696,000 dresses along with 5,680,000 suits and 92,328,000 skirts and some 19,859,000 coats.

Play around with that and you are playing around with one of the major forces, financially and sociologically, in the United States. It is definitely not child's play. When a recession strikes—whether part of a general economic pattern in the country or due to "fashion confusion"—it is serious. In 1970, unemployment in the women's garment industry was up from 5.9 percent to 8.2 percent in just two years.

"*Women's Wear Daily* began a campaign to force the Midi down on the industry," said Charles Zimmerman, vice president of the International Ladies Garment Workers' Union, the union that controls the garment industry across the country. Zimmerman is a Russian immigrant with an accent as warm and as thick as a fresh blintz. He is neat, tidy with the kind of little old man quality that makes people think of immigrant grandfathers and hard work and hard times. Indeed, that is exactly the way it was for Charles "Sasha" Zimmerman, who was born near Kiev in 1897. By 1913 he had fled Russia and the Jewish persecutions there and joined a sister already in New York. One of his first jobs in America was in the garment center as a knee-pants worker. With it came his first experience with unions, an experience that would stay with him for the next seventy-odd years. Soon after he began working, his shop—where the workers were mostly boys under the age of twenty—went out on strike. After it was settled they dumped their old union and joined the United Garment Workers. Zimmerman then discovered that out of their $7.25 union dues—squeezed out of their monthly salaries with a great deal of pain and difficulty—the union business agent was pocketing $5.00 of it. With Zimmerman leading the pack, the boys put up such a prolonged howl that the agent was sacked—something unheard of back in those early days of unionizing. Zimmerman—who was once described as the perfect union man: a blend of idealism and practical realism—has been doing that ever since then.

He is typical of the ethnic qualities the garment industry has had up until the last decade or two. Until then, the industry was primarily one of immigrants and immigrants' children. Eastern Europeans who immigrated to America and went into the only business their families knew: the garment business.

Zimmerman's office at the union overlooks the teeming turbulence of the garment industry. It is a confusing scene to the outsider, full of people and pushcarts, an endless sea of people ebbing and flowing up and down the streets and sidewalks. Racks of finished garments are being pushed by hand from manufacturer to showroom to department store to warehouse to trucks. Bolts of fabric spill out of trucks and carts. Models clutching large briefcases stride through this whole earthy scene wearing the uniform of the day, be it mini or midi, boots or cork-sole shoes, scarfs or tiny little crocheted hats. If lipstick is in, it's on. If it's out, it's off. Then the secretaries and salesmen and the unidentifiables. They swarm endlessly up and down, in and out, back and forth. "Fashion is not forced upon people," Zimmerman continued. "It took some time for the Mini to become popular—it didn't happen overnight. *Women's Wear* started their Midi campaign—I don't know why—this I cannot understand. They really are doing a great deal of damage to the industry. We suffer a lot because of this campaign of theirs. It has caused a good deal of unemployment." There. He said it right out, the V.P. of one of America's most powerful unions, the International Ladies Garment Workers' Union. OK. Fine. One man with one newspaper says he digs a longer look. How can he be held accountable for Mr. X's manufacturing concern going out of business and taking all the employees with it? To Mr. Zimmerman, and many of WWD's critics, the answer is sadly simple: "When there is so much confusion and protest against the Midi—women say they don't like it and they don't buy it, so manufacturers didn't know where to put the hemline and store buyers didn't know where to order them—WWD is advocating this thing." He leans back in his chair, raises his hand in a resigned gesture, lifts a shoulder for emphasis. "Such a bad year. We've never had such a bad year.

Workers are underemployed. Workers unemployed. It's terrible." Zimmerman is the kindly sort of man who makes you think that aside from the very real and heavy and sometimes sordid union activities—organizing, bargaining, digging, pinching, pushing, poking, and all the other daily activities of a professional union man—he worries about the human element of the business. Whether the babies are warm and the stomachs full and the hearts happy. He looks *concerned*.

The subject of *Women's Wear* has him wound up. "WWD lives in Paris," he says. "WWD is unfair to the New York fashion industry." If ever there was an American chauvinist it is Charles Zimmerman. When Zimmerman thinks of fashion he sees American flags waving and probably smells apple pie. He must carry some all-American mom in the inner space of his head, alternately getting encouragement and giving it. He is the original America Firster of the fashion industry. "It seems to me *Women's Wear* should be more interested in promoting American fashion industry," Zimmerman speculates. "Instead, what do they do? What do they do? I'll *tell* you what they do. They degrade it. They humiliate it. They tear it down. For the life of me, I can't understand it. They are really doing a great deal of damage to the American fashion industry. It is not for the union to butt into this, but I just don't understand it." He really doesn't. His head goes into his hand. A puzzle passes over his face. WWD—dumping on the garment center? Dumping on the fashion industry? DUMPING ON AMERICA! "They hurt the industry. They hurt our people. Why, there are over 200,000 people employed in the fashion industry here in New York. They are underemployed. Work two, maybe three days a week. Or the seasons are very short. Never have we had such a situation where workers run through their twenty-six weeks of unemployment. It's terrible. Terrible." The head goes back in the hand. "*Women's Wear*—it should be building up the industry. Instead, what is it doing? Tearing it down." Zimmerman gestures to a pile of clippings. "See—see what they do." The headline reads, "NY Is Rated Dud As a Fashion Hub." The story quotes the merchandise manager of a Montreal department store as he gleefully rips into the New York garment industry. Snip, snip, snip. The article cuts away. "Who is this guy anyway? A nobody. A nobody from Montreal." Another WWD story. An English merchandising man asserts, "American women are dowdy." Zimmerman waves these items like good luck charms with a hex on them.

There are others who couldn't agree more with what Charles Zimmerman is lamenting. The New York Couture Business Council, a group that represents forty-six manufacturers, is also tilting at the quixotic WWD. Formed in 1943, partly because of the blackout of fashion news from Paris and partly in response to the ILGWU's efforts to promote the "Made in New York" label, the council's major function is to represent the manufacturers in presenting two press weeks a year. During press week the member manufacturers present their collections for the hundreds of fashion editors from around the country. Out of this is generated a veritable flood of press—publicity for members, "for American" manufacturing.

Mildred Sullivan, director of the council, made a flaming speech in Omaha in June, 1970, at a gathering of newspaper fashion editors in which she charged that eighteen manufacturers had gone out of business because of the skirt length controversy. Vincent Monte-Sano, president of the council, picked up the fight a few months later when he addressed the January 1971 Press Week in New York. "The industry has achieved absolutely nothing in 1970," Monte-Sano said accusingly. "Confusion, distrust, and misguidance exist. It was a year that finds our industry in its darkest period since the Depression—a year marked by decline, indecision, and style disaster—and the consumer just wandering off doing her own thing." And who's to blame? Monte-Sano ripped off a list that would make any industry paranoid. The designers, he declared, for "letting fashion become a charade—a masquerade—a giant put-on." The union for its "head in the sand" attitudes, particularly concerning import controls (Monte-Sano felt the union was not strong enough in its support of stricter import controls). Fashion magazines for falling in line and often creating the "giant put-ons" each month. Anyone else, please? Do not go away.

Monte-Sano saved a special salvo just for—you guessed it—*Women's Wear Daily*, flatly asserting that much of "the crisis" on Seventh Avenue can be laid to WWD. "By the hypocrisy of WWD—who, hiding behind its often repeated statement, 'We only report fashions,' tried to ram, first the Maxi—a year ago—and then the Midi, down the throats of manufacturers, retailers, and the public alike. *Women's Wear* was out to prove that it could force the market in the direction it wanted. The public and Seventh Avenue be damned. It succeeded only in creating confusion, distrust, and resentment—and more publicity for itself than it could possibly buy. Nobody denies that the longer look was inevitable, but it should not have been force-fed but allowed to come down of its own volition and seek its own level—just as it did going up. The industry would have lived off this change for seasons—as it did on the Mini and other changes in the past."

Even WWD's John Fairchild agrees with the circular and cyclical nature of fashion. "Nothing is new," he asserts down there on East Twelfth Street. "Fashion operates in a circle." He swings his arms wide, almost tilting off his chair, describing a gigantic circle. Indeed there is nothing new. There are skirts and there are pants and there are dresses. They are long or short or somewhere in between. Beyond that—"it's planned obsolescence," says Jim Brady. "Fashion is change. Five years ago we went through the same problem in reverse with the Mini. Personally, I don't think any one length is aesthetically superior to another. Women just get bored wearing things the same all the time."

"The Midi had to come," Monte-Sano says, and Mildred Sullivan agrees. "The way it was reported and hammered away at—it fractured the market. The manufacturers were con-fused—this is an example of the tail trying to wag the dog. Where Fairchild tried to tell the manufacturers what to do." Monte-Sano paints a grim picture indeed of John Fairchild. "Fairchild is a Francophile," Mildred chirps in, "and I think with few exceptions he holds the American fashion industry in utter contempt." Monte-Sano picks up again. "Somebody said WWD was the cancer on the body of Seventh Avenue."

On and on the nonargument rages. Swirls around the offices like a brown fog. "I think the day has passed when people genuflect when they hear the word Paris," says Monte-Sano. "I think it's absolute crap, but just because it has a Paris label, John Fairchild still drops to his knees." So why don't the manufacturers rise up in rebellion? Throw down their scissors, march down to the Fairchild Building and string John Fairchild up with their tape measures? Stick pins in his effigy? Same old story. Fear. Paranoia. Other things to do.

Some—from the outside—have even suggested that manufacturers start their own newspaper, to compete with WWD on its own terms. In fact, Monte-Sano agrees with this far-out idea. "Right. I think the manufacturers should get ahold of some money and put out their own paper."

"The industry is too fragmented," Mildred insists. "They won't stand together and bar WWD from collections or refuse to take out advertising. They are afraid of *Women's Wear*. The manufacturers don't want to buck them and get into a battle." What's needed? A Super Organizer. An Abbie Hoffman or a Saul Alinsky. A razzle-dazzle radical to go in and shake up the designers. Shake up the manufacturers.

No sooner had WWD found itself hemmed in by the Midi Crisis than it began tootling away at other looks. Into WWD came some photos from Paris showing girls in short-shorts. SHORT-SHORTS! Shades of the 1940s. Betty Grable /on the table/. Uncle Sam Wants YOU! Rosie the Riveter. Frank Sinatra and Gene Kelly on shore leave. The Bronx is up/and the Battery's down. Oh, woweezowee. Fairchild couldn't quite go for "short-shorts." What does that mean? he wired Paris. Short skirts? Shorts? It just didn't sound right. No matter that entire generations not only wore them but would recognize the name. With utter disregard for history and tradition, John Fairchild wanted a new word. He hemmed and hawed and stewed. One day it came to him. On the subway. "HotPants!" he cried in the uptown Lexington IRT. Omigod, another one flipped out. His fellow travelers must have marveled at this well-cut and well-tailored man suddenly yelling out "Hot-Pants!" in the middle of the evening rush hour. Little did they know . . .

Then the campaign began. For weeks before the first HotPants hit the stores in New York, WWD was full of them. HotPants here. HotPants there. Everywhere HotPants. French HotPants. English HotPants. Spanish HotPants. Israeli HotPants. Maternity HotPants. Finally, the designers and the stores caught on, and another battle was won. And so it went during that year A.M.—After the Midi. HotPants, Knickers, CityPants, BootLeggers.

Jacques Kaplan did them in fur. Halston tie-dyed HotPants. Heads wore their tattered denims cut off and fraying. Grandmothers were set to crocheting HotPants. WWD chronicled The Ladies as they went shopping for HotPants. Then chronicled them as they went shopping *in* their HotPants. In satin, corduroy, suede, knit, cotton, fur. HotPants became the HotIssue. There it was again—the human thigh, exposed in all its natural beauty. Television crews, who only a few scant months before had been gloomily wading into a surfeit of Midi skirts, gleefully threw themselves into the sea of Hotpants they had been sent out to document. HotPants turned into one hell of a splash. If the country took a bath on the Midi, it was drowning in a sea of HotPants—and loving every minute of it.

As if the rest of the media were not falling lock step into line, touting its latest trend—WWD ran a full-page, HotPink ad in WWD touting you-know-who. "Who Heated up the Hotpants Scene?" the headline teased. Then came a historical list tracing WWD's involvement in HotPants.

September, 1970—WWD reports: "Short shorts make first appearance in French RTW ... the kind Betty Grable used to wear."

October, 1970— WWD coins the word "Hot-Pants"—"the newest way to play it cool for spring and summer."

November, 1970—WWD quotes top RTW manufacturers in U.S. and Europe: "HotPants—the short skirt replacement—the summer cooler."

December, 1970— In WWD: "Designers are busy making HotPants in New York, and from London to Los Angeles."

January, 1971— WWD surveys manufacturers and retailers—HotPants confirmed as a "hot item," with customers reacting quickly.

January, 1971— HotPants picked up by consumer media—*Time, Life,* ABC-TV; daily newspapers run HotPants stories.

"WWD didn't invent HotPants," the ad went on. "But we reported them first—September 22, 1970. We knew they'd be the 'hottest item' since fig leaves.... Come fall, HotPants may cool off ... but there will always be 'hot items.' It's the name of the game. Little firms get big, big firms get bigger—with items. You'll see them first in WWD."

As for HotPants—hurrah! It was merely a matter of giving the country what it wanted most: legs. Indeed, the country not only had said "No" to the Midi, but had stood there, kneecaps bared to the wrath and scorn of WWD, and yelled it out. In no uncertain terms and in the most effective polling place the American consumer has: the cash register.

The triumvirate at WWD was banking on what had been, up until that time at least, the most-known factor of all: the sheeplike acceptance of the American woman. "There are few American women with the guts to say what they want to wear and then wear it," Jim Brady said confidently at the start of the Midi Crisis. "Paris and Rome have decreed the longer skirts, and the U.S. will follow."

But lo! What did that most predictable of all known quantities—the American woman—do? She said no, that's what. Store after store around the country took a loss on the Midi as women rebelled against it. From sea to shining sea, women, and men, rallied to protest what they considered to be still another dictatorial move on the part of the fashion world to foist still another "look" down their throats. Or, in the case of the Midi, down their legs. They stayed away from the Midi in droves. The silence was deafening from one end of the country to the other. Then, when the alternative was presented to them, they jumped on HotPants like the football captain on the head cheerleader. Legs again. Skirts went up again, if indeed they had ever really gone down. Even WWD had to admit—in their own special way, of course—that all was not right down there around the ankle. Instead of referring to the heightened skirt as a m*n* skirt, WWD coined the catchword "HotSkirt."

"No faggot designer is going to tell me what to do with my legs," said one New York career girl. Well, now. "No more instant hip or Indian rip-offs," cried Blair Sabol, irreverent fashion columnist for *The Village Voice*. "Why do we need this business of a new way to look all the time? That's bullshit. We want to make our own embroidery and use the *Whole Earth Catalogue* as our *Vogue*. Fashion is a sociological movement and today—anything goes."

Indeed. Chubby fur coats, Joan Crawford platform shoes. Red lipstick, fuzzy curls. Embroidered jeans. Short skirts, long skirts. Prairie ginghams. Denim. HotPants. For a brief moment there was no uniform—a circle pin and a sweater set would have been just as appropriate as a pair of HotPants and a shrunken Jantzen ski sweater that exposed a navel and three inches of tummy. Because who's to judge what's Straight or Camp these days? Maybe that lady wearing her wig and her sweater set is really Camp. Who knows? And, thankfully for once, who cares? Wow! Freedom Now! At least for a little while.

And in the middle of it all—standing knee-deep in controversy, slogging through it like a G.I. through the mud— stood WWD. Invectives were hurled like stink bombs. Accusations were made. It was an emotional year, one that will not soon be forgotten in the annals of fashion history. At year's end, *Esquire* magazine gave *Women's Wear Daily* one of its Dubious Achievement Awards. "One maxi-hysterectomy to WWD for relentless nagging about the Longuette," read the citation. It is not hanging in the Fairchild Building, crowding out the ancestors that hang on the walls of the lobby at 7 East Twelfth.

5

To some of the uninitiated, journalism ranks right up there with sex for sheer mystery and glamour. Hot news tips. Climactic action. Muckraking in the garden of life. Ah, yes. *Front Page* and *The Name of the Game.*

Nothing—but nothing—could be further from the truth. Oh, true, some poor old *News* stiff still goes out and covers a fire and phones the story into a rewrite man. Periodically the *Times* can get to the parents of an upper-class girl murdered in a sordid Avenue B basement on the Lower East Side. But journalism today, with very few and rare exceptions, is not what some of us had the insanity to dream of when we were kids with dull pencils and Big Chief scratch pads. Journalism today is press releases and news conferences and carefully set up appointments via public relations officers. We stagger through a no man's land not so much of misinformation but, worse, of little or no information. Oh, when something pizzazzy comes along—Hippies or communes or counter-culture or riots —the mass media is tripping Carte Blanche card over coaxial cable to cover it. "I Was a Hippie For the S.F. *Examiner*." "I Smoked Dope at a CBS Pot Party." Like that.

Ah, but there are a few glimmers of that old glory shining through the murk and muck. A few intrepid reporters out slogging through their beats and racing back to knock out their stories while the second hand sweeps ever closer to deadline. A few hardy reporters who will go to almost any length to get a story. Take Brooklyn's own Jim Brady. Jungle Jim of the Fashion Forest.

Back when Jim Brady was head of the Paris bureau for *Women's Wear*, WWD was still having trouble getting photographs or sketches out of Balenciaga. He was the King of the Mountain in the Paris fashion world. *Haute couture. Haute mond. Haute merde*, baby. And if he was the King of the Mountain, Brady was Sisyphus the Boy Wonder, still trying to put WWD over the top. Balenciaga wanted none of the press. He was big and he knew it. He did not need the press and he knew it. Fashion was not the big business it is today, replete with stock mergers and diversification and boards of directors. Fashion then was a one man show and nobody knew how to run it like Balenciaga. *Sans* the press, naturally.

Just what Jim Brady needed. A challenge. A Balenciaga in his life. Somebody to run his Irish up against. Brady gets busy. Brady scouts out his location. Brady discovers there are rooms for rent in the buildings across the street from Balenciaga. *Voilà!* The rooms are *tout de suite* rented, Brady installs his crew armed with binoculars and sketch pads. While the Balenciaga *ménage* is pinning and basting and draping and hemming—Balenciaga cannot escape. The Brady Bunch across the street is peering and leering and sketching away. Haute news. Brady has broken Balenciaga.

On another occasion, Brady sent one of his girls out

disguised as a floral messenger. Destination: Balenciaga again. To see what she could see. It wasn't too fruitful—she only came back with the wedding dress details—but she did get a two-franc tip for her trouble, Brady gloats.

Hubert Givenchy was also a *haute couture* thorn in the side of WWD. He did everything wrong. Refused to give interviews. Refused to give sketch permission. Refused photographs. Often balked at seating the press altogether. Today, with the press as ubiquitous and taken-for-granted as tornados in Kansas during a hot spell, it seems strange—almost archaic—to realize there was a time when flashing a press credential was not a blank check for blanket admissions. The day before his 1964 collection, le Grand Hubert relented somewhat and decided to give WWD permission to sketch the collection that was being shown the next day for the first time. The collection for which buyers would shell out a neat $4,000 just for the privilege of putting their bottoms on those little-bitty chairs. The catch: sketching would have to be done from the street. So there was WWD artist Jack Geisinger, armed with sketch pad and pen, leaning on the hood of le Grand Hubert's *grande* Mercedes convertible which happened to be conveniently parked in front of the couture house. Givenchy's windows were open to let in some air and Fairchild only agonizes that it wasn't hotter "so the windows would have been open wider." (Later in the day, after Geisinger had been leaning and sketching with great diligence, Hubert's brother decided enough was enough. Swish went the heavy white satin curtains. What was a WWD artist to do but close up his sketch pad and fade off into the sunset.)

But wait—there is more to the continuing saga of the Fairchild boy, adrift in the Fashion Forest. As if Geisinger's body, sprawled across the Mercedes was not enough, a WWD photographer had also been lurking in the shadows on the Rue George V. Late in the afternoon when Givenchy emerged from his salon, he spotted the photographer and made a last-ditch dash to his car. Givenchy ended up in the middle of

George V, the WWD photographer in hot pursuit, while his mannequins stood on the balcony cheering—get this—the photographer. WWD got the shot, Hubert jumped into his car and shot off down the Rue.

Beyond renting rooms and investing in long-stemmed roses with which to disguise intrepid girl reporters, Fairchild and Brady—in turn—relied mainly on the American buyers who were in town. A few drinks at the Ritz, a few lunch tabs picked up at key three-star restaurants, and the boys could pick brains at leisure with pleasure. The buyers would hurry out from a collection and somehow manage to spill the beans to Brady. Sketches would be made, put on the wire and—*voilà*! Hours, days, and weeks ahead of the *Times* and the *Trib*. Months ahead of *Vogue* and *Harpers*.

In 1957 Fairchild, with his string of informers, got a sketch of Givenchy's newest silhouette and ran it on WWD's front page—weeks before it was scheduled to be shown to buyers. The new silhouette? It was callously dubbed "the Sack" by the American public. In 1960, WWD got advance word of St. Laurent's new silhouette, ran it on page one and described it as resembling "a toothpaste tube on top of a brioche."

When Princess Margaret and Lord Snowden visited the United States in 1965 (leaving a trail of unpaid bills behind them, including one for a pair of cowboy boots specially made by some little bootmaker in Arizona), John Fairchild figured an interview was in order. No way, said the Kensington Palace press aides. Just what Fairchild needed. When it was made known the Snowdens were to be guests of Philip Johnson in his New Canaan, Connecticut, glass house, the press thundered up in hordes. The Johnson frontage road was hip-deep in photographers and reporters all waiting for still another famous face whose death-bed wish would be a pox on all reporters. Jostling, pushing, shoving. Gaping pressmen who would probably much rather have been doing anything but loitering on a Connecticut roadside waiting for an English Princess and her husband. But wait—who's that guy over there? On the motorcycle. Wearing leathers. Yes—that one. My God—it's CHAUNCEY HOWELL! Vroom-vroom. There went Chauncey, at Fairchild's suggestion, roaring up to New Canaan on his BMW R60 to confront the Snowdens. Picking a rather isolated spot on the side of the road, close to the gates entering the Johnson yard, Chauncey took up his position. Up the road crawled the Royal limo. Bump, bump through the bodies. Suddenly, the limo braked to a halt. A little guy stuck his head out of the back window and started talking to Chauncey in a spirited English accent. Probably telling the nut off for showing up in motorcycle leathers to confront the Queen's sister and brother-in-law. Rather shocking. Rather *demodé*. Rather it's-not-done. But wait—what's happening? Who *is* that little guy? Talking to Chauncey. Pointing toward the house. Giving directions. Why—it's—it's—Lord Snowden, that's who—rapping with Chauncey. O, glory. *Honi soit qui mal y pense*. Seems Snowden is a motorcycle freak, see. Horsepower and leathers turn him on. Well, the upshot was that Chauncey was invited into the Johnson's glass house for a chat. And John Fairchild got one of the few exclusive interviews out of that whole Fantastic Voyage of the Royal Couple. And Chauncey had a real good time on his motorcycle. VROOM. And all that.

Then there was the time that Sal Traina, WWD photographer *extraordinaire*, spied Greta Garbo trying to walk down West Fifty-seventh Street in New York. Traina gave chase after Garbo, 35mm raised on high. The reclusive Garbo was, needless to say, reluctant. She fled. Traina followed. The chase was on. Garbo ducked into a boutique. Ditto Traina. Out zoomed Garbo. Out zoomed Traina. In and out the stores they went, first Garbo in the lead then Traina. To foil this Filmonster, Garbo shielded her face with a newspaper. The next day, WWD ran the results of this Keystone Kops chase: twenty pictures of Garbo trying to hide behind her copy of—*Women's Wear Daily*. Such is the high price of poetic justice.

WWD has always had an abiding interest in the various families who inhabit the White House, hovering around them like flies on the watermelon. The White House, however, is at times a great big shroud of secrecy. Talk about a credibility gap. It's a whole damn chasm. The Grand Canyon is a pothole compared to the White House when it wants to keep something secret from the public. Like the time WWD wanted a sketch of Lady Bird's inaugural gown, designed by John Moore. Pleading, cajoling, praying. Nothing worked. But, as John Fairchild put it, "We had to have that sketch." Mrs. Johnson swept into New York and put up at the Carlyle where, it was known, she was having fittings for the various inauguration functions. Coats and hats and dresses and suits be damned, Fairchild had to have the inaugural gown. In the end, said Fairchild, it was "very simple." Designers were sweeping in and out of the Carlyle for the fittings when one of them happened to see a sketch of what looked to be a fancy-dress ball gown lying on the floor. It had John Moore's signature and attached to it was a swatch of heavy jonquil-yellow satin. Before you could say "stop the presses," the sketch had mysteriously and miraculously found its way down to Fairchild and WWD.

There were other dustups with the Great Society. When Luci Baines was married, for instance, the White House once again got very close-mouthed about the wedding dress. Oh, there were vague statements about its being an old-fashioned creation, but nothing more specific. The release date for pictures and sketches of the wedding gown and the attendants' gowns was Saturday, the day of the wedding. Liz Carpenter, Lady Bird's press secretary, called in all the reporters assigned to cover the wedding for a briefing—a White House wedding has about as much security and intrigue and secrecy as a Laotian incursion or a Cambodian interdiction—passed out sketches of the dress and swore the whole bunch to secrecy.

And what do you know, three days before the official

White House release date, what should appear on page one of WWD but—you guessed it—a sketch of Luci's wedding gown. "I have lifted their credentials," Liz Carpenter announced. Big deal, sniffed *Women's Wear Daily*. As WWD semantically saw it, since they had purposely boycotted Liz's briefing—they were bound to no release date. Therefore, no release date existed for them to break. Since they had never been issued credentials, they claimed, how could the White House lift something that had never been given in the first place? Indeed.

Whew!

Then it all came tumbling down. The Washington *Post* reprinted what WWD had printed and the whole show was shot down. "How can I penalize the *Post*," Liz moaned. "I can't keep any paper from reprinting another paper's front page." (She was soothed in the knowledge, however, that the sketch was somewhat inaccurate and Lady Bird's ensemble was "totally inaccurate" as sketched by WWD.)

And how did WWD do it? Simple. They were on the phone as soon as the press briefing was over, picking a brain here, picking a brain there. Put them altogether, they add up to a sketch. It was a terrible brouhaha.

Not that all is frivolity and froth at the Fairchild Empire. They are not always dealing in derring-do that ranks only a hairs-breadth from pointlessness on the relevancy scale. Not at all.

When the Communist tanks rumbled into Czechoslovakia in 1968, crushing that country's brief springtime of freedom, among the few Western newsmen who got into the country and filed regular stories were two reporters from WWD. Gerald Dryanski, now WWD's Paris bureau chief, and Bernard Leason from the London bureau. According to Brady, Leason was on holiday in Majorca, completely and blissfully unreachable because he left no forwarding address and had no telephone. WWD was desperate because Leason, who once worked for Radio Free Europe, spoke Czech. Drat. And a crash Berlitz course wouldn't get a guy through a Prague menu much less across the border and into a good meaty story. Meanwhile, Dryanski was alerted and he proceeded posthaste to Vienna to prepare for the WWD assault on Czechoslovakia. And who should he bump into in Vienna? Intrepid reporter Leason, who had loyally hauled his body off the sun-drenched sands of Majorca, sharpened his pencil and his Czech, and was headed for the border. The two reporters entered the country—not as journalists, you silly people, but by posing as two textile buyers. From Minneapolis. Or Chicago, or somewhere. Tossing around such terms as "wool" and "worsted" and "suiting," the two stayed in Czechoslovakia for two weeks, filing for both the Fairchild News Service and Capital Cities Broadcasting. "They were not expelled," says Brady proudly of his two textile buyers. "They came out freely after we figured we'd milked the story for all it was worth." Oh, Fourth Estate. Oh, yeah.

Brady beams. He looks pleased. He is, after all, a self-confessed "editorial animal." (Daphne Davis of *Rags* puts it this way: "Brady is a publishing freak." Take your pick.) Life is made up of scoops. Get there first with the most. Damn the presses, full speed ahead. While other newsmen were humbling themselves at the border, there was the WWD duo running off at the mouth about textiles, all the while running down the biggest story of 1968. Five stars and a tip of the Hatlo Hat to the WWD crew.

One newsmagazine's Vienna bureau chief was somewhat less than enthusiastic over WWD's invasion of the Czechoslovakian story. In fact, he was downright rude. Snorting with derision. "*Women's Wear* and Czechoslovakia. The whole thing was absurd. They play it up for a few days and then drop it. If anybody wanted the continuing scoop on Czechoslovakia, they sure wouldn't get it in WWD. As soon as the sex appeal has gone out of a story, they drop it. Why bother in the first place? Besides, it doesn't have much to do with the garment industry, does it?"

And there's more. Like other publications, WWD wanted an interview with Mary Hemingway when Papa's *Island in the Stream* was published. But she refused all comers. Reporter Steffie Fields pursued Miss Mary to a ceremony, however, and got her to talk. When Pompidou went on his Russian visit, WWD was along even though the Russian Embassy rejected the applications of five other American journalists. Not only did WWD get a reporter aboard, they also had a photographer. Chalk up two for WWD.

Upon word of Nasser's death, Chuck Mitchelmore, WWD's Vienna bureau chief, made immediate arrangements out of Vienna to head for Cairo for the Arab leader's funeral. To his dismay he discovered that getting there was *all* the fun. Upon his arrival in Cairo he joined the hundreds of thousands of other funeral-bound journalists, mourners, curiosity-seekers, and trapped tourists. There was absolutely no room in any inn. Not to worry. Mitchelmore just bribed someone who knew someone who knew someone who knew someone with two bottles of scotch and two cartons of Kent cigarettes. God Bless America. And scotch. And Kent cigarettes.

The pranks and the barnstorming tactics may have subsided a bit these days—after all, the mission did not prove impossible. WWD was, eventually, noticed. And, eventually, some sort of grudging respect (some call it fear) was offered to the publishing upstarts from East Twelfth Street. They don't have to try harder any more. That bruised ego of the 1950s has become so healthy it often threatens to turn around and eat chunks out of itself.

Head honcho of the HotStory used to be Publisher Jim Brady. He ran the real show—the guy who came in and pushed the right buttons and pulled the right switches and activated the whole editorial machine at WWD. Arriving on the scene around nine o'clock, Brady sat at his metal desk (which was jammed head-to-head with his secretary's desk) and did his daily "critique" of WWD. Armed with a black felt-tip pen, he went over the paper making marginal notes on the current issue. "Buried" might denote an Eye piece that got lost on the page. "Brilliant" for a story on *The Wall Street Journal*. "Dull" for another. "Didn't understand" on another. Key words to tip him off when the editorial meeting started, every morning promptly at ten.

Once finished going over the paper, Brady moved across the wide-open spaces to the conference room, a cubbyhole right off the elevators, which offers a long table and some chairs and little else. Here, the senior editors of WWD, along with the art director, the photo editor, the out-of-town news director, sit down to discuss the current issue and map out stories and makeup for the next day. "I'm really a daily newspaper man," Brady once said pre-Hearst. "I can't wait to get one issue out of the way so we can start planning the next day's." Now that's a real Spencer Tracy remark, to be made with a flip-brim hat pushed back while the guy is rocking on his heels, hands in his pants pockets. Real newspaper guys talk this way with cigarettes dangling out of the corners of cynical mouths. *Front Page*. Oboy.

The editors come drifting in, and they are a decidedly mixed bag. Some are coatless, shirtsleeves wadded up in donut rolls around their elbows. Oh, right on—right out of the City Room of my mind. The City Room of all the journalistic dreamers who grew up believing printer's ink really did run in people's veins. Where reporters said such fearful First Amendment things as, "Take some dame along? Whatddya mean? I don't want any sob sister cluttering things up." Spencer Tracy and Katharine Hepburn. Ace and Scoop. One hot story after another.

Others of the Brady Bunch were a little more *au courant*. More With It. The Now Generation of journalism. High-vent suits, year-around suntans. Wide ties and Gucci loafers. You just know that in the summer they go to the Hamptons and wear their shirts unbuttoned and their loafers without socks.

It was a casual and chummy affair, with Brady doing most of the talking. He either liked the day's paper ("It has a lot of variety and a lot of snap") or he didn't ("Looks like wastebasket liner"). All very simple. Then he went through it, almost story by story. "If we talk about a designer who isn't a household word, we should identify him. Tina who? Tina Glop? That could be a pen name for Arthur Schwartz for all I know." The front-page story on Henry M. "Scoop" Jackson as possible presidential material. "No mention of the nonaggression pact for presidential hopefuls," Brady said, referring to the top-level meeting of Democratic White House aspirants held the day before. "Should have had an insert on that. Would have updated it."

Chauncey Howell was at it again. This time an interview with Walter Cronkite, Mr. CBS Himself. "Mr. Cronkite is rather upset with Chauncey's story," Brady announced. Brady was calm. Brady was cool. He would light another Between-the-Acts and smile through the smoke. "I told them to calm down. And be thankful for the story." There it is! WWD socks it to CBS! Local scrapper takes on the Big Boy from Uptown. Local Boy Makes Good! More Chauncey. "Chauncey covered a meeting at the Princeton Club last night. Gloria Steinem talked to the old grads. Chauncey said she made sense most of the time, but sometimes she got a little silly. I challenged him to go out into the alley." Smiles. Brady digs Steinem, see. Pages turn and rustle. "Doesn't look as if we talked to anybody for that retail story." The editor in question defended his writer. "It doesn't look that way. Where are the Blass quotes? Where are the Beene quotes?" Brady didn't like an Eye piece. "Terrible. We were supposed to have a reporter sitting outside that meeting to corner people when it broke up. This looks like a piece of telephone reporting." Christ! Schlock work! The Daily *Blat* approach to journalism. Whatever happened to the Good Old Days when the WWD reporter would be sitting outside the room—probably with a water glass between his ear and the wall—ready to pounce when the first victims came through the door? It gets worse. Seems Eye neglected to print a denial that hemlines were a topic of the meeting.

Things perk up. "Pages four and five were sensational." A

picture spread on London street fashions. "Look at that girl." Brady would pause. Looks at That Girl. Everyone else does, likewise. "Just look at her." Good old Jim Brady. Always an eye out for the finer things of life. "Beautiful girl." Brady might note that the *Times* liked John Wayne's latest oater, *Rio Lobo*. "Gail Rock thought it was a dog. I'll stick with Gail." That's it. Stick by Chauncey. Stick by Gail. Up yours, CBS. Up yours, *Times*. And speaking of the *Times*, June Weir has covered the opening of Giorgio di Sant'Angelo's summer collection. It was a Weir-do whiz, taking eight and a half minutes on the moving belt in the Burlington Building. One thousand people whisked past fifty of New York's most gorgeous girls wearing Giorgio's things. Rough suede, chamois, bits of fabric tucked onto body stockings and leotards. June Weir has covered the opening of Giorgio di Sant'Angelo's enthused. King of the Savages—in the Age of the Civilized Look. Brady would go along with her. "Did the *Times* cover it?" he asks. No. The *Times* covered the umpteenth collection of Mainbocher, 80. "Well—that's indicative of the *Times* to cover Mainbocher." He gave himself an assignment. "I'll have to write an Eye piece."

(And so he did. "REMEMBRANCE OF THINGS PAST: *The New York Times* has an admirable appreciation for tradition. Instead of reviewing the Sant'Angelo collection Thursday, the *Times* resusitated [sic] Remember-the-Mainbocher [sic] in its lead fashion story.")

Laos has been invaded. There was a demonstration in town the night before. "Did we know about this? Why didn't we cover it? We should be aware of these things, whether we run stories or not." Get on the ball. Shape up. No names are mentioned. They know who They are. Futures. June Weir summing up American collections for next day's issue. Big story on downtown Cleveland. "God," Brady moaned. "The whole idea of downtown Cleveland depresses me." Good solid retail story on page one. "That's it." Wrap it up. Pencils and pads are picked up. The shirtsleeves shuffled out. The high-vent suits left. Approximately fifteen minutes passed.

Back on their own turf, the editors parceled out the assignments. June's girls clustered around, a sea of midi skirts. News Editor Mort Sheinman and City Editor Si Lippa dispatched their reporters out and about town. Anthony Palmieri alerted his photographers. The day moved on. Brady, meanwhile, kept hands off. "I wander over to see what's going on later in the day—to see how page one is shaping up." But beyond that, he swore he kept his hands to himself. Late breaking stories are scheduled by the various editors themselves. Jim and John rarely acted—only reacted. Or, as in the case of the Midi or HotPants or the Civilized Look, did a little prompting. A nudge here and there. And a lot of judicious worrying.

Brady cared about his product, you see. "I'm an editorial animal." The phrase keeps coming back. He refers to his publishing days at WWD as "the six years I had WWD." It sounds like a disease. He worried over it, brooded over it. A mother hen with a black felt-tip pen. Every negative remark must have brought a prick of pain to this boy from Sheepshead Bay. It was *his* newspaper.

In addition to those daily critiques of the paper, Brady sat down on Friday and knocked out a weekly critique. A sort of *My Weekly Reader* of WWD's pluses and minuses. Some noted a late-starting change in the Brady manner. "He got very kind at the end," says one of the reporters. And in the past? "A real bastard. Sometimes."

The cover memo for the critique of the week of January 18 noted that "both the editor and the publisher were out of town last week and the paper looked better than ever. No connection, of course." See. Jim Brady is no ogre. Didja get that cozy humor? Camaraderie just oozing out. But there's more. "There will be a publisher's report this week, but then I will be in Paris and will skip a week. (Loud chorus of huzzahs off stage.)" Oh, God—journalism school never said it would be like this. There were supposed to be Bad Guys running newspapers. Tough guys who made the girls cry and grown men take refuge in corner bars. Who is this guy who can talk about a "loud chorus of huzzahs off stage."

And get this. "Must mention Chauncey Howell's piece on Mailer. I thought it splendid. Obviously it could have been written straight and could have been fine that way. Chauncey chose to be Chauncey. Personally I thought it came off. Was Mailer charmed? Who knows." Who cares. Who gives a damn about what Mailer thought—Brady liked it. Hushed murmurings around the office. "Psssst—Brady liked it. Chauncey, baby, you're in."

And the next week. "You would not believe the popularity of HotPants in Paris. But you gotta have legs."

Jim Brady is a GoodGuy!

But all was not sweetness and light when Brady finally got into critiquing each issue in this weekly report. "Focus on seniority system in Congress badly needed editing. Lively writing but shouted for control. . . . Story would have been so much more effective if edited into restraint."

"Marty Gottfried liked a play. Why not put it on page one."

"Ossie Clark story by London just so-so. Exciting, strange guy made to sound dull."

"Backpage . . . a bit pious toward the end. Sounds like recent TV mush on Vinny Lombardi."

"Backpage on [photographer] Arnaud de Rosnay . . . Arnaud's a bad little boy and story should have been more wicked."

"We seem sometimes to forget that the element of time is vital to daily newspapering. Today's page-one interview with Givenchy, exclusive and a week in advance of his show, makes no mention of that fact. Yesterday the page-one Valentino sketch was two days before the competition yet we did not so indicate."

"People really did care about Jim Brady," says one reporter. "His Newsletter was the ultimate status symbol around the office. People wrote specifically for him—hoping they'd get a good mention in the Newsletter. Very competitive." Others thought it was all a big joke.

Brady is probably right about himself. He most likely is an editorial animal. He knew every word in his paper. Then, it was on to the next day. East Lynn. A one-night stand, then on to something new and different.

"Several of the Eye pieces read like the Woonsocket *Call*," he complained on September 28. "Stroud's story on Nixons had no angle you couldn't find in a wire service report." A mental shrug. Oh well—"Can't win 'em all." Next. "Eye full of typos. 'Tout Paris' becomes 'toui Paris.' Sounds like someone is spitting." And then. "WWD ran Cairo sidehead on Nasser successor. Phony journalism this. We picked up UPI cable, ran it as our own. This isn't WWD practice."

The load was not always heavy, a burden to be borne through the publisher's day, carried with him to La Grenouille or Le Club or Elaine's. No, there were bright spots. Moments of joy to lift the spirits of the most hassled of publishers. "Gottfried's review provocative, gutsy. No critic doing better theater stuff than Martin these days."

Meanwhile, back on page one, "Picture of those Russian fashion leaders a delight. No wonder Brezhnev is difficult when he has Mrs. Brezhnev to come home to."

Well, it might not be *The New York Times*. But then again, it isn't the Woonsocket *Call*, either. Maybe working for WWD is like spinach and squash and rice and all those hateful childhood foods that Mom was always passing down the table to you. Maybe you learn to live with them. Or maybe it's like pizza and egg rolls and blood sausage—an acquired taste. Who knows—after a while, a reporter might just come to love the Bra and Girdle beat. Or Accessories. Or Pantyhose.

(Loud chorus of boos offstage, gradually replaced by a single clear huzzah from a guy named Brady, now residing uptown in the bosom of Mother Hearst.)

6

There are those among us who, for one reason or another, suffer from an incredible case of rampant insecurity. There are people who, unless guided (some would say shoved) into the proper decisions, might never make those all-important decisions in life. Where to eat. Where to shop. What to buy. Imagine getting up every morning not knowing what to do for the rest of the day. Not knowing whether to eat Here. Or There. Not knowing whether to shop Here. Or There. Not knowing whether to buy This. Or That. Face it—the decisions in Manhattan are endless. There are over 22,000 restaurants. Nearly 1,500 shops and stores selling ladies' goodies. And a selection of merchandise unrivaled. New York is the Sears, Roebuck catalogue come true. A person could go absolutely stark in New York just from the sheer overwhelming amount of decision-making that confronts one. Or, worse, reduced to an immobile mass of indecision that sits quivering and cowering unable to choose between Here and There. This and That. O, woe, New York.

But wait—there is hope. There is salvation. New York's Great Black and White Hope comes rolling off a New Jersey offset press five nights a week except holidays, Saturdays, and Sundays. Hooray. *Women's Wear Daily* tells all. Step right up and read all about it. Psssst—wanna good French restaurant? Stick by me, baby.

Most of WWD's helpful how-to-do-it (and where-to-do-it) hints are contained in the Eye and Eye View pages. Additionally, these are probably WWD's most controversial pages—and certainly those claiming the most outside attention for WWD. Edited by Peter Davis Dibble, who used to share some of the show biz assignments with Rex Reed, these two pages are nothing more than a pizzazzy potpourri of gossip, conversations overheard, short interviews, and minuscule pictures. They look very much like the Class Prophecy pages in a school yearbook with one and two-inch copy blocks (it doesn't take much more than that to get a rumor started, does it?) and pictures demanding either 20/20 vision or a pocket magnifier.

It was Eye that took off after Jackie O, chiding her for that "white strapless bra under her black T-shirt. How can a woman who spends all that money on all those clothes miss on something like that?"

"Peter was a great force in shaping the bitchy quality that Eye has," swears Daphne Davis, a *Rags* editor who keeps a sharp cynical eye peeled on the Establishment's fashion press. "Prodded along by John, of course."

"Peter Davis Dibble is such a prima donna," says one female on the staff. "He can be such a bastard. He actually has the balls to sit down and start teaching experienced reporters how to write that drivel for the Eye pages." Drivel. Dibble. Peter Davis Drivel? But there is a way to that man's heart, girls. "If you give him the same bullshit he gives you, you're OK."

For Ethel Scull this special drop of venom in the Eye: "Ethel Scull, of the taxi-strike Sculls, thought she'd upstage Mr. and Mrs. George Zauderer's dinner-dance . . . at the Metropolitan Club Sunday night by showing up in a black satin Body Stocking and ammunition belt. 'It's a cartridge belt, dear,' said hotshot Ethel. But no one really cared too much, they'd all seen it somewhere else before." Like that. (In Ethel's defense: That was no body stocking, it was a jump suit. It made the poor woman sound like a satin-clad Barbarella.)

And get this pot shot at Jackie O: "DROOPY DRAWERS: Jackie O went fur shopping Monday in New York at Maximilian. She's still wearing those pants for day. It's a nice costume, but really Jackie O . . . with all the time and effort you put into your wardrobe, can't you wear higher heels, or have those pants shortened so they don't droop like that?" Tsk. Tsk. Indeed, Jackie. Why do you cause WWD so much consternation? Don't you know they probably stay awake nights just so they can practice Freedom of the Press on you? Wondering whether you are out with your white bra under your black sweater? Or with your drawers drooping? God knows what you'll be up to next, girlie-O. Honestly.

Poor lady. It has gotten so she can hardly stagger up Madison Avenue under a load of expensive boxes without having WWD in there to make note of it. "MISTAKEN ID," read an Eye piece. "Madison Avenue people watchers are still chuckling about Jackie O walking down the street last week, loaded with red packages, but never turning her head left or right as everyone watched her. . . . She quickly got into a big black chauffeured car. But got out just as quickly. Seems it was the wrong one. Hers was parked across the street."

It was "O Week in Paris," WWD tootled one summer. There they were, Jackie O and Daddy O, dining at Maxim's. "Jackie flashed her profile and her ruby earrings" and "Daddy O his homely and endearing teeth." Yes, WWD re-stated a bit later on, "Daddy O is as homely as a frog." Jackie then did some shopping at Givenchy and there was the WWD photog, standing outside on the sidewalk snapping away. "At Chez Givenchy she preferred to try on the boutique things downstairs near the glass door rather than out of sight upstairs," WWD noted. And get this: "Sometimes in the store she appeared to be imitating the gestures of mannequins." Lordy, all those people who waste their time reading secretary's memoirs and nanny's memoirs and nurse's memoirs. Unshackle yourselves from a world of expensive hard-cover books. Read WWD instead. You even get pictures. And philosophical observations: "People are noticing how much Jackie O is starting to look like Maria Callas in AP's most recent photo from London," WWD mused one day, stretching a point like an overdrawn rubber band.

"Jackie O was all smiles as she breezed through the Pierre lobby Monday after a ninety-minute shopping session with Valentino," WWD noted last winter on page one with an accompanying three-picture spread of Jackie O striding through that lobby. But, WWD wanted to know, "does she really need more clothes when all New Yorkers ever see her in are those perennial pants, a turtleneck and one of her many coats?" Now there's the problem: what does she do with all those clothes? WWD confesses to being absolutely intrigued with this aspect of the world's most renowned SuperShopper: where *does* she wear them all? WWD wonders and ponders and asks interior questions and, finally, comes right out and asks it in public. Sadly, there is no answer forthcoming.

But there are other things. In 1969, Toni Kosover (her) and Denis Sheahan (him) collaborated on a two-page article on—vaginal sprays. Even Jackie O pales a bit in comparison. "What could be more artful than a sweet smelling vagina?" the two asked. Approximately 82,000 jaws must have dropped down and then gone up for grabs. It was a straightforward piece on the vagina. "Without a doubt," the two figured, "the subject of a woman's vagina has become a contentious area for manufacturers, advertisers, broadcasters, and everyone connected with making money out of it." These two were blowing the whistle on the vagina interests! "Let's face it, people are still uptight about discussing the vagina even if it is deodorized." By the end of the lengthy article, Toni and Denis quoted a Revlon spokesman saying, "We have a deodorant for men, which works for the male crotch, too."

Moving right along, Peter Davis Dibble and his Eye pages got hold of a confidential memo from Helen Gurley Brown, editor of *Cosmopolitan* magazine, on the subject of—ready?—breast manipulation. "We are doing an article," wrote Helen, "on how men should treat women's breasts in love-making. It will either help us sell another hundred thousand copies or stop publication of *Cosmopolitan* ALTO-GETHER!" She then asked for help and suggestions. "What pleases you in terms of having breasts caressed? What do you think men do that is wrong." Then. . . . "Any personal experiences you've had yourself . . . where somebody didn't *like* having her bosom caressed and then she was able to begin enjoying it?" Well, Dibble took one glance at this memo and ran with it. It hit the Eye pages and all over town people were doubling up with laughter. Curling up with envy. Falling apart. All but Helen, that is. While others around her were breaking up, she supposedly took one look at Eye and broke down. Needless to say, the Cosmo girl is still waiting for an article on breast beating.

For the first-timer, running full-tilt into WWD, especially the Eye pages, the experience is very much like a rat caught in The Maze. Puzzling, confusing, frustrating. You've got to know the language. Then, little by little, the maze becomes clearer. *Voilà!* A body can pick his way with ease through wry that is Eye:

BP: Beautiful People. Classy folks who spend their money in the right places, and generally meet John Fairchild's ever-changing criteria on what makes a P really B. (Jim Brady figures BPs are "people who take themselves very seriously. They consider themselves to be BPs. It's all very tongue-in-cheek; a big joke with us.")

FV: Fashion Victim. A woman who lets fashion wear her, instead of vice-versa. One who follows fads instead of dressing for herself. Or, as one manufacturer put it, "John Fairchild's opinion of someone who doesn't know her ass from a hole in the ground." Fashion-wise, that is.

SM: Social Moth. Best described in the words of that anonymous anal-oriented manufacturer (see FV): "An ass-kisser," i.e., one who is trying to brash his/her way into Society via money, connections, money, money. Does not really have the pizzazz to be the light bulb, so to speak.

Lunch Bunch or Ladies: BPs who regularly lunch at New York's better restaurants.

Restaurant X: Usually La Grenouille, a real nifty eatery.

Restaurant Y: The other zippy places for the BPs to have lunch. La Seine, Lafayette, Orsini's, La Caravelle. Sometimes Le Pavillon. Never, *never* Your Father's Moustache.

Restaurant Z: Usually La Côte Basque (sometimes these will be switched in a sort of test of the BPs to see if they really know where they have had lunch).

Restaurant Le Poop (or LeP or just plain Le): Le Pavillon, when it is not referred to by its full and proper name—Le Pavillon—or as Restaurant Y.

GOM: Grand Old Man. Snotty reference to designer Norman Norell.

VOM: Likewise snotty reference to designer Mainbocher, who is often referred to as "Remember the Mainbocher."

YOM: Young Old Man, meaning James Galanos. Whom they love. This year.

Mr. Fashion Right: Bill Blass.

Daddy O: Aristotle Onassis, Greek shipping magnate married to the former Jacqueline Bouvier Kennedy.

Jackie O: The former Jacqueline Bouvier Kennedy, now married to Greek shipping magnate. Daddy O (see above).

Her Drear: Princess Margaret of Britain.

Her Efficiency: Lady Bird Johnson during her term in the White House.

Her Goodiness: Pat Nixon, wife of the best friend Bebe Rebozo ever had.

Her Happiness: Wife of Albany's Master Builder, Nelson Rockefeller.

Queen Mother: Rose Kennedy.

Sexy Rexy: Rex Reed.

Midi: Midcalf length.

Longuette: Anything South of the kneecap.

HotPants: What Betty Grable wore on the table.

HotSkirt: Formerly called a Mini.

Tough Chic: Some might say Dykey. Others just see a heavy, masculine look, full of belts, nailheads, welt seaming.

SA: Seventh Avenue, center of the garment industry. The Street where most of the manufacturers and designers have offices and showrooms. (Does *not* stand for Sex Appeal. Necessarily.)

RTW: Ready-to-wear.

Civilized Clothes: What we got when we threw the Ethnic Look out of our closets and ended up with shirtwaist dresses and blazers.

All this fractured franglais once prompted Marylin Bender of the *Times* to write that *"Women's Wear* is larded with language that can easily be mastered by dropouts from freshman French who are confident because the stewardesses on Air France and the hall porter at the Plaza Athénée" can understand them perfectly.

But through it all, WWD remains consistent and faithful to what surely must be an interior motto, inscribed in printer's ink on the foreheads of the faithful down on East Twelfth Street. "Keep America Beautiful." A sort of jingoistic journalism that must keep WWD in a constant swivet, forcing it to stagger from one person to another, and publicly point out faults and *faux pas*. WWD, the watchdog of the fashionable public. Quivering at the end of its tether over hemlines and necklines. Bra straps and boot heels.

There are those lucky souls in the world, born unto the Middle Class in Middle America, who grew up being warned never to venture off the front porch without clean underwear because, after all, there might be an accident. And what would the nurses in the emergency ward think? And clean underwear of course conjured up smooth legs and fresh armpits. And what else was needed to make it through the Emergency Room of the World. But face it—eventually most people must leave the security of the front porch for the larger Lawn of Life, replete with perils and pitfalls and no one there to warn of clean underwear and satin-smooth armpits. Oh, what now America? Must we face a future of uncertainty? Damned forever to live under the specter of dirty linens? Fear not. *Women's Wear Daily* is out there, keeping watch. Keeping tabs.

America, how fortunate you are. Some countries must stagger around under the weight of ignorance, forever buried in the pit of know-nothingness. Blind to the wondrous joys of revelation and truth. While here, we in the U.S. of A. are staggering only under the all-powerful weight of WWD, the watchdog that is watching YOU. The super-snooper dedicated to the proposition that all people are up for grabs and if WWD should happen to hit where it hurts, you had damned well better not let out a yelp of pain because they'd squeeze just that much harder the next time. There are no alternatives, folks.

But it is a hell of a burden, you must admit. Coining phrases, dropping names. When *Women's Wear Daily* puts a cutline under a picture, that is usually exactly what it is—a cut line. Princess Margaret became "Her Drear" because, as Jim Brady explained. "The British Royal Family has a very old and honorable tradition of being dowdily dressed and Margaret is very loyal to that tradition. Margaret is dreary whatever she wears." Brady figured Pat Nixon is a real Goody Two-

Shoes, dismissed the Nixon daughters as being too dull to even think about. Would you wonder why WWD is sometimes called "The Godfather" of its industry?

Perhaps the sharpest cut of all came on September 1 of 1970. On September 1, WWD unleashed its list of "Fashion Victims." Former BPs all, it was a little like that cheerful Boy Scout helping the old lady across the street—and then mugging her when he got curbside.

"I'd been visiting with some very social friends," John Fairchild recalled when questioned about the Fashion Victim list. "And they were laughing and giggling about a list of fashion victims they had going. And I thought, what an idea for a feature. Call it 'Fashion Victims.'" Fairchild raced back to the office and fired off a salvo aimed directly at the fashion bombs of America. Boom-Boom-Boom. It was a two-page spread with an enormous black headline announcing that these ladies were, indeed, WWD's chosen FASHION VICTIMS. It was a screaming, blaring headline.

"Clothes do not make the woman," WWD somberly wrote on that day of infamy. "Some women think so and spend a fortune trying to prove it. But they end up as the Fashion Victim. Instead of being simply well dressed they become walking billboards for all the latest status symbols. They allow fashion to wear them rather than wearing the fashions that suit them." WWD then proceeded not only to list their chosen Fashion Victims, but to print pictures of each of them accompanied by extremely snide captions, thus reducing each of the ladies to the status of a throwaway gag. The punch line at the end of a very dirty joke.

Included in WWD's list were Mary Lou Whitney dubbed "Horse Feathers" in reference to the stable of racing horses kept by the Whitneys at their farm in Lexington, Kentucky; Lyn Revson, wife of Revlon president, Charles Revson, was *nom-de-plume*d "Ultima II," which is not only the name of a Revlon cosmetic line but also the name of the Revsons' sumptuous yacht; Ethel Scull, who allowed her summer house in Southampton to be used for a fund-raising benefit for the

Women's Liberation movement, was dubbed "Liberated"; Gloria Vanderbilt Cooper, a rich lady who is also a very well-known professional artist, earned the sobriquet "Collage" (That reference both to her then-current artistic interests and to the way she had of dressing, which was to put herself together with bits and pieces of clothing and accessories which, taken as a whole, formed an entity. See?); Countess de Romanones, the former Aline Griffith of Pearl River, New Jersey, and now married to the Spanish count of the same name (de Romanones) became "Spanish Moth"; Barbra Streisand, whose FV picture was a rear-view shot of her infamous Scassi see-through creation worn for the 1969 Academy Awards ceremony, was captioned "On a Clear Day You Can See Forever." Perhaps the cruelest cut of all was the naming of Margaret Truman Daniels to the list. Of being, in WWD's own words, a "walking billboard for all the latest status symbols." On and on the list went. Liz Burton became "Diamond Lil." Joan Kennedy was "The Golden Girl." Former *Harper's* fashion editor and Best Dressed Winner D. D. Ryan was "Tough Chic."

To John Fairchild and Jim Brady it was a big joke. When asked whether he had a guilty conscience over such an act, Fairchild merely laughed and scoffed. "Oh, of course not. Why should I? It was all a big joke. All very funny." Hmm-m-m? "Nonsense. They knew it was all a joke." Yeah, sure. Tell that to the lady whose face crumpled up six months later when she was asked about it. "John Fairchild is a very cruel man," she said, sitting in her sprawling East Side apartment. "We all know he's bitchy. We all know he's cruel. I subscribe to WWD but only out of self-protection. I suppose I would be better off if I didn't know what he was saying about me—maybe I'm just a raging sado-masochist to read it all the time—but somehow I feel I can protect myself if I know what is being said. Also—it's such a relief when *nothing* is said and believe me—I want to know when nothing is said so I can be relieved!" Her face uncrumpled a bit and she mustered up a wan if not wary smile.

Well, let's have a list. "So we all sat down and we all threw in names. We vetoed one another and the names we agreed upon stayed on the list," explained Fairchild. Only in America could a list of Fashion Victims be arrived at in such a democratic way. Do you think Hanoi would allow freedom of choice such as this? Brady saw nothing wrong with singling these Ladies out for this special drop of venom. "In fact, I'd forgotten about the list—I forget about all our lists, something new is always coming along—and one day I had lunch with one of them." One of Them. A Fashion Victim. *Quelle* courage, to walk into a restaurant with One of Them. An FV who lets fashion wear her instead of vice-versa. God knows what might have been wearing her to lunch that day. Repeat: *quelle* courage, Brady. "I asked her how she was and she said she hadn't been well." And what might the matter be, dear. "I've been suffering from Fashion Victim-itis," she told him.

Shortly after FVitis, Eye instituted something called "L'Institut de l'Ennui" in which WWD listed, in Brady's words, "the people we thought were the most boring people we knew." High on the list was John Weitz, who took one look at his name on the list and sent off a "long and florid letter—in French" to Brady. Don't you think Weitz was the littlest bit um, er—upset by the inclusion of his name on the list of those somewhat less-than-sacred members of L'Institut de l'Ennui? "Nonsense—John Weitz has a terrific sense of humor," said Brady. Besides, "he's a publicity hound."

(Weitz had his one-uppance after that l'Ennui come-uppance, though. A typo in the Eye column later referred to New Jimmy's in Paris as "Jew Jimmy's." Aha! Another letter from Weitz, this time accusing Brady of trying to "reopen the Dreyfus case." *J'accuse*, J.B.)

Even the younger generation is not safe from WWD. When Prince Charles and Princess Anne made a Royal Visit to the United States, one WWD headline read "Prince Charming and the Petulant Princess." The story pointed out that "the Princess was miserable" as she snubbed reporters and was in general a Royal pain in the arse who "looked consistently as if her jaw had been wired shut." Even the Royal lady-in-waiting came in for a load. WWD characterized her looking "as though she were chewing sourballs." And a Bronx cheer to you, too, ducks.

Now Caroline Kennedy may be spared a great many things simply by being the daughter of Jackie. Plus having Aristotle Onassis as a stepfather along with a phalanx of bodyguards, private secretaries, and Money available for this and that. Those little things that may crop up in life. She has been having expert skin treatments at Lazlo's since she was six so she probably won't have to worry about teenage skin problems. Or overlapping teeth. Or the frizzies. All those common complaints of most teenage girls around the country. But one thing Caroline Kennedy is not spared is a little nudging now and then from WWD. Something the Silent Majority of teenagers around the country will never have to worry about. There she was, off on an innocent ski trip with other members of the Clan. There was snow and sun and bowls of chili—and WWD. "Caroline Kennedy obviously doesn't go along with the democratic way," WWD noted in a two-page picture on the skiing Kennedys. "She avoided the chair lift lines by moving right up front, to no one's amusement." Oh, well, Caroline—you're just sharing WWD's burden with Mom and Princess Anne. The piece finished with still another swack: "What can you do?" asked one irate skier. "They really fit in here. And besides, all together they probably outnumber us." Most likely.

Few if any politicians running for public office give much thought to the effects of WWD on their wives and daughters. This is too bad. This should be uppermost in the minds of all would-be political contenders. They should check this off in the big check list in the mind: Can the females in my family stand up under WWD? After Tricia Nixon's Easter 1971 picture was flashed around the country, WWD had this to say: "TRICIA'S FASHION IMAGE: Tricia Nixon, 25-year-old daughter of the President, has been named 'one of the best dressed children in America'. . . . Miss Nixon has been nominated by a group of children's wear manufacturers for their 1971 'Goody Two-Shoes' award . . . said one manufacturer, 'She dresses as children should. She's definitely one of the best dressed subteens in the country.' "

Shortly before it laid the FVs on the world, WWD created the Sensuous Woman. "The Sensuous Woman," said WWD on July 13, 1970 (those dumb old Fashion Victims should have known what was coming but do you think they shaped up. Christ—they had a good two months to get themselves in shape. You cannot say, therefore, that WWD did not give them fair warning) "has it but doesn't flaunt it—she would never buy ostentatious diamonds like Liz Taylor. She may own a yacht manned by a lively young crew, but she'd never have bibb lettuce flown to her boat as Jackie O does." Tsk. And shame.

And for the runners up—those girls who were close to making the list—WWD printed a handy little advice section on how they too could become and remain a Sensuous Woman. Ah, now don't you fret little missy—Big Daddy is here to tell you about it. "Gloria Guinness, if only she would leave those strict little Balenciagas in the closet and let that Latin blood run wild." And "C. Z. Guest, if only she would put those Mainbochers out to pasture and get off her horse."

The one incredibly endearing thing about owning, or at least controlling, the company you work for is the freedom that it allows you. Oh, sure there are those pesky libel and slander laws. The threat of a source suddenly and constantly being in conference and unavailable. All of which could escalate to make you afraid to get on an elevator, cross the street, or eat soup. But beyond that, there is still the warmingly wonderful idea that this product is all yours. Yours to be toyed with, tested, tinkered with. And Fairchild uses WWD like a kid with a fresh supply of Lincoln Logs, constantly puttering and poking and fiddling and fixing.

When *Time* correspondent Peter Forbath accompanied

Fairchild to Bermuda as part of the reporting for the Fairchild cover story (*Time*, September 14, 1970) the two men plunged deep into a discussion of how sloppy airline food service was becoming. Harried stewardesses. Boring food. Little plastic knives and forks. Paper napkins. Not much better than customers at a Bickford's. Forbath allowed as how airlines ought to get their comeuppance every now and again for treating people like cattle. A few days later Fairchild showed Forbath an item in WWD sniping at the airlines for their less-than-inspired service and fare.

Fairchild is a confessed Chanel lover. Through all the fads and fancies "Chanel stayed pure," he says. "Chanel never got fooled by the Peasant look or the Rich Hippie look or the Savage look. Chanel was always so—so—Civilized." Thus, when Freddie Brisson and Alan Jay Lerner got together and gave birth to *Coco*, Fairchild rushed off to a preview and scooped his drama critic by running this Eye piece: "Hepburn is fabulous. But the show itself is a bore. The music isn't much. The lyrics are sometimes amusing, but those terrible little movie clips of Chanel's early life bug you. *Coco* is Katharine Hepburn's show, not Mlle. Chanel's. It's a Seventh Avenue knockoff rather than an original Chanel. Even the clothes (by Beaton) don't look Chanel." See—even if you didn't grow up to be a drama critic, it doesn't matter. Just as long as you own the newspaper.

Gossip is the True Grit of the fashion world. Like the Jolly Green Giant, gossip grows and flourishes and blossoms—and eventually gets published in *Women's Wear Daily*.

RUMOR! "Charlotte Ford, who is celebrating her birthday today, reportedly is about to announce her engagement to Tony Forstmann, a broker."

Then the denial: "THE TRUTH. Charlotte Ford, visiting her mother in Los Angeles for the week, says her reported engagement to stockbroker Tony Forstmann 'is news to me. It's absolutely ridiculous.' " Print it. Deny it. Print it. It could go on forever.

RUMOR! "Designer Chester Weinberg has been spotted carrying pins into 530 SA and the SA grapevine reports Chester and brother Sidney will be on their own come fall. Although Chester is 'no comment' on the matter, Eye hears they're in the final stages of dickering with the Parnes boys . . . who reportedly have Chuck Howard up for grabs." That was a two-for-one shot in the dark.

RUMOR! "Paris is full of rumors about the Boussac empire. The latest is Boussac will unload the rest of Dior to Moet & Chandon and that Chandon will keep the rtw operation but drop the couture operation."

RUMOR! "In London they're saying that Mick Jagger has finally decided to marry. The bride, they say, is a South American beauty—Bianca de Nacias—who used to be friendly with Michael Caine and Eddy Barclay."

RUMOR! "Truman Capote is said to be thinking about selling his Palm Springs home."

Then there was the time a magazine fashion editor attended an East Side party also graced by Rudolf Nureyev, who arrived breathless and flushed after a rousing performance, wearing a black leather jacket and "escorted by five young men who couldn't keep their eyes off him." When the fashion editor asked Rudi if he would pose in a fur coat for her magazine, Rudi allowed as how he would and said he just loved leopard. She responded that their publication didn't run pictures of furs from animals who were becoming threatened with extinction but "would sable, mink, or otter be okay?" Rudi drew himself up inside his black leather jacket and asked her "Would pubic hair be all right?" Whereupon the fashion editor told him, "It takes too long." Fairchild heard the story from the editor, laughed himself into a fair fit, and ran it.

Those who didn't know Fairchild and Brady and their own particular brand of brashness might have figured that after the Genesco dustup of 1965, the Rumors Wanted sign would have gone down from WWD. Not on your life.

"Bonwit Teller here is scouting the nation's retail scent

[sic] for a topflight merchant to assist William Fine," WWD stated flatly one front page in 1971. Two paragraphs later they quoted Fine as saying, "All this talk about Bonwit Teller is a lot of childishness. Someone is trying to put together a number of unrelated pieces. It has become a bore to keep denying these reports because they are not true." See how it works? WWD hears rumors. WWD checks rumor out. Round and round it goes. The old circle game, WWD style.

WWD isn't the only Fairchild publication to deal in rumors—and have to deal with the aftermath of rumors. "Your standards of journalistic responsibility amaze me," Eugene N. Beesley, president of Eli Lilly & Co. said in a telegram to the late *Drug News Weekly* in 1964. This was after DNW printed the rumor that Lilly was contemplating selling its pharmaceutical products directly to retail drug chains. This was heady news to the drug industry and the Lilly Company was outraged. "Had your front page story been cast as reflections of a gossip columnist, that would have been one thing; but to print the rumors which you did as news 'reliably learned' is quite another."

"If there is a rumor running around the market, it should be made available to our readers," one Fairchild publisher once told *The Wall Street Journal*. "We'll usually print it." Even when it's denied, he said.

Sometimes the imagination down at the Fairchild Building runs amok, though. Take the case of the East Coast blackout in 1965. When the lights came back on, WWD ran a front page story based on a rumor they had gleaned that the power failure was due to a "test of a revolutionary weapon to destroy enemy missiles." Leapin' Lizards! WWD readers must have figured The End had come. As WWD called the mis-shot, it was "a highly classified project called 'Fireball'" which in all likelihood drained the East of its power by siphoning off the current in order to shoot electric beams into space. The Pentagon—naturally—denied all. Sci-fi buffs were transported. The down-to-earth types slapped their thighs and their guffaws were heard echoing eerily up and down Seventh Avenue. And Fairchild? "We overplayed it," he said at the time. "It should have been treated as only a theory and it didn't deserve page one."

When Jim Brady hustled off to Paris to help cover the 1971 spring collections, he not only reviewed St. Laurent's clothes, but he did a quick rundown on Yves's friends as well. "Look around the Maison St. Laurent," Brady wrote, "at the subcultural influences at work on a sensitive, creative person.

"There standing in a corner of the salon, shooting pictures during the collection is a young man called José Vilela. He's obsessed by stars, wears them all over the clothes he designs for himself. St. Laurent's collection has been full of stars since José left New York and came to live in Paris."

And more friends. "Lulu de la Falaise, whose image is a sort of marked down version of Marisa Berenson" plus a "young Cuban ballet dancer" along with a few others "help form his [Yves's] view of the world." Little wonder then that "the house which used to boast the most beautiful mannequins in the world now seems to be staffed by consumptive versions of 'the little match girl.' "

When the 1971 Paris collections were over and the dust had settled, WWD re-stated its new fashion position: that we were in for a period of Civilized Clothes for the Civilized Woman. "Women are secure enough to wear clothes that are natural and not some figment of a designer's imagination," wrote WWD. "What woman wants to be an Indian except an Indian? What woman wants to be a whore in public except a whore? What woman wants to be a man except...?"

Out of all this highly personal and subjective journalism have come a number of notable personal feuds between WWD and various individuals in and around the fashion world. Most remarkable among them was the one-and-a-half-year feud with designer Bill Blass. During those eighteen long, dreary months

Blass was, in his own words, *persona non grata* at WWD. Prior to that time, relations between the publication and Blass were warm and cozy. They would share lunches at Restaurant X and Blass would see that WWD got good seats at his showings. Nobody is saying for sure how the falling-apart occurred but the fallout was thick and heavy. WWD's version is that through a simple clerical error, the paper was dropped from Blass's invitation list and, therefore, since they weren't invited to collections, how could they cover them? (No matter that they covered Givenchy even though he locked them out for eight years.) The Seventh Avenue version is that one of Blass's colleagues told June Weir that he, Blass, had willfully withheld a yummy piece of gossip from WWD in addition to which he spoke out and damned the paper in front of other people. It is difficult to determine which of Blass's supposed sins is the worse—withholding information or proffering an opinion.

Sometimes it seems that those Out of Favor are far more numerous than those who are In Favor. Mollie Parnis is dubbed Pollie Harness by WWD and considered everything from irrelevant to silly by them. One version goes that she didn't divulge the contents of Lady Bird's White House wardrobe—for which Mollie was designing a great many pieces—and WWD was miffed. Jim Brady allowed as how he thought Mollie was miffed because "I think it had something to do with our writing she was eavesdropping on the Duchess of Windsor and she was so mad she banned us from her collections." Then there is Pauline Trigère. Trigère went on the *David Susskind Show* early in the Midi Crisis and had the shocking gall to damn the Midi skirt right there in front of everybody—including Jim Brady, who was also on the show. Well, omnia gall est divisi and Pauline was forthwith cut out and packed off. With WWD's reputation for reaction and retaliation, a professional organization should have assembled a crowd to stand outside the studio and wave a morbid farewell to Pauline as she disappeared, once again, into oblivion.

The official WWD version runs like this: "Oh, nonsense." Then it continues. "We don't mind healthy criticism down here," said Brady. "After all, she said it right there in front of me and you have to respect her honesty."

Susskind once insisted to Brady that designers were "frightened to death of you [WWD] because you have a way—when a designer doesn't get aboard your train—you ridicule them. You give them names." "Some people are afraid of us," admits Brady. "Mollie Parnis and Pauline Trigère admitted it. I think they are very silly ladies—pixilated ladies." Besides, one very good reason for not covering the Trigère collections Brady says is because "Madame Trigère has no influence on American fashion." As for Mollie, ditto. "We don't think she's that important. Besides, she doesn't like us."

When the *Ladies' Home Journal* came out with its list of "America's 75 Most Important Women," Trigère was on the list. Little wonder, that Eye in an item headed "Poll Cat" called Trigère's inclusion the list's "one bad joke."

Just like the ladies, even the gentleman giants tumble. John Fairchild was so enamored of Norman Norell in the 1960s that he devoted an entire chapter to him in *The Fashionable Savages*. "Behind all this perfection and fashion power there is a fine man named Norell," Fairchild exulted, after describing a Norell 1964 collection. Today, WWD doesn't even bother to cover Norell. "Norell is no force these days," Fairchild says, boredom glazing his eyeballs. "No influence at all." Right or wrong, to refuse to consider Norell in the fashion world is a little like a drama critic refusing to review a David Merrick production. WWD now dismisses Norell with the sobriquet of Grand Old Man which they often boil down into initial form—GOM.

With all the controversy on *Women's Wear Daily*—both in what it is and what it says—opinions about it are as wide-ranging and far-reaching as opposite ends of the rainbow. To be confronted by *Women's Wear Daily* is like being confronted with a female impersonator. It is difficult to determine exactly what it is. It is equally difficult to gather a consensus about something as—well—indeterminate. It is a task, however, that most people are well up to. Getting up an opinion on *Women's Wear Daily* is as easy as getting mugged in Central Park.

"WWD is a highly constructive irritant," says designer John Weitz, who considers WWD a very "necessary gadfly. My hat is constantly off to them even though their scars on my forehead show." The tweed pattern on his John Weitz jacket is fairly standing on end. Fairchild? "He's a latter-day Hearst: You write me the news, I'll build you the war."

Bill Blass admits WWD is "surprisingly well-known. Almost every one of my clients around the country subscribes." Part of its success he feels is because it is not only a monopoly but, because of the dearth of newspapers around New York City, it can also act as a daily. But is it fair? "Wel-l-l-l—personalities enter into it but I think for the most part there is an honesty." Well. So much for that. Besides, "it's snappy." Beyond that, "I don't want to talk about it."

Weitz sees much of what WWD says and does as part of an ego problem. To Weitz *Women's Wear* is somewhat "like the wealthy girl who, after having gone to bed with someone, wonders why he did it. You know—after a simply orgiastic night—will he call again? And then she is surprised when he does." Weitz considers himself a pal of Fairchild.

See that guy over there? The one who blushes. Geoffrey Beene—your opinion of *Women's Wear Daily*. Fair? Accurate? Beene blushes through his blush. Of course, it's not fair. "And it's frequently inaccurate." Especially at this moment. "When they covered my last collection, I didn't feel they gave a valid critique and I let them know it." The blush deepens. This is scary. *Newsweek* reports that no designer will bad mouth *Women's Wear Daily*. Visions of knives slipping silently down out of the heavens and quietly cutting Geoffrey Beene to ribbons dance in the head. He continues.

"We had a real falling out a couple of times. They were particularly anxious about Lynda's wedding dress and the fact that I wouldn't give them a sketch." It got to be a very sticky thing, what with *Women's Wear* hustling about trying to get the lowdown on Lynda Bird's gown. Beene contends, "I'm fond of everyone who's on the paper, particularly at the top. Weir, Brady, Fairchild—they are personal friends." It's the little ones Beene doesn't approve of. The little girls fresh out of finishing school or design school or wherever. "They're not adequate fashion reporters," he sniffs.

Halston Frowlick, who was once the head hat man at Bergdorf's and did Jackie's famous fur beret for the 1961 inauguration, is now a full-blown fashion designer, complete with an uptown boutique and scads of uptown clients. Halston figures Fairchild is a genius. "He revolutionized the whole fashion press. If he hears of a good story, nothing—absolutely nothing—will stand in his way of getting to the source."

One of Fairchild's best pals is French-born designer Jacques Tiffeau. Tiffeau is much like Genevieve—the French bird who nested on the old Jack Paar *Tonight* show for many seasons—the longer he lives in America, the worse his English gets. "Fairchild," he once said, "has ze power of ze devil!" He pictures June Weir as "a nun with a knife in each pocket." Religious parallels aside, Tiffeau says the whole situation with Fairchild and WWD is often very confusing. "One day he love you—ze next day he hate you. I say something in *Time* magazine—" Tiffeau shrugs inside his white work smock. The palms point ceiling-ward. The head droops down over the shoulder. The mouth makes a questioning little *moué*. *Qu'est-ce que c'est?* Tiffeau and Fairchild lunch together frequently, but Tiffeau is never sure what is going to be in WWD about him. "Zey have a new girl to take care of Tiffeau every year. I say ze Midi is ze ugliest thing I evair see—next day zey say Tifman say so and so." Tifman. Tiffeau. A computer gets blamed, the buck is passed faster than a bullet, faster than the speed of sound. Tiffeau sits in his studio overlooking Seventh Avenue, wondering when the blow will fall for his *Time*-ly remarks. It must be very much like waiting for the guillotine blade to fall. Fall it must, Tiffeau figures, as surely as reaction follows action. For Tiffeau, along with most people, feels that a slip of the tongue rates a slap heard round the garment industry. Designer Pauline Trigère never reads it before going to bed, "because I can't sleep."

Reaction to WWD's actions is not confined solely to the guys slaving over those hot sketch pads on Seventh Avenue. Social movers and shakers and other industry professionals also have their opinions about WWD. "*Women's Wear* is bitchy and tasteless," says Mrs. Gilbert Miller. "I told John Fairchild years ago that he had no manners." It is a little bit like the family grandmother taking the wayward son into the library for a confrontation, powder dry and pearls a-quiver.

For just about every on-the-record, there is an off-the-record. Fear strikes deep. The garment industry is a business of asides, furtive glances, and throat clearing.

"WWD is a potential heart attack for the fashion industry," a prominent designer says off-the-record for *Newsweek*. They speak, disembodied voices on the telephone, hiding behind their fear like veiled women on the streets of Arabian cities. Another wonders "who appointed John Fairchild the high executioner of high fashion?" To another, "WWD is the typical female gossip: after a while she turns bitchy."

Jackie Taub, head sportswear designer over at Jonathan Logan, summed it up when it looked as if the Midi just might catch on, "If they can pull it off, more power to them. I think they do a tremendous job of covering the industry and the markets. After all, it's Fairchild's paper."

That just about says it.

Women's Wear Daily is many things to many people. To some it is a vital source of industry information. To others it is a titillating peek behind the scenes of a glamour-packed world. To some it is a pretentious pain in the neck. A plain girl with delusions of glory. The girl with a terrific personality who thinks she can become Homecoming Queen if only she tries harder. The upstairs maid who wants a shot at the banquet hall—or the master bedroom.

The union, the council, many manufacturers, and industry-related organizations take a Jewish Mother approach, thinking it should be strictly an industry paper whose major function is to bolster up that industry. Pat it on the back when its feelings are hurt. Would you like some chicken soup? Eat, eat. Enjoy, enjoy.

To the social set, it doesn't go far enough in its gossip—especially to those who are In and not smarting from its pricks and pokes.

To Capital Cities—well, as Daniel Burke of Capital Cities points out: "*Women's Wear* has never been more successful commercially." Daniel Burke at Capital Cities points out. "But whether it is in danger of evolving further and further away from an advertising medium into which advertisers want to continue to pour support is a question that has to be continually evaluated and re-evaluated." As the boys over at Capital Cities see it, "It may at some point turn out that there is room for two publications. One that is more like what it used to be and one that is even more like what it has now become." Burke remains convinced that "it has to continue doing its original job—a newspaper aimed at the trade—or it can anticipate defaulting that job to someone else who will come along and do it very gladly and willingly. It is a problem of definition and direction. It was once very pedantic and very dull—but it might not have been at all pedantic and dull to a man making a make-or-break decision about investment or inventory or purchase of fabric or that sort of thing."

And so it goes. But in America, where the ultimate question is "Does it make money?" John Weitz would seem to be correct. "If Fairchild Publishing is making money—they're fine. If they're not making money—they're not fine."

It's that simple. And that difficult. After all—the Beautiful People do not buy ads.

Blair Sabol, who used to write a fashion column for *The Village Voice* and is an editorial consultant for *Rags*, is a bit more blunt. "WWD is full of shit. Especially the front pages. It's *Women's Wear* talking to *Women's Wear*." Sabol says the front pages—fancy sketches, Eye, double spreads on Hot-Pants in Paris—are the fluff and froth. The back pages are where the action is. Where it's at with WWD. "The back pages go absolutely against what the front few pages are saying," she says. They talk about the real industry. "*Women's Wear Daily* is bitchy—I'm something else again. WWD will put people down for dumb reasons. There's a lot of dirty politics on Seventh Avenue. A lot of payola and politics. A lot of lunches at Restaurant X and Restaurant Y and all that crap. That's not fashion and that's not fashion writing.

"These designers are scared shitless of WWD, no matter how much they try to deny it. They're intimidated by this piece of rag that comes out every day that can make them or break them. They are being reviewed—like by Clive Barnes and they figure they'd better be nice to these people or they may get a knife in their back." Blair figures, "You're either on the bus or off the bus, as [Ken] Kesey says—and those people down there at WWD are off the bus. I asked Brady once, where are you guys gonna be in ten years? I'm concerned for you." Blair Sabol is tall, with a Jewish Afro and good-looking in a Fillmore East sort of way. "I don't see my generation reading you, I told him. God knows—my generation hates you because you represent what they're blowing buildings up over. I'd love to see some little revolutionary put Brady up against the wall. Christ—how does he get up in the morning without a guilty conscience. Writing about those stupid dumb things like what they served on TWA. Food reviews! How does he relate? It's an insult to the times we live in to have a publication like that. *Women's Wear Daily* is just part of the problem and not the solution. Their political coverage—now that's all right. I mean, at least they're getting into heavy stuff. They're really trying and I respect them for that."

The amateur psyching that goes on about *Women's Wear Daily* is very reminiscent of the 1950s when the Beats put on their black leotards and their Greek shoulder bags and spent endless hours throwing back cheap red wine and trying to understand heavy-handed German expressionist movies with subtitles, bad sound, and a grainy quality to the film. WWD is the German expressionist movie of the 1970s. Heavy, fraught with meaning, undertones and overtones and undercurrents. "They're on a power trip," swears Blair. "*Women's Wear Daily* really believes they're in competition with *The New York Times.*"

Daphne Davis, *Rags* contributing editor, says, "Politics is chic. But you know what—Fairchild and Brady have alienated the mass manufacturers, and let me tell you—it's the mass manufacturer who keeps Seventh Avenue alive. It's not Oscar. It's not Geoffrey Beene. It's not Donald Brooks. Besides— Oscar's clothes at Saks are always reduced. And those fucking sequins are always coming off. Those chi-chi/Frito/Puerto Rican clothes—I'll just bet John Fairchild and Jim Brady never go into Saks and look through what's left over from Brooks and Beene and Oscar and everybody else." Back to the home sewing center. Secure those sequins.

"Jim Brady has a very funny accent," announces Blair. "He sounds like a Kennedy."

"He wants to be a Kennedy," asserts Daphne. "He wants to be Social Register. He's like the Irish cop whose son makes good."

"That attitude is all over the paper: 'Please accept me. I want to be in with the heavy people.' "

"Actually, Jim is the kinder of the two when you're alone with him," says Daphne in Jim's defense. "He'll talk on a wide range of subjects. But as far as WWD is concerned, Brady's line is, 'Well I'm reporting the news.' Well, marvy, man, but the way you've reported the news—it's like with a sledge hammer."

WWD is the perfect target because of all that up-front publicity which puts it into the public eye. WWD is sitting and smiling smugly, while the pot shots zoom in.

But the whole issue boils down to just what WWD is—and what its function is. "WWD is a very sore point with the industry," says Leo Orlandi, Ben Shaw's partner in an unabashed empire-building operation that has seen the two men buy into such operations as Geoffrey Beene, Donald Brooks, and Leo Narducci. (Additionally, they are keeping an eye on Norman Norell and Giorgio di Sant'Angelo.) "At one point it served an important function as a dress industry periodical Today it's an amusing newspaper that prints opinions designed to create dissension and controversy." Leo Orlandi, who started out in the business pushing hand trucks and sweeping up garment industry shops, figures WWD "is just not serving its function today. It's a fashion newspaper. It doesn't serve the dress industry. Yeah, sure, it's John Fairchild's ego trip. Oh, it's a fun newspaper—I enjoy reading it. Every day I enjoy reading it." But mostly, what Orlandi objects to is the way in which WWD handles its fashion coverage. "There they are—sending young people to cover the collections. You have to be a critic to cover a couture collection. How can a young kid do it?" Orlandi asks. His shoulders point straight up in bewilderment. What's wrong with these kids today? "They don't have the sophistication or background to analyze a collection." This is a charge heard time and again about WWD: they are sending kids in to do a grownup job. Sending the second string in when the first team should be thundering through the doors.

Norman Norell is ignored completely. He is considered by many to be the top designer in America. His pal, Jimmy Galanos—the Golden Greek from California—is a whole different story. Galanos flies in from L.A. hauling his collections with him. WWD is ready and waiting, sending in June Weir herself to interview Galanos and oversee the photographing of the collection. Wham! Two full pages devoted to Galanos. *Nada* to Norell. Not even second string.

Even WWD takes perverse delight in rapping its own knuckles, which they do publicly in their Letters to the Editor column. One bright, sunny April day, long after the Midi crisis had peaked and begun to slide downhill, the following venom spilled out of the WWD letters.

Sirs: Your article about Tricia Nixon is about as low as journalism can sink. . . . If there was another trade paper, I would discontinue yours, as of now. It's time you take stock of who you want to sell your paper to—the "do nothing" jet set, or as an informative paper to the retail merchant, as it used to be. Because you can't represent both.

Sirs: I am a constant reader of WWD for the past twenty-one years—but find it impossible to continue reading your paper any more, as the garbage you put in it is not worthwhile reading. The article I am enclosing [Note: on Jill Johnston, self-professed Lesbian writing for *The Village Voice*] is not fit to print. . . . I am just wondering whether your staff are Homos and Lesbians as they seem to enjoy writing such articles . . . in fact, bragging about them. Believe me, I am not a narrow-minded person.

Sirs: In your March 26 issue, as usual you are wrong again. . . . HotPants is not the No. 1 best-seller in Atlanta—pantsuits are—and as per usual your newspaper hasn't written one thing right in the past year.

Brady loved reading and running these letters; he felt they stirred up more controversy. Besides—it sells newspapers. And after all, isn't that the Good Old American Way?

But the real heart of the matter is Seventh Avenue, N.Y.C., U.S.A. The decision-makers are here; the trendsetters; the sleek, smooth designers; the con men; the rip-off artists; the salesmen. Once you've made Seventh Avenue, you've made it.

Tucked in among the rapes, the garbage, the traffic, and junkies in New York is influence. The power and the glory in theater, publishing, journalism, advertising, television—and Seventh Avenue. Sew a seam in San Francisco—fine. You might be healthier and live longer, but you'll most likely never make it unless you figure out a way to peddle it on Seventh Avenue.

If the garment industry is a sly maiden, luring the fabric freaks who dwell among us, it is also an industry encompassing many identities. It is, for example, the smooth, slick commercial manufacturer. Jonathan Logan. Susan Thomas. Suzy Perette. Sue Brett. Mr. Mort. Sportwhirl. The dresses that hung in Sillik's Dress Shoppe back in Albion, Nebraska. The dresses from J. C. Penney's and Sears, Roebuck that saw generations of us through Eighth Grade Graduation, Honors Convocation, Junior Class Plays, and finally, High School Graduation. A Jonathan Logan to get through Rush Week at the university. For those first few insecure weeks in New York City—Jonathan Logan, you were there. Comforting. Bringing security. Yes, we knew. Things would be all right if Jonathan Logan was there in your bedroom, girls. We knew. Faith was a Jonathan Logan. God bless America and Jonathan Logan!

But the garment industry is also the one-man operation. The knockoff artist who reads his copy of *Women's Wear* every day, reads John Fairchild's mind as it lies right out there on page one, and continues through to his back pages. HotPants. Knickers. Jump suits. He can look at the sketches, the photographs, turn the whole shebang over to his pattern maker, and faster than you can say "Sister Susie Sewed a Simple Seam Sitting at the Seaside," the first pair of HotPants is ready for sale. And weeks before the larger manufacturers have had a chance to gear over their manufacturing. Months before the designers have had a chance to show a collection.

Then there are the designers. Oh, the designers. High fashion. Don't they conjure up visions? Kay Thompson striding through *Funny Face* urging the world to "Think pink!" Lanky models. Photographers who tap dance as well as they take pictures and then marry the model at the end of the last reel. Pass the popcorn. Pass the corn.

Yes, America has designers. Seventh Avenue is where they live. American designers are a strange breed. To some of the uninitiated, they would seem to be the Yankee counterpart of the French designer. In some ways they are extremely similar. They design four so-called *couture* collections a year, each collection consisting of eighty to a hundred pieces. The prices range from expensive to absolutely outrageous (generally ranging from $200 to $2,000-plus). The press and buyers are invited to private showings and then the press goes back to the office and writes little stories about the collection they have just seen while the store buyers (hopefully) sit down and write big orders for the collection they have just seen. As in Paris, American designers are celebrities and personalities. And, as in Paris, they have a following of ladies that would leave a celebrity seeker breathless. Actresses, society types, wives of Very Important People.

But there are subtle differences: for one thing, French designers are still considered *haute couture*. If *haute couture* is taken to mean custom-designing and custom-fitting clothes for the private customer—nobody, but nobody, makes that mistake about American designers. For another, European designers are still designing for private customers with designer ready-to-wear as a necessary but secondary evil. American designers are strictly businessmen, heavy into ready-to-wear. Mass producers—although certainly not on the scale of a Jonathan Logan—selling, for the most part, large quantities to stores rather than to private customers.

It is generally agreed that Seventh Avenue pizzazz is the sole property of the Designers. This is a small, select world—covered passionately by *Women's Wear Daily*. Keeping up with WWD's favorite designers is about as difficult as predicting the weather. It fluctuates. It varies. It changes constantly. Some are definitely In—Bill Blass, Oscar de la Renta, Geoffrey Beene, Galanos, Valentino, Giorgio di Sant'Angelo. Some are definitely Out—Norman Norell, Mainbocher, Pauline Trigère, Mollie Parnis. Some are teetering—Yves St. Laurent. As for being In or Out of favor at the court of WWD, it is vastly preferable to be In. Much more comfortable.

Among the most In of designers in the WWD Inner Sanctum these days is Valentino, lovely, beautiful, gor-ge-ous Valentino. He can do very little wrong in the eyes of WWD. Valentino most typifies all the stereotypes about the male fashion designer: He is drop-dead gorgeous; a real Italian stereotype in the best sense of the word. Teeth like Chiclets marching across his face; straight nose; nice hair; terrific body; great tan. He wears suede pants and his shirt unbuttoned the requisite three buttons plus a gold cross on a chunky chain. A copper rheumatism bracelet. Loafers without socks. This guy could do more for the Italian image than all the mass gatherings at Columbus Circle.

Valentino Garavani was born in a small town near Milan in 1932. Mama and Papa Garavani had visions of their boy becoming a doctor, but Valentino had other ideas. At seventeen, he dropped out of school and left home—with parental permission, of course—and headed for Paris. Within six months, he had a job with the couture house of Jean Desses, where he stayed for six years. He left with Desses's chief designer, Guy Laroche, who opened his own salon. Valentino went with him and worked with Laroche for two years. All this is not bad training for a kid from Milan. By 1960, Valentino was ready to quit working for someone else. He ditched Laroche, Paris, France, and went back to Italy. He headed straight for Rome, where he opened his very own couture house on the Via Gregoriana. By 1962 he was well on his way.

Valentino might have been puttering around in a world of VVVVV's the rest of his life if it hadn't been for the century's Super Consumer, Jacqueline Kennedy. So loyal had she become, in fact, that when the time came for her to become Mrs. Onassis, Valentino did her wedding dress.

Not that Jackie O is Valentino's only customer. Hardly. The ladies who put their bodies into a Valentino are impressive, to say the least. Audrey Hepburn, Princess Lee Radziwill, Mrs. Henry Ford II, Vicomtesse Jacqueline de Ribes, Gloria Guinness, Mrs. Charles Wrightsman. Not your ladies who shop off the rack at Penney's.

Valentino is a peripatetic sort. He flies back and forth from Rome to New York so much he finally broke down and snapped up a little Manhattan pad *à terre*. But it is on Capri that those who dream of fashion designers as living some sort of mythic existence—one that imbues them with all the glamour and aura of movie stars and other sorts of celestial celebrities—find a certain sort of voyeuristic joy. In December of 1969, Valentino socked out a reported $400,000 for a villa in Capri, then proceeded to put into it more than $150,000 worth of repairs, redecorating, and refurbishing. His white limestone villa that caused Fashion Writer Eugenia Sheppard to gush, "It's the first thing on the island that every visitor longs to see."

The villa is off a narrow alleyway about a mile from the port—and up fifty torturous steps. The villa itself is built on three levels and decorated with lots of vinyl-covered walls and plexiglass and white marble floors on the first level. Plants and vines, bougainvillaea, creep around the gardens. Purple curtains cover the windows on the outside.

There is a Moroccan tent room on the first level, draped and pillowed, and *très* sexy. The second level contains guest rooms and extra rooms. Valentino and Giancarlo, his equally sexy business manager, have separate apartments on the third floor.

The thing that really knocks visitors out is the little touches, like the gold leaf ashtrays that measure two feet across on the cocktail tables. Jim Brady once remarked, "It seems a shame

to stub out a butt in one and you find yourself looking for a
convenient pants cuff to use instead." Oh, wow—you can take
a boy out of Brookyln, but you can't take Brooklyn out of the
boy. Atta boy Jim Brady. Servants run around in white gloves
serving pizza on gold trays, turning beds up and down, running
baths. Terrific!

The closest thing the American designing community has to
Valentino is Oscar de la Renta. Oscar also has those sugar-
lump teeth that flicker and flash in a usually constant smile.
He is also tall, with an exquisite body and an equally exquisite
skin color.

Oscar is a native of the Dominican Republic. "Most of my
uncles were in the diplomatic service and my father was in
insurance," he says vaguely. From there Oscar went to Spain
to study painting and the next logical step was Paris. Here
Oscar wound up as an assistant designer in the House of
Lanvin. After two and a half years with Lanvin, Oscar was
ready for New York. He got a job designing for Elizabeth
Arden, replacing Castillo. He sketched away, built up a stable
of contacts, and in 1965 struck out on his own. The ladies
thundered off after him into the dawn of his independence,
clamoring for his clothes. Today he sells to all the Kennedy
girls (minus Jackie O) plus Babe Paley, Anne Ford Uzielli,
and the Duchess of Windsor. There was a big splash in the
fall of 1967, when, after the première performance of *Camelot*,
three women walked through the doors of the Americana for
the benefit bash each wearing an identical Oscar creation.
Ebullient Suzy Knickerbocker promptly nominated it the
"Dress of the Year" in her New York *News* column the next
day. The Dress, a metallic brocade, seemed ordinary enough.
Short sleeves, an obi sash at the waist, a full floor-length skirt,
a demure neckline, and a $500 price tag.

In October, 1967, Oscar slipped down to City Hall and
married Françoise de Langlade, former editor of French
Vogue. She is a good friend of the Rothschilds in Paris and a

fashion whiz in her own right; it could have been construed as the fashion wedding of the decade. (Since so few designers get married, it no doubt *was* the fashion wedding of the decade. Maybe the *only* one.) Anyway, they make a good team. Françoise is a striking woman with a broad streak of French charm and earthy humor about her. She has a big wide smile that never seems to slip from her face, and she wears her hair pulled back in a simple bun and little or no make-up. But she is a power to be reckoned with, say those who know her. Cross Françoise, and you'll answer to Oscar.

The de la Rentas are everywhere; they are the most visible of the designer set—partly because there are two of them, partly because both are so striking, and partly because they just make the scene. Pat Kennedy Lawford sponsors a charity fashion show in the Dominican Republic and Oscar is along showing his clothes. Serge Obolensky organizes a super-junket to officially open Paradise Island in the Bahamas and Oscar's clothes are the ones (along with Pucci's) that come floating down the runway. The de la Rentas seem to lunch every day at Restaurant X, although at separate tables, thus doubling their visibility.

"Socializing helps," Oscar once said. And nobody worked harder at proving it. "When a woman buys an expensive dress, she wants to know whose dress she's buying, just for the sake of vanity. It helps me to know people. I know that when my friends go to shop, they will ask for my clothes first."

Oscar was also very generous to those good friends/customers. As one of Oscar's models recounted, "You wouldn't believe these women—they actually come in and get a dress one afternoon, wear it that night, and return it the next day." Oh, well, the lady wore the dress, Oscar got the publicity. From time to time the whole thing backfired. "One day ———— ———— did that and the dress was ruined." Seems she had a perspiration breakthrough all over the dress's armpits. Even Society Ladies are RealGirls. And RealGirls do Real Things. Like sweat.

Oscar's trademark is a lush richness; brocaded fabric overlaid with embroidered beading. And if he sometimes looked as if he were into the Rich Hippie look—lots of baubles and bangles and contrasting textures and patterns—it was because he was probably there first with it. And WWD loves Oscar and his clothes. "De la Renta Great," a headline thrills, after what WWD considered to be still another Oscar smash last year. Oscar received a "Great" rating in WWD's Fall Scoreboard for 1971. Oscar, smart businessman that he is, knows how to be enthusiastic, too. "What *Women's Wear* does better than any other publication is get the whole feeling of what women want to wear. No fashion designer really creates a look," Oscar says. "They merely interpret what is already in the air. And *Women's Wear* is great at feeling things out."

Oscar was at his peak during the late 1960s when there was one splashy charity bash after another. Endless functions reported endlessly in the press. WWD reporters sitting cheek-by-jowl with the *Times, Vogue,* AP, *Newsday.* Everybody wanted a piece of the action and to those involved in the scene then, no piece of flesh was too big or too insignificant to donate to what they considered a worthy cause—especially if it was photographed and written about.

While houseguesting at Newport, Oscar met Mary "Minnie" Cushing, daughter of the super-rich, super-social Howard G. Cushings. She was interested in fashion, wanted to work in it some way. Oscar knew just the place. Before anyone could holler "Minnie, you're mad!" she was zipping through Seventh Avenue traffic on her motorbike, bound for glory at Oscar's. She acted as his receptionist, publicist, and general all-around Girl Monday through Friday. When Minnie left to marry the handsome, dashing photographer Peter Beard—then stationed in far-off Kenya—her replacement was Ames Cushing, Minnie's sister-in-law by dint of her marriage to Minnie's brother Thomas. "Darling Ames" was the way Suzy described her. A cute, open little blonde, Ames did ditto duties for Oscar that Sister-in-law Minnie did. Few who know the operations of the couture business on Seventh Avenue say it hurts to have a social type acting as your assistant whatever.

If Oscar introduced the art of socializing to the fashion world, it fell to Bill Blass to take it out of its amateur standing and perfect it into nothing short of a profession. Bill Blass was *everywhere*, but *everywhere*, during the 1960s. A ball with Louise Savitt. Lunch with Cee-Zee Guest. Drinks at Chessy Rayner's. Like that. "Bill's great thing about clothes was that he was the first designer to go out and lead the social life," said Louise Savitt, whom Blass escorted about frequently when she was ceasing to be Mrs. Savitt and before she became Mrs. Freddie Melhado. Even though the scene has changed gears and now sits idling in the driveway waiting for something to happen, Bill Blass is still out there socializing, albeit in a very 1970s way: Bill Blass is out to Lunch.

"New York and San Francisco are the only two cities I know of where people dress for lunch," Blass stated flatly one morning. "The thing about La Grenouille, La Côte Basque, and those restaurants is that they have a club atmosphere. Everyone knows that if they are in New York and they want to see people they know, they go to lunch." To one of the Big Three or Big Four: La Grenouille, La Côte Basque, Le Pavillon, Lafayette. "And now that I travel so much I must say I want to go there. It's a way to catch up. From a designer's standpoint it is valuable to know what the Italian princesses in town are wearing."

If Valentino and Oscar are drop-dead handsome in an ethereal way, William Ralph Blass is handsome in a sort of wide-open all-American-boy way. Stocky, perennially suntanned, and incredibly groomed; the Marlboro Man of SA. Furthermore, Bill Blass has blue eyes that rival Paul Newman's. One would guess that if the two were ever to really eyeball it for the Blue Prize, it would be nothing short of a Mexican standoff.

The image of Bill Blass hit its peak last year when his line of men's grooming gear—called, of course, Blass—went into full swing. A full-page ad in WWD had a headline that screamed, " 'Bull' says Bill." Then a serious picture of Blass. Furrowed brow, stern jaw. "Most men's grooming stuff around today is a lot of you-know-what," Bill's man-to-man copy said. "Especially the fragrance. (It just doesn't separate the men from the girls!) So what's the answer?" BLASS! that's what. And then a list of he-man goodies. No-Sweat Anti-Perspirant . . . Men's "Other" Deodorant Spray . . . Great Hunk of Soap . . . 100-Proof Cologne.

Blass was born in Ft. Wayne, Indiana, where his father owned a local hardware store. "I did do some caddying in Ft. Wayne," is as much as Blass will admit about youthful attempts at capitalism. And since Blass is the ultimate Seventh Avenue capitalist—into bed sheets, bath towels, men's grooming gear, men's wear, rainwear—one wonders where the instincts came from. "I wanted to be a designer from the time I was a small lad back there in Indiana," Blass admits. "Because of what I wanted to do I happened not to have a very pleasant adolescence and childhood. I knew what I wanted to do and it wasn't so much a matter of disliking Indiana—or Iowa or Nebraska—as it was a matter of wanting to get someplace where I could do what I wanted to do. The whole process of growing up in Indiana seems unreal. Indiana wasn't the worst place to grow up in. Everytime I try to talk about this it comes out wrong. It's just that—well, if you want to grow up to design clothes, you just can't talk about it in Indiana. Does that make sense?"

As Blass puts it, "It was a matter of biding my time." But in the meantime he had been selling sketches to Seventh Avenue by mail even before he left Ft. Wayne. "I'd look in *Vogue* and *Harper's* and see the names of manufacturers," he explained. "Then I'd send them a batch of sketches and they'd buy them." He was fifteen-years-old then, playing football in Ft. Wayne and selling dress designs to Seventh Avenue. At seventeen, he was out of Ft. Wayne faster than the Wabash Cannonball. He went straight to New York. And stayed. And boy—did he make it!

After dropping out of Parsons School of Design, Blass

worked as a sketcher for David Crystal. Then came World War II and the Army where he was with a camouflage unit peopled with a lot of artists.

(Then there's the Apocryphal War Story out about Bill Blass and his escapades: when people wondered why Blass always looked so good in his khakis it was discovered that one week after enlisting, he reported to Brooks Brothers and had his uniform altered TO FIT. So there, Dogface.)

After the Army, Brooks-tailored uniforms and all, Blass settled into Seventh Avenue for good. He worked as a sketcher for Anna Miller, sister of Maurice Rentner. When her business merged with Rentner's, Blass went along as Number Two designer. When Rentner died eleven years ago, his business was bought out by two businessmen—with Blass as a partner, vice president, and chief designer. In 1970 Blass bought out his partners and set himself up in business as Bill Blass, Ltd.

Bill Blass has come a long way from Ft. Wayne, Indiana, replete with hardware stores and high school football teams and an adolescence seemingly best forgotten. Today he lives with his valet in Sutton Place with neighbors the likes of Charlotte Ford Niarchos. "I live on the top floor of an apartment building," is the Blass way of describing his penthouse pad. He flies thousands of miles a year—doing charity fashion shows, giving speeches, opening collections for those 280 accounts around the country, buying tweed in Scotland for his men's wear line. Buying and selling, Blass is in there.

There is no doubt that the notorious WWD-Blass feud has been patched up most securely. "Blass Collection Hailed as Winner," ran the page-one headline after his 1971 fall collection was presented. "He obviously topped the Seventh Avenue fashion parade," WWD stated. Then they promptly hailed him to the top of their Fall Scoreboard with a "Great" rating. (At the bottom of the list were Boutique Donald Brooks and Jacques Tiffeau with "Ahem" ratings.)

"He could sell the eyelashes off a hog," was the way Ruth Preston, New York *Post* fashion editor, once put it. Every once in a while he can snatch a weekend at his "fishing shack" in Christmas Cove, Maine. "That's where I can escape," he sighs. "There is absolutely no one up there. No pressures. Nothing." Just fresh air and sunshine. Peace and quiet. "He has an image as a party boy," Fashion Publicist Eleanor Lambert once explained, "but three or four times a week he's simply home in bed—collapsed." It's a tough life, but Blass has it made. His one hang-up: "I haunt Army-Navy stores," he confesses. "Look at this." He sifts through some items on a chrome garment rack, comes up with a train brakeman's jacket in navy blue denim. "Look at that detail," says Blass, pointing to the intricate double-stitched and triple-stitched flat fell seaming. He was transported by that heavy, durable LEE jacket stuck among chiffons and silks and voiles.

Ranking right up there with Blass is Geoffrey Beene. WWD loves him and his clothes, and he makes money.

Now Geoffrey Beene is about as far from being the stereotypical fashion designer as is possible. He is a short cuddly man in his forties, who wears glasses on his round moon face. He blushes with amazing regularity and speaks softly with more than a trace of his native Louisiana in his speech. He looks and sounds as if he would be more comfortable swatting flies down on the bayou than sticking pins in dress samples on Seventh Avenue.

Where Bill Blass is casual, confiding, man-to-man, Geoffrey Beene is the quintessence of politeness. He sits prim and straight in his chair—*wearing* his necktie instead of flinging it nonchalantly over a filing cabinet. He listens to questions, responds softly.

Another down-home boy, Beene hails from Haynesville, Louisiana (population 3,040), a town more noted for oil wells than for producing fashion designers for New York City. "Everything I remember about Haynesville is extremely pleasant," Beene says. "It was a normal black-eyed peas and grits life." His parents divorced while he was still a child. He went off to Henderson, Texas, to public school, then returned to Louisiana and Tulane University to study—medicine. "I spent three years at pre-med and then did one year at medical school." He dropped out. "I didn't like it at all," Beene drawls. "I didn't have the dedication for medicine." Besides, "the first year of medical school is always cadavers, which I didn't find too inviting."

His family was mad as hell. "They couldn't believe that after $20,000 worth of education I would give up, so they sent me to a psychiatrist. They thought I was mad—and they still do, I think." It figures. Beene comes from a line of medicine men—a grandfather and two uncles. At his family's urging, which he confesses he didn't find too hard to take, he split for California and his "rest cure." There went Geoffrey Beene, corn-pone accent and all, into that hotbed of celluloid decadence. And here is where it all began. Oh, California! What did you have in store for this youngster from the South, the simple son of an automobile salesman and a millionaire's daughter? He got bored and applied for a job as a window dresser at I. Magnin's. Beene worked there for two years, tossing off a sketch or two every now and then. There was Our Hero, decorating his windows by day, sketching by night, and who should see those sketches and get terribly excited— none other than the president of Magnin's. "He suggested I go to school—so I did." It was a good excuse to go to Paris, which he did, studying for two years at the Chambre Syndicale.

After leaving Paris, there was no question about what came next: New York. All those lives, converging on New York. Almost like a radio drama, isn't it? Fairchild comes in from New Jersey, Brady takes the subway from Brooklyn, Oscar arrives circuitously from the Dominican Republic, Blass takes a troop ship from Ft. Wayne, and Beene comes in from I.

Magnin's window via med school and the Chambre Syndicale. Complete strangers, slipping into town from different directions.

Beene arrived in New York in 1954 and found a job at a custom house uptown. He describes it as mainly "picking up pins," a job he lost when he accidentally dumped a load of mayonnaise on an antique chair. From there, it was a short step downtown to Seventh Avenue where he worked for several houses. Eleven years ago he got a job with manufacturer Teal Traina and worked for his firm for seven years. It was not a pleasant experience for our boy from Haynesville. "Traina refused to give me label credit and I thought since I'd made him—financially and fashion-wise—I deserved it." Traina, unfortunately, did not agree, so: "I found backing and started my own business." In fact, Beene was so miffed and worked so quickly he left without seeing the last collection he had designed for Traina.

The Beene business has grown from a simple couture house to a large conglomerate, now owned by Beene, Ben Shaw, and his partner Leo Orlandi, which takes in $6 million a year. No wonder. Prices range from $110 to $600 *wholesale*. There is Beene couture, Beene Bazaar (lower price boutique clothing), Beene bags, Beene men's wear. Geoffrey Beene is in Big Business. He looks longingly over his shoulder from time to time, sighing up through his Cardin suit coat about The Good Old Days. "It was so much more fun then," he confesses. "It's gotten so big now. I am so aware—constantly— of the tremendous overhead that has to be met. I can't always be as fanciful in design as I normally would be."

Notables who have been known to toss a Beene or two on their backs are Gloria Vanderbilt Cooper, Mrs. James Stewart, Diahann Carroll and, of course, Lynda Bird Johnson. Beene did Lynda's wedding dress, a simple Princess-line gown. He sighed again. "You know, it wasn't so much the Secret Service that ever bothered me about Lynda's wedding dress—it was the press." There is something about a celebrity's closet that fascinates the press and the public, an insatiable desire to know exactly what is in there and where it is being worn.

Beene, a bachelor, lives with his twelve-year-old dachshund Hans in a *maisonette* on East 69th Street in New York. "Well, it gets called a *maisonette* because it has its own front door and back door, but it's really just a duplex in this whole huge compound of apartments. How many rooms? Well, let's see. One, two, three, four, five, six—about seven I guess." It's a whole mixed melange of antiques and stark modern simplicity. Modern paintings are strewn about, splashing color all over the walls. Beene also has a summer house on Long Island.

When he returns to his 1-2-3-4-5-6-7-room *maisonette*, Beene doesn't immediately change into black tie and hit the town. "I'm tired." When he does stir around in the after-hours, it's either to go to a movie or have a few friends in for dinner and—Monopoly. "I play Monopoly in five languages—Dutch, French, German, Spanish, and English. It's a silly thing, isn't it? Such a simple game, but it's fun." Actually, Beene figures he's antisocial. "I refuse to go anywhere that requires a black tie. If I'm obliged to wear it, I hesitate to go. I think it's pagan to dress in those monkey suits.

"I go back to visit my family, but I get so bored when I get back I can hardly stand it over a day. I need stimulation that I can't get from a small town in the South." And what does Haynesville think of its famous son? The man who puts clothes on presidential wives and daughters? "They poke fun at me." It figures. "They think I'm snobbish, which is perfectly ridiculous. I've just outgrown the community. I'm still interested, but there are so many more things that are important to me. Haynesville is an oil boom town, completely wrapped up in itself. They become so involved with *little* things."

To that end, his mother usually comes to New York rather than Beene returning to the scene of his youth. "She comes up for every collection, and we go to museums and galleries and see some shows. It's much more fun that way. Besides, she's such a fan of mine."

Another WWD favorite—this year—is James Galanos; it wasn't always thus. In fact, Galanos himself pulled the old double shuffle and banned *Women's Wear* from his collections for years. One story has it that Jim Brady himself flew out to California, where Galanos bases himself, and came back in triumph. WWD has been enthusiastically covering Galanos ever since.

Galanos was born in Philadelphia of middle-class Greek immigrant parents, spent most of his life in a small New Jersey town. As Galanos once put it, "With three sisters it was easy to learn dressmaking." He began with simple designs at age thirteen. He ended up in New York, floating around trying to find a job and after four years of having doors slammed in his face, he cleared out and headed for Paris. Galanos went to work for the now-extinct design house of Piquet. He returned to Seventh Avenue ready to give it another chance. Doors all over Seventh Avenue politely but firmly closed in Galanos's face for four years.

It didn't take much to convince a creatively starving Galanos to Go West, Young Man. Once in California, Galanos met designer Jean Louis, who figured the kid had talent, but unfortunately Jean Louis had no job for him. He did, however, scrape together a loan to set Galanos up in business. Done. Working with one assistant in a tiny room, Jimmy Galanos was—finally—on his way. Like Bill Blass, he devoured *Vogue* for names and addresses, picking out the names of stores whose ads appealed to him and who carried clothes similar to what he was designing. Galanos would write the stores, inviting them to stop by his shop and see his things whenever they sent a representative to California. They did. Little by little, the Galanos enterprise picked up steam. And a little money.

Finally, it was 1954. And Galanos figured it was time to

give New York another chance. He packed his simple sample bags—thirty-five designs in all—and headed East. (He knew vaguely when the other collections were being shown, so he got a reservation for around that time.) It was Democracy in Action again. A boffo perf. At the end of three weeks, Galanos packed his bags—plus $400,000 worth of orders and his first Coty Award nomination—and headed West again. The rest as they say, is show biz—er, um, ah—fashion history. The Coty is given for outstanding fashion design achievement and Galanos has gone on to win Coty (1954) after Coty (1956) after Coty (1959) and now he lives in the Coty Fashion Hall of Fame. He has won the Nieman Marcus Award for "distinguished service in the field of fashion," the National Cotton Council Award, Filene's Young American Designer Award, the NBC "Today" Award as the "most creative designer in America," and the London *Sunday Times* International Fashion Award for the U.S. of A. It's a long way from New Jersey, right?

Even while WWD was snugging itself into the Civilized Look last year, wrapping itself up in a cocoon of blazers and pleated skirts and shirtwaist dresses, they couldn't help but succumb to the one vagrant gypsy left flashing his wares in The Forest. There he was, Count Giorgio di Sant'Angelo daring to use color. Daring to use flamboyant patterns. Daring to show legs and breasts and thighs, and just about anything else that smacks of human anatomy, albeit covered in one of his fanciful creations. Working in rough suedes, jerseys, cottons, patches of chiffons, Sant'Angelo was about as far from a blazer and a shirtwaist dress as rock music is from a Bach cantata. "Sant'Angelo is wild," Fashion Editor June Weir enthused.

She was absolutely right.

There is nothing ordinary about Giorgio di Sant'Angelo. He goes about his business (which is designing everything from

HotPants to gloves and scarves) in anything from jeans and no shoes to blue velvet Edwardian suits dripping with chains, necklaces, bracelets, rings, and ringlets. He is *everything* people want to think about fashion designers. Wild, exuberant, fey, temperamental. He wears *ruffles*! Bill Blass might be all male-y in tweeds and plaids. Geoffrey Beene might keep his necktie on. Oscar might never let his suntan slip—but Giorgio wears *ruffles*. And low-slung shirts. When he bends over you can see his nipples! And low-slung pants. And ringlets in his hair. And wraps his waist in silken sashes. "I was the first to walk around with my shirt open to my pants," he claims. Sweetheart!

Giorgio di Sant'Angelo was something of a mystery man when, in 1967, he won his first Coty Award for accessories. Nobody, but nobody, knew who he was. With the possible exception of Diana Vreeland, who helped discover him, and Eugenia Sheppard, who did one of the first interviews with him. His background reads like the dust-jacket blurb on a bad novel. Sant'Angelo was born in Florence and he spent his time floating between family compound there and the family ranch in Argentina. He studied architecture, then industrial design, and finally got into ceramics. While kicking around the family farmstead one summer, he packed off some of his ceramics and entered them in an international competition. He won, which meant he got to spend six months studying sculpture in the South of France with Picasso. During his stay with Picasso, he sat himself down—just like that—and whipped off some animated cartoon sketches. Well, before you could say *Fantasia*, he was off working for the Disney studios in Hollywood. There were a few snags. First of all, Giorgio spoke absolutely no English. There he sat, sketching away while English flew around him. After fifteen days, Giorgio quit and headed for New York City. He bought a copy of the *Times*, pored through the Want Ads, and got a job in a small textile design studio. From there he moved to designing hotel interiors. Then he discovered plastics. Little did he realize this substance would ultimately turn out to be his Big Rock Candy Mountain.

There is nothing inherently sexy about plastic. It is usually associated with things like coffee-can lids and cottage cheese containers. But with Giorgio, it was something different. He took plastic and fashioned it into jewelry. While working for du Pont, he did a collection of jewelry and who should come to a showing of the stuff but Diana Vreeland, editor of *Vogue*. Was she excited? She used up four pages in *Vogue* getting excited about it.

Plastic and Diana Vreeland got Giorgio into fashion full time. He promptly rented a studio, started churning out the accessories—jewelry, belts, scarves, gloves—that won him his Coty Award.

From there, it was a short step to sweaters, pants, shorts, skirts, dresses—all of which Giorgio now does, but with his own special flair. His designs conjure up American Indians, Balkan peasants, rich hippies. This year a big item in his show was the body stocking, adorned with clippings and drippings of brightly colored chiffons. Last year it was Indians complete with feathers and beads. Even Giorgio's HotPants were distinctly his: rough cut pieces of suede and chamois that seemed to be ripped, then wrapped around the body. "I don't believe in twenty-seven different pieces of construction and nine different linings," Giorgio once said. "I don't want my clothes to be able to stand up without the body inside them." He lives in a dream world peopled with gypsies, peasants, Indians. "I love the individuality of young people," he claims. "I can design for them." Rich old ladies? "I have nothing to say to them." It is indeed difficult to think of a pearl-ridden dowager in any of Giorgio's creations.

Giorgio is a mover and a shaker; he's into movies, sets, costumes. He likes to work on live bodies, and sometimes will have the ladies in his life over gussying each other up in whatever bits and pieces of fantasy catch their fancy. Half the time they play Dress-Up too long and never get to the parties. "Fashion is in the streets," insists Giorgio, following the lead of both John Fairchild and Blair Sabol. "Clothes are too expensive today. Who can spend $1,000 for something. That is ridiculous." His prices are generally $100 to $200 and "I think that is too expensive." His fashion hero? Jonathan Logan.

Another all-American boy who came thundering out of the Midwest to take on New York was Norman Norell, born Norman Levinson in Noblesville, Indiana, the youngest of three sons of a haberdasher. When Norell was six, his family moved to Indianapolis, where he lived until he came to New York at age nineteen.

Norell became interested in fashion through the theater. His father would stick theatrical posters in the window of the shop, Norell would bum the resultant free passes and play hookey from school to see the shows. Ah, vaudeville. Norell loved it, especially the costumes. When he finally got to New York, he enrolled in the Pratt Institute of Design—and dropped out. He tried Parsons School of Design—and dropped out. He then found himself spending most of his time in the cavernous New York Public Library. "I suppose I went there partly to get warm," he says. "My apartment was so cold." Well, once there—in out of the wind and rain and snow—Norell closeted himself with costume books. Stacks and stacks of costume books. The librarians took a kindly attitude toward the skinny little guy with the midwestern accent. It didn't take long before Norell began "fooling around with theatrical sketches." He submitted some to a local movie-making outfit that was shooting in New York—sketches that were accepted and eventually wound up on Gloria Swanson. Lights! Action! Cut! Print it! Norell was in business. He ended up designing costumes for the Ziegfeld Follies and more for movies. Then he got a job at Brooks Costume Company, where he spent years whipping things up for vaudeville shows and burlesque shows. By age twenty-eight, he had moved on to the Hattie Carnegie company, becoming her chief designer. In 1938 he even designed a pair of sequin shorts worn by Paulette Goddard. What a stir. "Restaurants wouldn't let her in." Same old story. The association with Carnegie lasted thirteen years, until "we had a huge fight over a sequined skirt for Gertrude Lawrence." Norell lost and promptly quit. He was immediately picked up by a manufacturer Anthony Traina (Teal Traina's uncle) who offered him not only a job—but a deal: your name on the door, less money; no name, more money. Norman may have been a skinny kid out of the Midwest, but he was no dressmaker's dummy. His name quickly went up on the door, and in 1941, Traina-Norell was launched. In 1960, when Traina retired, Norell was more than ready to go out on his own. Which he did with a flourish, with one of the most respected and expensive fashion lines in America. By 1970 a Norell suit cost $1,700 to $1,900. And the ladies were snapping them up like girdles at S. Klein's. Coats were hitting $1,300 to $1,700. Dresses *began* at $700. Not that his customers can't afford them. (Ever hear of Lady Bird Johnson being strapped for cash? Or the Duchess of Windsor?)

But the times were catching up with Norell. The only designer who has had both the integrity *and* the business to stay relatively singleminded (the only sideline Norell has is marketing a perfume bearing his name), in 1970 Norell found himself backed into a corner by a combination of spiraling costs and the economic slump. Fashion potentate Ben Shaw came in and figured out there were ways to do things better and not sacrifice quality. He immediately began implementing plans to make things even better. One of Shaw's first moves was to cut Norell's prices by one-third. SALE! BUY NOW! DRASTIC REDUCTIONS! Not that they'll compete with Gimbel's basement. A one-third cut on a $700 dress doesn't really relegate it to the sale rack. Five hundred dollars is still a lot of dough for a dress. "I've devoted my whole life to quality," Norell said when the announcement of his price-cutting came. "I realize it's not as important now as it once was, but I'm too old to change." But one thing even Norell agreed upon: prices had gotten out of hand. That first collection he did for Traina-Norell was the most expensive of its day. Suits went for $159, dresses were $95. "A long cashmere evening dress covered with spangles was $110—and there were an awful lot of spangles." By cutting Norell's prices, Shaw figures business will boom. "We expect to do twice as much business." Shaw, meanwhile, is negotiating to buy the Norell business.

Although fussy about his ladies, Norell confesses to being something less than a perfectionist when it comes to himself. He is very casual about his own clothes. "As long as I'm neat and clean." You could spot Midwest from that remark alone. It's the old front porch/emergency room response. Norell is so casual, in fact, he once went to a cocktail party wearing the jacket of one suit and the pants of another.

Norell says, "When I was young I had a horrible temper. I was the worst child that ever lived. I threw things and yelled and kicked. I was always sick as a child and my mother let me get away with murder." When he came to New York, there were no handy targets. He didn't know anyone and therefore had no one to yell at—"so I just got over it." About the only time he shows any temperament is when collection time rolls around—then it usually manifests itself in a somewhat clenched-teeth attitude that turns into a migraine headache as soon as the show is over. One night he got so distraught he threw himself down on his showroom floor and declared, "I'm going to clean this goddamn floor before those goddamn dresses get dirty." And he sent out for a bucket, a sponge, and some Ajax. He scrubbed for a half-hour. The goddamn floor got clean. And the goddamn dresses didn't get dirty.

Norell, a bachelor, is something of a loner. His first love is his work, and he is most unhappy when he isn't working. "We're his family," a long-time Norell model once said. He rarely takes time away from his office, unless it is to show his collection or travel to Paris to see what's going on. He lives lushly in an East Side townhouse, a resplendent duplex full of Roman hangings, Louis XVI antiques, and Ming porcelains from the T'ang dynasty. The apartment is his pride and joy—and a far cry from Noblesville, Indiana. Or Indianapolis. All of Indiana, for that matter. The running of the duplex is left in the hands of a maid, however. (Once, when the maid went off to Europe for a visit, Norell was stuck trying to run the place himself. "I can't even cook," he lamented. "The only thing I can make is coffee." He nearly went crazy—especially trying to keep that goddamned kitchen floor clean. He scrubbed and scrubbed and scrubbed—and "I just ended up with mud.") "I've always been a hard worker," he says. "And I've gotten where I am only by hard work." That is about as solid and sensible middle western as one will find these days. A Goldwater Republican, he loosened up just enough to approve of most of LBJ's policies.

In 1965, Norell was operated on for cancer of the vocal chords. He recovered but today talks in a low voice. Always a shy man, this makes it even more difficult for him to meet strangers. Not that his shyness keeps him from being anything less than an individual.

So there they are. Fashion designers. And all along you thought they lived in *Vogue* and *Harper's*, awash in satins and chiffons. Nonsense. They are alive and well and living in WWD; just plain working men living on their pin money. Designing everything from ball gowns to genital spray. Just plain RealGuys.

8

If the fashion designers—those pretty fellows with their suntans and their couture collections and their fat price tags—are the whipped cream of Seventh Avenue, there is a lot of butterfat down below ready, willing, and able to be packaged and put on the market.

Take heart, America—your sartorial salvation lies in the hands of the manufacturers of Seventh Avenue. Mass production—Jonathan Logan, Sue Brett, Joan Leslie, Junior Sophisticates, Susan Thomas. With factories and contractors all over the place, these firms are responsible for most of the clothes the women in America wear. Mass Cult or the Mid Cult. They deal in volume. Where Geoffrey Beene's many divisions might bring in $6 million, Jonathan Logan, in a bad year, is still in the counting house and counting at $266,713,000. A quarter of a billion dollars. That's a lot of dress business. A lot of cotton. Wool. Skirts. Pants. Blouses. Seams. Zippers. Buttons. All of which makes Jonathan Logan the biggest manufacturer of ladies' garments in the country. With some fifteen major divisions, Jonathan Logan, with that $266 million in sales, is a giant in an industry where more than half the firms have an annual sales volume of less than $1 million and where the life span of a company is less than three years.

David Schwartz founded Jonathan Logan some thirty years ago "when I bought out a business with that name." He is described by one showroom manager as being, "the kind of person that gives Seventh Avenue a bad name." Ah, well. Few who have dealt with David Schwartz will dispute this charge. But then you don't get to be chairman of the board by being a nice guy, now, do you? Not in the garment industry, anyway. Schwartz, who stepped down as president in 1964 and was replaced by his young son, Richard (Cornell '60), was born poor but honest up on 112th Street in Manhattan. The son of Russian Jews who emigrated to this country, he attended New York public schools, worked in the printing business (hauling linotype plates), then became a messenger and delivery boy for a relative who worked in the dress business. On cold days he stuffed newspapers under his coat to keep warm.

"In 1928 I made the first rayon dress in this business. I'll bet you didn't know that, did you? The first rayon dress. I made the first Bemberg dress, too. Bemberg fabric for $1.57½ a yard. That was forty-three years ago. It was navy with big red flowers on it. $1.57½ a yard. You couldn't find it for that price today." When he decided to go into business for himself, Schwartz accumulated a few thousand dollars, found a loft already housing a dress manufacturing firm—named Jonathan Logan—and bought them out. Rather than change the name on the door, Schwartz kept it because he liked its tone. The business, like Topsy, kept growing. Schwartz almost sold out to Glen Alden Corporation. At the last minute, he decided not to close the deal. "For my children's sake." What he did, instead, was go public in 1960. Besides, "I wanted to see how big I could get." Well, he made it.

Richard Schwartz graduated from Cornell and came into the family business, but not from the bottom up. "From the bottom up? That's silly. Why should the boss's kid work his way up? He had lots of good ideas. I paid good money for his good education—he should use some of it, not waste it pushing carts and wrapping packages."

The difference between the chairman of the board and the president of the company seems to herald the coming revolution in the garment industry. It is old *vs* new, noise *vs* quiet, hustle and hurly-burly of the old ways *vs* the subtle and sharply-honed corporate qualities of today's big business. David plays gin rummy and bridge; Richard plays chess and rides to the hounds. David dropped out of high school; Richard is pure Ivy League. David is hand-held scissors; Richard is IBM computers and laser-beam cutters. "My son, the president—he runs the business today," says Schwartz senior.

The garment industry has something for everybody. There are clothes so expensive only the Very Rich can even think about buying them. Clothes so cheap that, as Michael Harrington pointed out in *The Other America*: "America has the best-dressed poverty the world has ever known." Clothes for hippies and heads. Clothes for old ladies and young ladies. Clothes for skinny people and—clothes for the fuller figure! Make that the inhabitants of Fat City. For the lady who is in no way willowy and could never be mistaken for Audrey Hepburn, even if she stood behind a tree and talked in a whispery, slightly English accented voice. There is even a manufacturer whose major cause in life is designing for the Fuller Figures among us.

He is Leonard Shtendel. He is the Little Caesar of the Big Woman. He works out of Philadelphia and Hialeah, under such names as LeDamour and M'Lady of Miami, manufacturing for the sizes 38–52. Now Leonard Shtendel is probably providing the biggest public service in America today. And if he makes a couple million dollars while he's at it, do not censure him. Praise him. While other designers and manufacturers stay away from the nation's fat ladies in droves, Leonard Shtendel cares. "They should be able to wear everything they want to. If bright colors are fashionable, why can't ladies of the fuller figure be able to buy them? If HotPants are In, why can't they buy them and wear them?" Some purists—WWD among them—might object that a size 52 in HotPants is not esthetically appropriate. Leonard Shtendel and M'Lady of Miami say: Let the lady decide. "We make HotPants wider than they are long," he says.

Leonard Shtendel did not get into the fuller figure through any sort of high-blown altruism. No, that came later. About $2.5 million per year annual sales figure later. LeDamour began strictly for expediency's sake: "It was 1948, see? A recession year, right? I had a college degree in economics and nowhere to use it. So I figured I had to have something safe, right?" So it hit him—large-size women's bathing suits. "See, that was when nobody cared about fat ladies. They all wore big black bathing suits. I could have a big line made up, if they didn't sell that year I could hold them over for the next, right? My stock wouldn't be out of date." He checked the idea over with his fiancée; she said yes. They were married, packed up their snuggies, and shuffled off to Miami Beach for a combination honeymoon-selling campaign. "The marriage lasted; I sold out my bathing suits." He's been in business ever since.

"You know—somebody has to do it." Leonard Shtendel is the social worker of the oversized. He really cares. Does Oscar care about the fuller figure? Not on your life. Does Geoffrey care about the fuller figure—the figure that's fuller all over?

Not a bit of it. But Leonard Shtendel cares. He figures a fat—you should pardon the expression—lady has just as much right to wear snappy, up-to-the-minute clothes as anybody else. "She looks in the mirror—she doesn't see a fat lady in size 52 HotPants," Leonard insists. "She sees a size 10. Well, maybe a size 12. You know what? The catalogues? For Lane Bryant? The models are all size 10. Size 12. The ladies, they look at those models and they think, 'That's how I'll look,' and when they put the clothes on—that's how they see themselves. Isn't that wonderful?" The Miracle Worker. Lay off that Diet Mazola, ladies. Throw away your Light 'n' Lively. Leonard Shtendel is here—and he loves you just the way you are!

He must be doing something right. Every week, 25,000 garments ranging in size from 38 to 52 go out of his factories. That's nearly 1.5 million a year! He and his designer, Billie Donaldson, put out four lines a year and about 300 different styles for the Ladies of the Fuller Figure. Bathing suits up to 66-inch expansion.

Yes. Something for Everybody. Even if the body is size 52.

WWD finally recognized that Mid-America did indeed exist, out there in the Vast Wasteland West of the Hudson. Jim Brady himself sat down and said so one day late in 1970. "Sometimes I think we get carried away with the following WWD has among name designers, chic stores, beautiful women," he told the staff. "But do we do a good job of covering the K-Marts, Penneys, Korvettes, *et cetera*? They're big retailers, hundreds of times larger than many of the pacesetting stores we cover." Oh, Jim Brady. Man of the People. Saviour of the Middle Class. All those folks caught with their nothing down and ten dollars a month plus 12 percent carrying charges. Now you're talking! WWD took up a new cudgel. We must "let them know we realize they're out there and alive." Alive and well and kicking—and making it in WWD.

Since Brady's memo, WWD has got into the whole mass

market of chain stores, catalogue operations, and discount houses.

The mentions of the Big Three retailers—Sears, Roebuck, Montgomery Ward, J.C. Penney—came in a flurry, fast and furious. "Sears Acceptance Net Gains" and "Sears to Step Up Expansion Pace" and "Sears Eying New Fields" and "Penney Chief Approved Pants—But Hot Pants?"

A month later, Brady was so pleased his suggestion had been heeded so well, he could start ladling out some praise. "Mort Sheinman's Penney, Sears, Monty [sic] Ward interviews most significant," he announced October 9. "When the Big Three take a stand on fashion, it means Middle America will follow."

Even Fairchild, who probably has never set foot in a Monkey Ward store, much less worn a Sears, Roebuck necktie or a pair of J.C. Penney jockey shorts, got the message. "People want inexpensive clothes. Clothes that are priced so people can afford to buy them." He leans back in his chair. "I would guess," he pondered, "that a designer like Oscar will be doing a collection for Sears, Roebuck and J.C. Penney's before long." It wouldn't be surprising. Blass does sheets and towels. Oscar has already done a mattress ticking for Simmons. Why not a collection for Sears and Penney's? "These days, women who have money don't want to spend it on just a few clothes. They want a lot of clothes." Fairchild's predictions? "I see inexpensive ready-to-wear doing a better job in the creative areas. Snappy and better clothes for the money."

Ah, yes—J.C. Penney. Yellow and black tile-front stores where you could buy everything from overalls to nursing bras; salesladies who got a perm every six months and wore flowers on their collars or handkerchiefs pinned to their left shoulder. Today, Penney's is much more plush and lavish, but it still services the same basic customer. According to Gaylen Hoganson, merchandising manager for women's apparel, that comes to about 85 percent of the consumer market. There are approximately 1,700 Penney's stores across the country, plus mail order services in thirty-seven states. In a year, Penney's sells well in excess of sixty million ladies' garments across the country.

There arose in the Psychedelic Sixties, however, a whole new set of alternatives to even the high-fashion designers and the manufacturers of Mass Cult. Americans saw boutiques. Boutiques to the right of us. Boutiques to the left of us. Boutiques had been around in Europe, notably Paris and London, forever. Not having the massive department store approach to buying and selling, the Europeans long favored the small-shop approach. The whole concept of the little dressmaker stitching away in her atelier was a reality—only the 1960s saw a slight shift in philosophy. The whole explosion of the Youth Culture—complete with the deification of rock stars and the stoning of a young population—remade the boutique culture into its own image.

The 1960s came exploding onto the public conscious like a freaked-out Fourth of July celebration. Somewhere around 1962 when the Beatles made it out of that cave in Liverpool, it came to pass that a whole new counter-culture was born. It was a young culture with lots of money, lots of leisure, and easily bored. The inhabitants of this counter-culture were constantly seeking out new kicks. Freedom, individuality—a sort of assertive self-expression came to pass in the 1960s. Young people were thus courted by politicians, the mass media, and American merchants.

It was a rapidly-changing scene, this "boutique" culture that swept across the country in the mid-1960s. A person could get a whiplash just trying to keep track of whose store was still open and whose had closed down over the weekend—or overnight, in some cases. (One boutique owner even closed over a lunch hour. She locked the door, bought a hot dog, and never went back.) Boutiques might close from poor business management to boredom to a fight with a boyfriend. Princess Zorch, alias Carol Hollett, is a survivor of those Good Old Days of the mid-1960s, albeit not in her original form. Princess Zorch of the Hot Shit Manufacturing Company. Carol was just a George Washington University graduate who had done time teaching at the Phyllis Bell Charm School in Washington, D.C. Then she ended up in New York working for Wilhela Cushman, then fashion editor of the *Ladies' Home Journal.* "I wore hair spray and a bra and seams in my stockings. I can't believe it," she says. By 1965 Carol found herself living in a loft on West Houston Street, trying to figure out what to do with herself. "It was a common dilemma with Village chicks then," Carol says. "Here we were—Women's Lib hadn't come to rescue us. We were like all those goddamn suburban ladies in *The Feminine Mystique*—only we lived five flights up in a loft—who were bored and miserable but didn't know it. Most of us got into the scene for two reasons. One, to get a little bread, two, just to be doing something. Fortunately, all of us could sew." Carol, as Princess Zorch, ran a shop called The Ninth Street Emporium and General Store on Ninth Street, which sold her original designs along with others that she took on. "*Women's Wear* called us 'The Boutique Makers' but we were just trying to earn a living the best way we knew how without working for *Vogue* patterns or *Ladies' Home Journal* or typing for some goddamn insurance company or something." In one form or another Carol/Princess Zorch survived until the 1966 subway strike. "That really closed it up tight." With the subway strike on, the Bad Guys were less mobile. Carol and a number of other small stores were robbed countless times. "I just shut the door and took off for Woodstock." Today, she's moved uptown—but only physically. Her long mane of 1960s red hair ("I wore it in a French twist in the fifties. A *French twist!*") has given way to a WASP Afro. From the simple shifts of the 1960s, she is now into hand-painting important Afghanistan coats. "I'm choking to death on this goddamn acrylic junk—but it's still more fun than *Ladies' Home Journal.*" Those were comfortable days,

Door. Everybody's best friend. She bites her fingernails, talks a mile a minute, often looks weird, in a cuddly sort of way. And she has a *terrific* personality.

Betsey Johnson does not look like a fashion designer. "But who wants to look like a fashion designer," Betsey laughs. "Clothes really don't mean a damn. I hate fashion," she says. "And I hate to take it out of real life. And I hate people who put labels on fashion. Fashion editors and Seventh Avenue people tend to name things. A skirt length, for example. Christ—when you name things it has to come in and go out of style. For me there's no particular skirt length—just a lot of different lengths."

Betsey Johnson is truly a child prodigy; she got her start at *Mademoiselle, Vogue, Glamour.* She was not born with a silver thimble in her mouth. A product of Terryville, Connecticut, she attended Pratt Institute, then dropped out and headed for Syracuse, Class of '64. She entered "everything in sight" in the *Mademoiselle* Guest Editor contest and was assigned to the fabrics editor. From there it was a short step to working full time on *Mademoiselle* after graduation.

While working at *Mademoiselle,* Betsey began supplementing her salary by making body sweaters at night and on weekends. She wore them to work, advertised them by taping notes in those various ladies' rooms at 420 Lexington Avenue—headquarters of the Condé Nast publications empire. She sold them to anyone who would fork over the ten dollars.

Fashion editors were intrigued and wore them around town. They were sensational hits. "I was sick!" Betsey cried. "Where could I go with them? What could I do with them?" Face it: a good Oo-o-o-o-o, even from a fashion editor at *Mademoiselle,* isn't worth a tinker's damn on the open market. Praise won't pay the rent and there is not an A & P in the country—no matter how altruistic they make themselves out to be with ecologically secure detergents and returnable soda pop bottles—that will take an enthusiastic Oo-o-o-o in exchange for a turkey pot pie.

Enter one day, almost on cue, Paul Young with an idea for mass-producing boutiques and boutique items. Edith Raymond Locke at *Mademoiselle* turned him on to Betsey and from that point on it's—history! "Everything was so accidental," Betsey said.

Betsey Johnson may not have given the world the cure for cancer, but she did get things moving in a whole new fashion direction. Back when she started with her skimpy little T-shirt dresses and body sweaters, the world was still snugged into dresses that looked as if they had been constructed by the Army Corps of Engineers: heavy welt seaming, high little armholes that pushed a lady's armpits right up under her ear lobes. Simple to look at, but a masterpiece of construction underneath it all. Linings and inner linings and facings and inner facings. Seaming, top stitchings, welting. If a thread ripped, a person needed a mechanical engineer to get it fixed. Things were not made—they were constructed. The fashion designers were the hard hats of the garment industry. Onto this construction site stumbled Betsey Johnson, with nary a dart or a welt seam in sight. Flippy little skirts, comfortable armholes, body-hugging dresses. With Betsey Johnson, getting there was *all* the fun. The silver fish dress, made of silver acetate. It looked like the magic ball that turned round and round and skittered out all those fragments of light over the Marathon Dances of the 1920s. The Noise Dress, a simple drift of jersey with big metal grommets around the hem that jingle-jangle-jingled when the wearer walked. The Slip Dress, made out of the very same stuff that basketball uniforms were made out of—and looking very much like a basketball jersey: low-slung armholes, low-slung neckline, high wavy hemline. The Do-it-yourself Dress, a piece of clear plastic dress which came in a can complete with all sorts of goodies to tack in, on, and around the dress.

By late 1967 the Paraphernalia people were splitting off, one by one. "It had turned into just another big business," Betsey says. "The money people came in and everything else went out the window." Paul Young left and ended up in London running a boutique. Betsey quit and ended up free-lancing for a year. Then, she and two Paraphernalia pals—Bunky (Barbara Washburn) and Nini (Anita Latorre)—came up with $250,000 worth of investors to open a store stocked with their own line of designs. "It was awful. All the investors wanted to do was go public!" It is a wail from the heart. "As soon as big business walked in and it had to make pots of money—it went down the drain." They dropped the project, Betsey headed for San Francisco and designed for Alvin Duskin for a year. That was even more depressing, so she moved back to New York City.

And who should she end up with—the Alley Cat people. Alley Cat had been started in 1965 by none other than Leonard Shtendel when he discovered, lurking among those layers of fat, the Youth Market. He was willing to give what Betsey wanted—which was freedom, control, and label credit. So this highly unlikely duo went into business together. Additionally, Betsey, Bunky, and Nini own and operate a boutique of that name on the East Side, lavishly stocked with Alley Cat designs plus funky other stuff that keeps them all happy. And solvent.

"I like to design. I like to make people happy with my designs," says Betsey, stomping around in her red T-shirt, her pink cotton harem pants, and her lace-up suede wedgies. "And I figure—if I can mass-produce my designs with any sort of quality and at a good price, I can make just that many more people happy, right?"

These days, WWD loves Betsey Johnson. June Weir takes her to lunch at Orsini's. John Fairchild mentions her name. "WWD picks the Women of the Year, who understand today's mood," they wrote in a pious singling out of the women in fashion, including, of course, Betsey Johnson. "On both sides of the Atlantic these are the trendsetters, designers who get their Sensuous message across in everything from coats, suits, and dresses to sportswear and knits."

"My clothes are people," Betsey told WWD. "Their animals, what they eat. My customers should only buy what they cannot make themselves, for just a little bit of money." On January 7, Betsey was given the coveted page-one illustration slot with a sketch of a do-it-yourself dress in white muslin outlined with red piping. The idea? Do something with it yourself. "Betsey's aware of the fact that more than a few people are sewing their own clothes, embroidering their own accessories, appliquéing their own jeans," said WWD. "And, that's right up Betsey's alley." It wasn't a Donald Brooks fur blazer or a pair of Halston HotPants. But it sure showed WWD was with it.

"Betsey Johnson, that clever girl, has done it again," WWD thrilled in still another front page feature of the February 18, 1971, edition—in full color. "She's come up with the newest direction in summer dresses." Sketched was a comfy Betsey dress with low-slung neckline, floppy sleeves, and a loose, long skirt—made up in nylon tricot. *Nylon tricot?* That's *bedroom* stuff. What old ladies' *panties* are made from. There was Betsey Johnson, hot into nylon tricot—and there was WWD, hot into Betsey Johnson for her ideas. (Betsey's nylon tricot was bright poison green with enormous shocking red cherries printed on it. Flying yellow zonkers—what a switch for nylon tricot.)

Betsey may be Fairchild's and WWD's Big Hero, but she has company: Carol Horn, the shaggy-haired designer for Benson & Partners; Pinky (Wolman) and Diane (Beaudry) of Hang-Ups; Liz Claiborne of Youth Guild; Jeanne Campbell of Sportwhirl; Luba (Marks) of Elite, Jrs.; Meredith Gladstone of Crazy Horse. These young women are the antithesis of the male designers. For one thing, they are strictly into sportswear. "My look is basically Plain Jane," Maxime de la Falaise told WWD. "The sort of basic clothes women can wear all the fabulous belts and handcrafted things with." Face it: you could hardly wear a handmade macramé belt with one of Oscar's chiffons.

"I stick to basic shapes, then follow the current mood," said Carol Horn. "My clothes are geared to whatever the mood of that particular day is."

The difference between today and that yesterday of a few years ago is the attitude. The Woodstock Nation came down from a super-high and started working. Five years ago, although there was quality and imagination, it was simple. Ordinary fabrics made into ordinary things—cotton, wool, and silk into dresses, skirts, and capes. Today it's much more flamboyant. A lot of leather—leather that is stitched, stenciled, painted, braided, patched, appliquéd. A lot of nylon tricot again to be appliquéd, stitched, stretched, patched. Velvet to be appliquéd, scorched, tie-dyed. Fanciful and far-out. And a lot more mass production, at least compared to the do-it-yourself scene of five years ago.

Not that the heads' version of mass production is anything like the ILGWU version of mass production. "We play the radio loud," said Jeff Stuart of Hideout Manufacturing, a leather manufacturing concern in Los Angeles. Ten people who gather in a loft, turn the radio on to an FM station, and stitch away. It's not WWD they're reading—it's the L.A. *Free Press*. Fifteen people, calling themselves Annabel Lee Time, do likewise in Philadelphia, turning out nylon tricot shirts and dresses with appliquéd designs—very cosmic. Very fanciful. Wide lips spilling out stars. Castles with clouds sitting comfortably on hilltops. Cosmic designs. Fairy-tale storybook designs. "We're not in it for money. We're not looking to become a large manufacturing company. We just like to make pretty things."

It's the Underground Seventh Avenue. The hip alternative to Jonathan Logan. There are designers, manufacturers, sales representatives, stores that buy them. And even a fashion magazine irreverently called *Rags*. Sniggin Piggin and their relationship with Fein Things is about as direct a parallel to

Seventh Avenue as can be found. Sniggin Piggin is a design and manufacturing firm operating out of a series of crumbling Victorian apartments in Providence, Rhode Island. Most of the gang are former members of Georgie Porgie and the Cry-babys, a rock group from the late 1960s. "We needed weird clothes when we were in the group," explained Judy Higgins, the wife half of Sniggin Piggin (and responsible for the "iggin" portion of the name). Judy played bass, her husband Danny played guitar. Heading up Fein Things, the hip manu-facturers' rep group, is Paul Fein, aided by his wife Gloria. "We handle ten or twelve funky manufacturers. Stick with me and you can outfit a whole boutique with my crowd," says Fein. Among them, Sniggin Piggin, now into appliquéd capes and pants done in lightweight upholstery velvet. "Last year was a bummer. Tie-dye—and the dyes wouldn't arrive. Cro-chet—and the thread wouldn't arrive." Jeff Antin, who has his "factory" in Woodstock, does absolutely incredible work with chamois-colored suede. Antin, who looks more like a bash-ful Marxist scholar than a suede freak, commands upwards of $300 for his creations, most of which are custom made for The Stitching Horse, an unbelievably expensive leather bou-itque on Manhattan's East Side. A wrap-around suede skirt. Delicate and airy, butter-soft suede. Bits of suede nicked with a sharp knife, producing an embroidered effect. Wild stuff. Jeff was also into music but, "I was starving." So he got some leather and started working. No dropping in and out of Pratt or Parsons. No two-year stints at the Chamber Syndicale. And no penthouse apartments in Sutton Place, either. The factory? "Mostly kids who are good but can't get jobs anywhere else. You know—hair and things." Kids who wear jeans with hand-embroidered peace symbols on the ass and flowers running around the belled bottoms. Like that.

Two young handicrafters—George Fasbinder and Frank Rubino—hand-painted skirts and pants and vests and peddled them out of a pushcart on Eighth Street in the Village. Man, no bread in that venture. They worked around and discovered a way to mass produce it using their original designs silk-screened onto the leather. Through a lawyer they found backing—a guy who owns parking lots and auto-repair shops and has weekend delusions of being Hip—set up a factory on the East Side where sixty young workers gather every day over containers of coffee to silk-screen away.

In some cases, this is pretty big business. Intricate and difficult designs translated into leathers and velvets. Patchwork reptile skin belts and boots. Patchwork satin shirts. The rock influence is all-pervasive. It was the rock groups, in their attempt to break out of matching weskits and sport coat outfits of the 1950s—white buck shoes and D.A. haircuts—that did it. That plus the whole wild mad psychedelic scene of the mid-1960s. The whole world dropped a super-tab and went sky-high, off on some swirling trip in a magic ship of the mind. A super-trip of exploding colors and fantastic visions. If acid rock was a "product of its time," then so were the clothes the groups wore—and the clothes their fans wore. Any time a T-shirt with the likeness of Jesus Christ stenciled between the nipples can sell in the millions, you can bet there are a lot of people around dressing in something besides letter sweaters and Sta-Prest slacks.

If life on Underground Seventh Avenue is cool, the real Seventh Avenue can be hot as hell. Make no mistake about it: fashion is a cutthroat business. Ulcers are as prevalent on Seventh Avenue as they are on Madison Avenue. A designer who is limited to only four collections a year not only has to anticipate but he cannot afford to take chances or to be whimsical. To experiment. With rising labor costs—estimated to be up 50 percent in the past ten years—and an economic slump, the 1970s did not start off with a bang. Some of the best names in the business went under. Patullo-Jo Copeland, Hannah Troy, Samuel Winston. "Women just don't want to spend a lot of money on clothes today," Winston said, after liquidating his Seventh Avenue couture house. He found out the hard way that most ladies—perhaps the BPs excluded—do not want to fork over $400 to $1,000 for an outfit.

"We were priced right out of the market," said Ellen Brooke, who decided to close her sportswear firm in late 1970. The biggest reason: labor costs. "When we began, we went from $150 to $200 wholesale." And when she shut the front door? Those same wholesale prices had zoomed to $300 and $400. No matter how much nice old Charlie Zimmerman has to say over at the union—the ILGWU must share the blame with everybody else.

Cheap knockoffs and a market that suddenly finds itself flooded with what started out to be a status item—be it Midi skirts or HotPants—run into trouble. Saturation leads to boredom. Women walking down the street seeing thousands of HotPants in window after window, some being of the shoddiest quality imaginable because they were so quickly knocked off, will eventually get bored. Meet yourself coming and going, like a loop of film run and rerun over and over again *ad infinitum*—a lady gets bored. The world moves so fast—the lady gets bored. HotPants in February. So whats new for March?

It's a $24 billion business, and that means get there first, get there fast. Rake it in. Then on to something else again. It is a mass market waiting to be served. It is at once fickle—easily bored and wanting constant entertainment—and cautious. Even the boutiques find this. There is money around to be spent, even in a recession, but it winds up being spent in weird ways. A dude will wander around wearing a $3.00 workshirt from the Sweet-Orr store down by the docks, an old pair of Levi's that probably cost $7.00 five years ago, and $80 patchwork snakeskin boots. Try explaining *that*. It's that old double shuffle that is driving the fashion industry up the wall. The *double entendre* that would take a pack of youth marketeers and social psychologists the rest of their lives to figure out. "Things have changed you know," says Marsha, of the old Abracadabra boutique. "People have a kind of social consciousness now. They don't give a shit about clothes—they're really frivolous and unimportant."

One of the most dismal aspects of the fashion business are the knockoff artists, the rip-off gang. Fashion designs cannot be patented or copyrighted. Design something, and if it's good, just feel flattered somebody stole it from you. Nobody is safe; few people are above it. It operates at all levels.

Princess Zorch was into pantsaprons—aprons with legs to be worn with slacks—back in the mid-1960s. They were sold in chi-chi little stores around town, featured in *Mademoiselle*. Like that. Jackie Kennedy even snapped up a few pair. Then the orders from one of the East Side stores stopped coming in. "I wandered in one day to see what was happening and to get some money the shits owed me—and there was a whole goddamn rack full of pantsaprons. Only they weren't mine." The store had a little workroom going in the back staffed by four Puerto Rican ladies—sewing up pantsaprons carefully knocked off from her originals.

Couture houses in Europe charge exorbitant amounts for the privilege of watching a collection. Entrants are screened as carefully as security risks in the Pentagon. The reason for this profitable paranoia is to save themselves from the knockoff artists. The unscrupulous guy who would not be caught dead buying an original, but would kill himself attempting to copy it and sell it.

The boutiques in the Village and over on the East Side are jammed on Saturdays. Some of the bodies belong to legitimate customers—folks who will actually trade in legal tender for a garment. The rest? Manufacturers over from Seventh Avenue to see what they can see—and sew. When the more successful boutique owners go on buying trips, representatives from department stores tag along after them to see what is being bought. It is more cloak-and-dagger than a Hollywood movie.

Hip boutique owner leaves shop in London side street. Over there—the character in the shiny suit and the shades. When she's safely outasight, he slips across the street and darts into the shop. What'd she buy? What'd she turn down? I'll take some of those—forget those.

There it is. Seventh Avenue. It's sixty million garments in 1,700 retail stores—or loud music in a leathergoods loft in Los Angeles. Dresses for high school graduation and bridal showers and bridge clubs. Flamboyant dress. Quiet dress. The Best Dressed List and the best dressed poverty in the world. Something for Everyone.

9

For one brief moment, all American women were free, free, free. Not just hippies or freaks or rock stars. Everybody. "Over my dead body!" the women of America chorused, as they sat around in their pantsuits waiting for SA's greatest crisis to crest. And crest it did, with the advent of HotPants and their overwhelming vote of confidence for the American leg. It was, to most women, the final vote of no-confidence to the Midi that they felt some conniving cartel had been desperately attempting to drape over their dead bodies. It was like kicking a dead horse. But the body was not dead, you see. Only rigid with barely controlled outrage.

Maybe it was Women's Lib. Maybe it was the whole stand-up-and-be-counted mood that swept over the country. Maybe it was just part and parcel of the whole enormity that America had become, turning people into punch cards and their destinies into printouts. Perhaps the colorful, flamboyant individuality that manifested itself during the late night of the 1960s and the early morning hours of the 1970s was merely a reaction to bigness. To the kind of conformity that had pigeon-holed us until we squealed with pain and finally with outrage and finally said Nevermore in sweet but firm tones.

Perhaps it was escapism. As designer Pinky Wolman put it, "People really want to escape from the recession, school strikes, and taxi increases and go back to the glamour of Bette Davis and Rita Hayworth." Maybe that was it. Maybe it was just the regression that saw thousands of women putting on red lipstick and platform wedgies and curling their hair again.

Or, maybe it was just fun: a gigantic costume party that saw cowboys and Indians and hookers and pinup queens all gathering at the river for one super-fantastic trip into never-never land where it didn't matter one whit what you wore just as long as (1) it was what you yourself chose to wear and (2) it made you happy and comfortable. It was, finally and once and for all, an individual ego trip. *Vogue* and *Harpers* and, yes, even *Women's Wear Daily* be damned.

In its own Civilized Woman way, WWD came closer than anyone thought to capturing what was really happening out in America. The slick fashion magazines were still dictating—WWD at least took some pictures out on the streets. HotPants were closer to where it was eventually at than the Midi ever hoped to be. To its credit, WWD finally figured that out.

Not since Dior pulled out all the stitches in 1947 and ordered the women of the world to unite behind longer hemlines had the post-War world been so preoccupied with fashion. Cover stories, talk shows, dinner conversations—not a day went by when America was not caught up in some sort of dialectic dialogue over the state of fashion. And why not? It is a big business and getting bigger. The designers are now celebrities in their own right, with a whole new pack moving up swiftly and nipping at their all-too-vulnerable heels. The

youth market, refusing to be hemmed in by either convention
or capitalism, is busting at the seams. And just as June Weir
said—we all wear clothes. And everybody is getting into the
act. Designers, the press, social historians, social psychiatrists.
And why not, if what social historian James Laver says has any
truth at all to it. "Fashion has its roots in the collective
unconscious," he contends. "The hopes and fears of a whole
society are reflected in the cut of a dress." Maybe. Look at the
Silent Fifties. A duller period in American fashion history
would be hard to find.

Skirts had plunged in 1947 and down they stayed with nary
a frolicsome calf exposed to leaven the dull days in America.
Circle skirts and circle pins. Political repression and fashion
repression. Dull days in Washington. Dull days for girl
watchers. Fear makes fools of us all. "The climate of opinion
that generates long skirts is not a socially liberal one," pointed
out Wisconsin history professor William O'Neill.

There are no laws governing what we Americans wear, but
that has never stopped a zealous do-gooder yet. Roy Rogers
and Dale Evans can wear their American flag cowboy suits—in
sequins yet—on nationwide television. Abbie Hoffman gets
busted for showing up in an American flag shirt. Clive Barnes
and LBJ and Bobby Kennedy's kids can let their hair curl way
down past their ear lobes, but the Chicago Seven had their
heads shaved "for sanitary reasons" two days before they were
released on bail. It's not so much what the Silent Majority
wears as what kind of pressure it puts on others to conform.
As Gloria Steinem puts it, "It's those Germanic,
stick-and-carrot urgings toward Americanism and propriety
that will be the test."

But it is not all just pop psych, fun and games, this
philosophizing over fashion. James Laver, a London museum
curator by profession and fashion analyst by extension, sees a
direct parallel between women's clothes and the amount of
sexual and political freedom and/or repression in a given
society. When skirts are up, repression is down. And vice

versa. In times of great freedom and a relaxing of strictures, clothes have kept apace. During the 1920s when women were getting the vote and getting jobs, they hiked their skirts and bared their legs. They shrugged into a pair of step-ins and threw away their Victorian corsets. Skirts came down during the Depression, hiked back up during World War II, when women were working and were self-reliant, what with the men gone off to war and jobs that desperately needed filling. Down came the skirts when the men came home and it was, once again, decided that a woman's place was truly in the home. And the 1960s—when the Spock generation grew up and broke out—saw skirts go zooming up faster than a speeding bullet.

As Dr. Joyce Brothers pointed out, "Studies have verified that the hippie garb of college students reflects a more liberal attitude toward social change than that of more conservatively dressed students."

In his book *They Became What They Beheld*, anthropologist Edmund Carpenter talks about clothing as "social weaponry." To him "it defines sexes, classes, age groups; fashion is therefore infallible. Violations threaten the social order, producing fear, shock, anger." As he sees it, in the Good Old Days, "Mass production of identical goods required mass consumption of identical goods. Current fashion was like currency: private dress was counterfeit." Nobody walked around in anything but what everybody else was walking around in. Circle skirts and circle pins. "Private dress was as unacceptable as a three-dollar bill. Fashion was obedience to public form. A woman wore one kind of dress or another kind of dress simply because it was done. By everybody. Not because she wanted to, not from personal selection, but simply because this was what all did. Fashion was a big package deal: Container Corpse of America."

Carpenter, the Pete Hamill of the anthropologists, expresses slightly controlled outrage. The antithesis to WWD's thesis.

All over the country, America found hundreds and

thousands of her citizens getting up off their collective bottoms and leaping to their feet in celebration of their identity. I AM ME! cried hundreds and thousands of voices, attempting to impress somebody with their very own specific qualities of individuality. I am me—a person, a mother, a son, a consumer, a voter.

Maybe it was that first tab of acid dropped by the Leary-Alpert adherents up at Harvard. Maybe it was that one toke of pure dynamite Acapulco Gold that broke the back of fashion conformity. Whatever it was—Flash! Bam! Alacazam! Out of an orange-colored sky came flying a screaming yellow zonker marked ME! I! I exist because I am.

"This whole nostalgia thing, I think, is just part of the whole disaffection with what things are at the moment," says Dr. Robert Campbell, associate director of psychiatry at St. Vincent's Hospital in New York. "Technology and urbanization have not worked for us the way we thought they were going to. In fact, they turned out to be absolutely ghastly. The youngsters today are much brighter than we are, you know. They don't have the hangups we do. They are much more interested in going back to other values—values that mean more to the human being. To the individual."

Liberation was the keynote of the time. Liberation meant mini skirts and mini skirts meant some kind of leg coverings that would enable a girl to bend over without causing governments to collapse and strong men to go into cardiac arrest. Liberation meant it was more comfortable to wear pants in winter. Liberation meant boots were a lot more practical than shoes for fighting concrete, weather, subway crowds, and the Sheep Meadow in Central Park.

"It's quite chilling to open up the pages of *Women's Wear Daily*," wrote Gloria Steinem in *New York* magazine during the Midi crisis, "and find them full of the new knee-concealing garment called the Longuette," As Gloria saw it ,"this dowdy skirt length" is all over WWD. "It's as if the

Silent Majority of France and America had got simultaneously fed up with styles dictated by what were, according to both *haute couture* and suburban standards, the outcast groups: the poor, the young, and the black. Manufacturers are hurrying back to styles set by the affluent, the perpetuators of Convenitonal Wisdom."

In a study of the youth market, one ad agency discovered that fashion does indeed filter upward: upward mobility in fashion. The first group to wear leathers publicly were—the bike hoods. The castoff cast-outs of the local high schools. The guys with the greasy D.A. haircuts and dirty fingernails. Now who wears leather? Well, Jackie Kennedy Onassis for one. That long black leather coat of hers came right straight from the Hell's Angels. The first ladies to popularize wigs in this country were the ladies of the night with their lacquered orange sausage curls tremblingly towering skyward like a Dynel version of the World Trade Center. And denim? Farmers and construction workers and railroad men. The working class reaches of society. Now Bill Blass rummages in Army-Navy stores and swoons over stitchery on brakemen's jackets. Geoffrey Beene and Jacques Kaplan use denim in their collections. Saks Fifth Avenue spends a fortune advertising denims from St. Tropez.

French author Jean-François Revel argues that the radicals in America are truly pro-American. Maybe the only true Americans. A true revolution, Revel figures, is "a social, cultural, moral, even artistic transformation where the old values of the old world are rejected, where relations between social classes are reconsidered, where relations among individuals are modified, where the concept of the family changes, where the value of work, the very goals of existence are reconsidered." As he sees it, the revolution began in the mid-fifties with civil rights and has marched right on with black power, women's lib, anti-war, environmental issues, and more recently, the eighteen-year-old vote, the defeat of the SST.

And nowhere was this new American Revolution more evident than in what America chose to wear in the early dawn of the 1970s: anything, everything, nothing. All of these, none of these. For once, Paris and couture and the so-called fashion designers and the press were not only ignored, but were told to Shut the Hell up. Hang on to your love beads, freaks; all is not lost. Wear what makes you happy. Blessed be the tie that does not bind, bend, spindle, or mutilate!

10

For years WWD—nay, the world—has been preoccupied with the Very Rich. Now, the Very Rich are really not much different from, say, you and me. They are just richer. Or, as Ernest Hemingway put it to F. Scott Fitzgerald once in a discussion on this very topic, "They have more money." It is a sensible enough argument.

In its early infatuation with the Very Rich, WWD was a veritable fountain of enthusiasm. A BP could barely head for the Ladies' Room without a retinue of WWD reporters and photographers in HotPursuit. WWD reporters lurked in the corner taking notes. Photographers staked out their subjects like Efram Zimbalist, Jr., staked out fugitives on TV.

Among the people WWD loves are Charles and Lyn Revson, in their twenty-nine-room digs on Park Avenue. (He's the head of Revlon, the folks who gave us Fire and Ice lipstick and matching nailpolish. And lots of other cosmetic goodies. She is his wife, sometimes a BP. Once an FV.) Enormous marble floors stretch throughout the place. Massive English chandeliers dripping shards of glass and light all over the place. Yards of leather-bound books in the library. A beige marble bathroom stocked with dozens of Porthault towels. Matching gold-leaf His & Her sinks. Gold faucets. A kitchen that can make do for 100, designed for them by Stuart Levin of Le Pavillon. One whole twelve-foot wall of stainless steel doors. Refrigerators. A green ballroom, full of gilt chairs, that can handle 150 BPs at once. It takes seven butlers just to run the joint. On and on it goes. Their yacht, the Ultima II, is the world's largest specially built private yacht. (Which knocks Ari's old tanker, the Christina, right in its midsection. After all, it was *converted*.) A crew of thirty-one to take care of the celebs that the Revsons haul around with them. A house in New Rochelle for country weekends.

Now, right off you should sense there is a great difference between the Very Rich and the Very Social and, say, you and me. As Charlotte Curtis puts it, "Society is anything that can't be nailed down."

Take those homes for example. They are, for the most part, fancy. The Very Rich seldom make do. If it is the difference between the real thing and a copy, it would be a safe assumption that they will snap up the real thing.

Over on the East Side, the Wyatt Coopers make do in a five-story private townhouse. There was a time when a WWD reader could not pick up his paper without having to wade through inches of copy on the Wyatt Coopers. She is the former Gloria di Cicco Stokowski née Vanderbilt now Cooper. They were everywhere—but everywhere—together. They were even named to the Best Dressed List together. The press loved them, but no one more than WWD did back in the heyday of the BPs. Gloria and Wyatt are collectors. They have more *chachkas* than both Elliot Gould and Barbra Streisand put together and then multiplied by two. Walking into the Vanderbilt-Cooper townhouse is like a mail-order catalogue come clangorously to life. The most famous room, of course, is the bedroom. One has the feeling of being sucked straight into a mosaic. It is absolutely terrifying. One false step and you are lost forever, off on a Fantastic Voyage condemned to wander the rest of your life unseen and unnoticed in the pattern around you. The bedroom is Gloria's masterpiece collage. It is the world's largest patchwork quilt. Patchwork on the bed. Patchwork draping the windows. Patchwork on the walls. Patchwork *on the floor*. Yes! Yes! The floor is covered with pieces of fabric, pieces of quilts, pieces of pieces all patched together and pasted onto the floor and then painted with high-gloss varnish. Seven coats, preferably. And then waxed. And waxed. And waxed some more. It is incredible. There is not one quiet moment in the whole room. The pillows are patchwork. The pictures on the patchwork walls are patchwork collages. Even the doors have patchworking on them. The recesses in the walls are outlined with patchwork. My God—part of the patchwork is stirring. Coming to life. Standing up! Oh, it's you, Gloria. Wearing— patchwork. What else?

(One is always tempted to ask the question: What if Gloria and Wyatt get sick of patchwork? What then? Whole floors must be ripped up. Whole walls must be cut out. Miles of patchwork must be torn off beds and chairs and windows and carted off. This could be an ecological disaster rivaling only the Johnstown Flood.)

Then there are Sonny and Mary Lou Whitney. The Whitneys. WWD runs hot and cold on the Whitneys. One day, there is Mary Lou nice as you please in Eye. Next thing you know, she's been named to the Fashion Victim list. Either way, the Whitneys are interesting. And Rich. The Whitneys. Yes, there is a name to set hearts racing. (He's the one who got that small airline off the ground in 1926. He called it Pan American.) They have a big horse farm in Lexington, Kentucky, a Fifth Avenue duplex, a house in

Saratoga, New York, a hunting lodge in the Adirondacks. A house they don't use in Marineland, Florida (they prefer the local motel). Two new houses in Spain. With all those houses, the Whitneys have more openings and closings in a year than David Merrick. Summer in Kentucky. Up to the Adirondacks for the Saratoga racing season. To New York and Florida and Lexington for winter. Oh, hither and yon. For the move to Saratoga, the Kentucky staff will usually do. The horses go by truck, the staff by car, the Whitneys by rented jet.

As for those various C. V. Whitney abodes, the horse farmhouse in Lexington, Kentucky, is unlike most horse farmhouses the normal person is apt to come up against. For one thing, you can barely smell the horses. For another thing, the house has some twenty-odd rooms. (Interestingly enough, even though the farm and racing stable were founded by Sonny Whitney's grandfather in 1896, the old man did not pass the farm along to sons and grandsons through inheritances. Sonny had to wangle a deal with his father and buy the place in 1930 for a reported $1,260,000. Now, that is a lot of dough even for a horse lover.) It fairly rumbles with family tradition, although Mary Lou admits some were easier to stick by than others, especially the one calling for the traditional Whitney Cream barns, the dark brown fences, and the Eton blue and brown racing colors. As for Sonny's father's habit of parking the family Pullman car in the middle of the farm—well, that just had to go. For one thing, there are no more private Pullman cars.

Up in the Adirondacks, tucked onto 100,000 far from cozy acres, is their cottage in the woods. Mrs. Whitney calls it "unchic," but those who have visited there confess that it is an experience guaranteed to produce absolute contentment. It is relaxed, informal, and terribly, terribly beautiful. Lakes and trees and fresh air and blue sky. Sonny in his faded jeans and old sweater hits the lake whenever the mood hits him and catches a batch of fish which are promptly cleaned and served for whatever meal comes next. It beats Chicken Delight. For most of August, home is Cady Hill House, a four-story number in Saratoga, New York, and once a stage-coach stop between Albany and Lake George. Cady Hill House is the Whitney headquarters for racing season at Saratoga. And for those brief moments in Manhattan? For shopping or lunching or theater-going? The Whitneys hole up at their Fifth Avenue duplex, just the place to kick off your shoes, change clothes, and prepare for the next move.

And just so the kids won't get disoriented, what with all that packing up and packing off to one house or another, Mrs. Whitney keeps their rooms in the various houses and farms and camps done in precisely the same way. It beats spending half a day looking for your socks.

To get and keep all these far-flung empires organized, Mary Lou Whitney uses card files. Complete with three-by-five-inch ruled cards and little notched alphabet dividers to compartmentalize you neatly into A to Z. Exactly. In that magic box? A record of the five hundred Christmas presents for staffers and other helpers—together with what went out to them before. A file for each child—the four she brought with her (hers) plus Cornelia Whitney (theirs)—recording medical and dental checkups, wardrobes, school info. A file on help in the various areas where they live. Who supplies liquor, tents, flowers, maids, linens, laundry services. The Whitneys do not just go to an area—the Whitneys assault an area.

To those of us who can barely write out a grocery list for the corner A & P—much less remember to take it along with us—Mary Lou Whitney is, well—either a wonder or a bore. Either you consider her to be absolutely marvelous and a whiz at what she's doing—which is, after all, playing the wife of C. V. Whitney—or utterly stupid to do what all that Whitney money could pay to have computerized. Well, why not? It just depends on your views. Whether or not you think Mary Lou Whitney should be liberated from her file-card box. Throw off her A to Z shackles and live like the rest of us.

Down Palm Beach way is Mrs. Marjorie Merriweather Post. And if WWD still has a heroine these days, it is Mrs. Post. She is treated with a kind of awe-struck kid-gloves respect as she faultlessly presides over the Palm Beach scene. A charity ball with Mrs. Post in attendance rates prime space in WWD. So grand does Mrs. Post live that it has all been left to various museums when she dies. For openers, there is Mara-Lago, Mrs. Post's legendary home in Palm Beach, Florida. It looks as if the Smithsonian has already taken possession. It is a cozy bungalow consisting of 115 rooms and chockablock with buzzers, gongs, and various other summoning devices. (After all, one could hardly yell in Room 115 and expect to be heard back in Room 1.) When sudden squalls drenched the weekly square dances that Mrs. Post is famous for, she had a Moorish pavilion constructed which can dance nearly two hundred with ease. There is a golf course, a tunnel to get family and guests under the highway to her own private beach. Every nook and cranny is filled to the brim with furniture, clutter, patterns on marble, wood, fabric. The huge table in the middle of the main drawing room is stuffed with pictures: the family, celebrities who have visited, presidents, statesmen. A chess set is ready to go in an alcove two steps above the main floor. Dozens of lounges and chairs encircle the patio, which runs around the crescent shape of the house in the back. The guest bathroom to the left of the main entrance—off an entrance hall that could sleep fifty—is as big as a normal two-room New York apartment. Mostly all marble. It is a spooky house, dark, mysterious, and endlessly tantalizing, stuffed with Dutch delft, Adams and Louis XVI furniture. It is the kind of house that makes a visitor wish for a guide, a guidebook, a pair of sturdy shoes, and then a whole week for uninterrupted snooping. For roughing it, Mrs. Post has her hunting lodge in the country, Camp Topridge. Now, Camp Topridge boasts one of the finest collections of American Indian artifacts to be found in America. And it takes a man and a woman four hours a morning just to clean the room holding the collection. The Smithsonian gets the whole shebang. Located in the Adirondacks, forty-two separate buildings make up Camp Topridge. It is not at all like a Boy Scout camp. It is not even like a Girl Scout camp. In fact, it is like no camp in the world.

Guests are usually ferried to Topridge in the Merriweather. (Mrs. Post sold her yacht, the Sea Cloud, and bought the Merriweather, figuring it was much more practical in this jet day and age. The Sea Cloud, a veritable floating mansion, was built in Germany in 1931 for $1,225,000 and carried a crew of sixty-two.) Guests are taken across Lake St. Regis by uniformed boatmen, then transported up to the guest houses at the summit of Topridge in a private, awninged funicular.

For city life, there is Hillwood in Washington, D.C., a magnificent Georgian mansion. The Smithsonian also gets that windfall along with its rare Gobelin tapestries and one entire room furnished with antiques from Imperial Russia. (One of Mrs. Post's four husbands was Washington lawyer Joseph P. Davies, Franklin Roosevelt's ambassador to Russia. Mrs. Post made headlines when it was learned that she had quantities of frozen foods and 2,000 pints of cream shipped to the embassy in Moscow.) The staffs work eight-hour shifts around the clock. A yen for cookies and milk before dawn? Push the buzzer. Hair a little windblown from hiking or swimming or boating or golfing or just plain crushed from lolling in a chaise longue? Get the resident hairdresser. Need a car? Push a button and a car is at your disposal. Maids, masseurs, manicurists. Three chefs at Mar-a-Lago: one for meats, one for pastry, one for candy. The little things: Around the trees at Mar-a-Lago—white sand, so that the dogs won't come in with dirty feet after they've relieved themselves on the palm trees.

One of the ladies who was long a WWD heroine, but who found herself tottering on the brink of acceptability of late, is Gloria Guinness. It is WWD that has changed—not Gloria G. The Guinnesses (he is related to the Guinness brewing clan but is more into banking and airplanes for his multi-millons) still lay claim to six homes plus their yacht and a veritable private air force. There is that seven-story mountain in Paris, a villa in Switzerland at Epalinges-sur-Lausanne (with a bowling alley in the basement), a stud farm in Piencourt in Normandy, a mansion near Palm Beach at Lake Worth, Florida, for winters, plus a weekend retreat in Acapulco. Plus a suite at the Waldorf Towers for those infrequent weekends in New York. The yacht is a 350-ton number and the Guinnesses usually have their three planes—somewhere—at their disposal, including a helicopter to get Mr. G from the Lake Worth house to the golf course in Palm Beach. "In a way," Mrs. Guinness once sighed sitting around her Lake Worth pool, "it is a very bourgeois little life we lead. So many people think it is difficult keeping all these homes, but I believe it is easier to keep six than one." Besides, she reasons logically—a logic needless to say of only the Very Rich—"you can't possibly spend twelve months at any one place." Since both Mr. and Mrs. G hate luggage, they have neatly dispensed with it. Instead, they keep complete wardrobes at every home they touch down in. The Guinnesses are rarely caught without their traveling retinue, which generally consists of two chefs, a kitchen maid, personal maid, valet, and three chambermaids.

The Lake Worth house is a wonder. Not one of your droopy old mansions with no imagination. Get this: Florida Highway A-1-A runs right through the middle of the Guinness property, which fronts Lake Worth to the west and the Atlantic Ocean to the east. Just to make sure old Highway A-1-A wouldn't get in the way too much, the Guinnesses have a wide tunnel under it connecting both sides of the property. And again, like Mrs. Post's, not your ordinary old tunnel. Not at all. Mrs. Guinness turned it into a little traveler's rest stop. A home away from home, just in case the trip from the ocean side to the lake side is too much for the traveler, unencumbered although he might be with no luggage and no customs worries. She had it decorated with hand-painted screens depicting the four seasons (the four seasons as known outside of Palm Beach). Here and there upholstered furniture is scattered invitingly along the way. The whole tunnel is stuffed with loads of plants and bright flowers. The house? More rooms than Gloria cares to count.

And for those who thought Mary Lou Whitney was the living end in organization, she may be rivaled by Gloria Guinness. "We don't have to wire ahead to tell the staffs we are coming," she once said. "My people know when to expect me." And to get back and forth in those long hauls? Why, their private turbojet of course. It used to seat fifty, but they've worked that down to ten by taking out the seats and redecorating it inside with Louis XVI antiques. Well, Eastern may be the Wings of Man and United may have Friendly Skies, but there is something unalterably appealing about plying the ocean in your own private turbojet replete with Louis XVI furniture.

It goes on. God does it go on. Robert David Lion Gardiner owns his own island called, appropriately enough, Gardiners Island. There it lies—nine miles long and three miles wide—in Gardiners Bay, stuffed full with wild turkeys, deer, duck, pheasant. Enough bird life to drive an ornithologist to drink. Whoops—there goes a wild turkey. Did you catch that osprey. My God, I think I just missed a heron. Robert David Lion Gardiner is, fortunately, a millionaire who can take care of such things. That old island, constantly being sought by the Feds for a national park, has been in the family for over three hundred years and R.D.L. is not about to let it slip out of his freckled hands without a hassle. For one thing, he truly loves being lord of the manor. "I can even behead people," he announces proudly. The island boasts a nineteen-year-old manor house which, even neophytes will admit, is not very old for a manor house. It is, however, the fourth such manor house to grace the island and it really is a nice one. Not some tacky split-level. Gardiners Island is some trip. For just plain puttering around outside the house, there is also an empty jail, a blacksmith shop, a windmill, and a family cemetery. Enormous stands of eight-hundred-year-old oak trees. The island was bought by Lion Gardiner from Chief Wyandanch of the Montauket Indians for "some red setter dogs, trading cloth, and beads" according to R.D.L. Being something of an acquisitive gent, the old guy went on to snap up about 78,000 other acres from the Indians of which the present Robert Lion still lays claim to some 5,000. Some has been developed residentially, while on some of it stands the Gardiner Manor Shopping Center in Bay Shore, Long Island.

On Gardiners Island, there is a mossy stone marker announcing that "Capt Kidd's treasure was buried in this hollow and recovered 1699." Every once in a while, when pressed to do so, the current lord of the manor will hold a gold chalice up and announce as how it is part of that buried treasure dug up on his island.

Not that all of the Gardiner time is spent at the manor house. Hardly. For time in the city, there is that Fifth Avenue duplex replete with a Gobelin tapestry that is almost as large as Central Park. It stretches a good ten feet down the main wall of the drawing room. By anybody's standards, that is one hell of a Gobelin. And for dinners? Black tie, of course. Often served on the Gardiners gold dinner service, which is kept in a New York bank vault between courses. (Ladies count your blessings. Can you imagine scraping gravy off a gold dinner plate?)

On a somewhat less grand scale are the Manhattan dwellers, often preferring apartments over private homes. They are sort of the Welfare branch of the BPs. Not that they are any particular sort of slouches when it comes to the way they live. It just isn't quite as grand as, say, a 115-room beach house in Palm Beach or a 100,000-acre country place in the Adirondacks. Or your own island. Not that Bob and Ethel Scull are complaining about their eleven-room apartment on

Fifth Avenue chock full of their multimillion-dollar pop art collection. Nor are they complaining about the six rooms at the warehouse that keeps the rest of their collection for them—the part they don't have room to display on Fifth Avenue. Nor are they complaining about that new house they built recently in East Hampton. It's one built like a Roman atrium so they could display all their outdoor statuary. "It's exquisite," Ethel says about her summer house. Or their 177 acres in Connecticut that they haven't quite figured out what to do with.

To help Ethel get it all together in her eleven rooms, she has only three staffers in New York. "I've cut down on that," confessed Ethel, a very pretty lady with very sexy streaky hair and neat long legs. "I only have three living in here in the city. I take them out to the country with me." Her cook, her maid, her laundress. "It's silly to have more. The more you have, the harder it is for them to get along." Plus some come-in help when necessary. But keeping up the Sculls' digs is no mean feat. All that art work. All those things on the walls, on the tables, standing on the floors. Son John striding through the apartment—it is spacious and sweeping—goes through a doorway at the wrong angle. "Watch the shirt dear," Ethel warned, as he banged into the stuffed shirt by George Segal. "Oh, yeah. Excuse me," he mumbled politely at the shirt. And the furniture. It's white. Now that is not only heretical in New York, but incredibly courageous. Ethel had her place air conditioned (it wheezes sometimes), then stuck masking tape around all the windows to keep New York out. Once a year, she and her gang go through the apartment cleaning everything because even with air conditioning and masking tape, walls get dingy and you can't exchange pictures without leaving big outlines on the walls. "What a chore," she sighs. But, it is a labor of love.

Other simple folk are Bob and Ethel's friends Bill and Chessy Rayner (She was Chesbrough of the Chesebrough Ponds people. You know, the Seven-Day Beauty Plan and all that.), who have a simple little six-room apartment on Park Avenue decorated by Chessy. (She also works for a living, heading up the decorating firm of MAC II with her bosom pal Mica Ertegun.) Of course, there are some compensations. Like the beach house they built last year in Barbados, "furnished with cheap bargains from Puerto Rico," as Chessy puts it. Simple, but nice. And their "tiny, tiny" teensy little house on Long Island for summers.

Other than a come-in housekeeper, Chessy makes do by herself. "Oh, I hire some outside help if we have a particularly fancy dinner party—the Irish Mafia my mother's been using—but mostly I do it myself. It's easier. I hate to be tied down to whenever a cook wants to cook." Besides, both Chessy and her hubby are no amateurs in the kitchen. They have two cookbooks already published, are working on another right now, a meat cookbook. Chessy hits the streets every morning at eight with the family Labrador, Ginger. By ten, she's at work with MAC II out combing the furniture market "and eating lots of lunches at Schrafft's" around the city.

Around the corner is Mica's place, Mica being Chessy's pal and partner in MAC II. She is also the Rumanian-born and Swiss-educated wife of Ahmet Ertegun, president of Atlantic Records. They have a four-story private house to be looked after, so Mica relies on a live-in Portuguese couple. It is hard to say how many rooms the Erteguns have because Mica spent two years knocking all the walls down, most of which she didn't replace. The main floor just goes on and on and on, from Eighty-first Street clear back to the garden.

And the Guests—Winston and CeeZee—are still considered very chic even after having to sell off their porcelains to tide them over a bad financial spot back in 1967. The Guests may have had to sell their figurines and WWD may have kept CeeZee off their Sensuous Woman list, but the WWD photog will still snap away when she emerges from lunch at the Colony. A black-tie dinner at the Guests' still rates an Eye mention. They even had to sell their snazzy Sutton Place digs and move into simpler quarters at Park Avenue. But there is still home—111 acres on Long Island—Templeton in Old Westbury.

Now, insofar as the American myth is concerned, Mary Lou Whitney is one example of why hope springs eternal in both civics textbooks and the American heart. Why the Great American Dream machine may creak and groan and appear to be headed for the scrap heap and thus do even further damage to America's ecological horizons—but is always, at the last minute, rescued and resuscitated and somehow revitalized. Mary Lou Whitney was born in Kansas City, Missouri, one of four daughters of Mr. and Mrs. Harry Robert Schroeder. It was a simple, quiet life out there in Missouri for the Schroeders and their daughters. Papa Schroeder was a real estate lawyer and a tax man. He provided a good, sensible, solid atmosphere for the ladies in his life. When little Mary Lou grew up she headed north, to Iowa City, where she attended the University of Iowa and majored in dramatic arts. Back home in K.C., she worked as a radio disc jockey during World War II. Who would have thought that the cute little blonde spinning those platters, flipping those discs, would one day get tuned in to the Whitney millions. What a groove, hepcats and zoot-suiters. After the War she married Frank Hosford, an insurance man, and had four children. The Hosfords moved to Scottsdale, Arizona, where Mary Lou did a half-hour television show five days a week. Early in 1957 Mary Lou then moved to California where she landed a film contract with—the plot is moving very fast right about here—C. V. Whitney Pictures. It beats hanging around Schwabbs, right? There she was, up on the silver screen in such forgettables as *The Missouri Traveler* with another unknown, Lee Marvin. By August of 1957, Sonny (billed as "millionaire, sportsman, industrialist, and motion picture producer Cornelius Vanderbilt Whitney") offered a public statement to the press, announcing he had asked for a divorce from his third wife to marry—can you wait?—Mrs. Mary Lou Hosford of Scottsdale, Arizona. And there it is folks—a little magic. A little glitter. Sure enough—old Sonny, always keeping an eye out for good horseflesh, had spotted cute little Mary Lou up there on the big ole screen and taken an immediate liking to the little filly. As Mary Lou (then billed as Marie Louise Hosford) tells it, she was whipping up a little soufflé in the kitchen of her California home when the telephone rang and it was good old Sonny popping the question. Naturally, Marie Louise Mary Lou was so excited the soufflé fell all over the place.

Even Ethel Scull was not born with a pop art painting in her mouth. Not at all. Ethel and Bob worked very hard for what they have today. Ethel was born Ethel Redner, a simple Jewish girl from the West Side who went to P.S. 9 and then Julia Richman High School and finally on to Parsons School of Design. Bob Scull is another all-American New York boy, educated in the public school system and earning money by painting signs and posters for neighborhood stores. He eventually ended up studying industrial design—over a period of nine years in night school—and was a partner in a struggling young industrial design outfit when he met Ethel. Flash, bam, pow. It was love at first sight for the two art-struck New Yorkers. "I think I love you," says the balloon over Bob's head. "Oh-h-h . . . " says the one over Ethel's. Just like the comics. They were married in 1944 and lived in a one-room walk-up around the corner from the Museum of Modern Art. There was Ethel, hauling her own groceries, hauling her own laundry, shoving her own vacuum cleaner, dusting her own window sills. "We practically lived in the museum those first few years," Bob says. They scrounged up their membership fee, would entertain in the museum dining room. In 1952, Bob confesses to buying a "spurious Utrillo," which, when he discovered it might have been a shady transaction, he promptly whipped back to the gallery from whence it came and put it back on the block—realizing a $50 profit. "I was hooked. We decided then and there that this was for us and we started to put every extra dime into art." Which meant: "I spent a lot of time sitting on packing cases," laughs Ethel, "while we spent our money on art." Suddenly it was the early 1960s and Scull was by this time a taxi tycoon. And POW! WHAM! WOWEE-ZOWEE! the Pop scene struck. And the Sculls were in business. Bob, who haunts artists' lofts and studios, found he was absolutely zonked by what he was seeing in the early '60s. The Sculls began snapping it up and suddenly they found themselves major celebrities. Today, that eleven-room apartment across from the Metropolitan Museum of Art is stuffed with Warhols, Lichtensteins, Oldenburgs, Rauschenbergs, Johns, Poons. Ethel figures they own more than 150 paintings with only thirty of them hanging in their apartment at a given time. Fifteen sculptures stand in the apartment—including George Segal's famous plaster work of Ethel seated on a love seat with Bob standing behind her. Additionally, there are ten sculptures in the garden at East Hampton plus various and sundry drawings and paintings inside. The Sculls rotate that art collection every year, a job that takes nearly two weeks.

It continues. Marjorie Merriweather Post may be the lady of the manor in various and far-flung estates, but it could have turned out quite differently. Papa Post was a frontier merchant, cowboy, traveling salesman, medical student, land developer, farmer, cattleman, oilman, inventor, tinkerer, adventurer. He could have easily wound up like a lot of restless dilettantes at the end of the 1800s: broke. He didn't. In 1895 he discovered a coffee substitute. He called it Postum and began peddling it door to door. From there he moved to something called Grape Nuts. In ten years the Postum Cereal Company was worth $5 million. When he died in 1914, Marjorie Merriweather Post's inheritance was reported to be in the vicinity of $20 million. By 1958 her estimated worth was over $250,000,000. She needs it. Her yearly living expenses are said to hit $2 million per. Not that Mr. Post did not prepare his only child for the hard task of manipulating and multiplying the millions that would fall her way. She recalls how he often left word for young Marjorie to go to his office after school. "I would go and I'd usually find a group of men in his office. I would go in and sit in a corner and listen. I had to keep absolutely still. But after the conference was over, Daddy would ask me a great many questions about what I'd heard and what I thought of each decision that had been made. I would answer as best I could." She was ten years old. God helps them who help themselves.

In one respect, the BPs are very much like all the rest of us: now and again, they like a free ride. Show them a free ticket and they will be shrugged into their sables and their designer labels faster than a politician can change his mind. One of the biggest free rides to come along in an age was when Col. Serge Obolensky—former Russian prince, former Cossack, former husband of Alice Astor, former husband of the daughter of a former Russian czar, former hotel president, former parachutist for the U.S. Army, current eighty-one-year-old *bon vivant* in New York City and Super-Publicist—organized a Super Trip to Paradise Island in the Bahamas in 1968. Trips like this are called "junkets" and they are usually done for "openings." There are many things that can be opened via a junket. For openers, hotels can be opened. Restaurants can be opened. Casinos. Collections of designer clothes. Usually what is opened are countless bottles of champagne. The Trippers in the BP set are simply wild about champagne. The best kind of junkets are openings of hotels, simply because they are usually out of town. (A BP probably wouldn't walk across Sixth Avenue to open a Hilton Hotel in New York, but watch the stampede if it is someplace out of town. Especially if it is winter and the sun is shining on it.)

This junket of Serge's was quite a blast. It was to junkets what the Cities' Service Band of America used to be to marching bands all across America: a goal. America had a new pastime—junketeering—and Serge was ace in his class. Three chartered jets flew BPs in from around the world. One from New York, one from Hollywood, one from Europe. Destination: Paradise Island, a 685-acre playground right across the bay from Nassau. Mission: to open the Paradise Island Hotel and Casino with a bang and a blast. Serge had rounded up 362 of the most B of the Ps and in they winged, armed to their capped teeth with titles, wig boxes, suntan lotion, and great expectations. Take a deep breath: Princess Peggy d'Arenberg (now Duchess d'Uzes; once, simple Margaret Bancroft, Standard Oil heiress), Count and Countess Crespi of Rome, Count and Countess Romanones of Spain, Mr. and Mrs. C. V. Whitney, Mr. and Mrs. Loel Guinness, Mr. and Mrs. Robert David Lion Gardiner, Wendy Vanderbilt, Mr. and Mrs. Huntington Hartford, Lady Sassoon, the Duke of Bucchleuch, Viscountess Astor, the Maharaja and Maharani de Jaipur, Her Royal Highness Princess Lalla Neza of Morocco, Marchese Emilio Pucci, Princess Luciana Pignatelli, Mr. and Mrs. André DuBonnet, George Plimpton. The Hollywood crowd included Carol Channing, Art Linkletter, Janet Leigh, Cliff Robertson, Dina Merrill, Walter Wanger, Henry Mancini, Kevin McCarthy. Notable press folk were Earl Wilson and Suzy. It was incredible. There they were, lining up for their free tickets, hugging and kissing enroute their free hotel rooms and going into ecstasies over their free Bloody Marys. In case all that sun got to be too much—or all that gambling in the Casino, or all those Bloody Marys—Serge provided a fleet of chauffeured limousines to toot the guests around the island or across the bridge and into Nassau for a little duty-free shopping so the girls could save a buck or two on French perfume. But Saturday night was the Main Event, the moment everyone had been wating for. A fancy-dress dinner dance. Meyer Davis played for the waltz crowd, a rock group wearing aluminum foil for the younger set. The champagne was provided by one Obolensky account (Piper-Heidsieck); the wine was Dubonnet, of course. A fashion show by Oscar de la Renta and Pucci. Carol Channing told anecdotes. Art

Linkletter told jokes. After the ball, gambling in the Casino until dawn.

Sunday was an R & R day, with everyone lolling around the pool until departure time in early evening. Promptly at 9:45 the first Piper-Heidsieck cork of the return flight popped off. Count Crespi cheered. Mrs. Earl Wilson wanted to hijack the plane and head it back to the warm Bahamian sun. To divert her attention, Serge's assistant, Alexandre Tarsaidze, threw an empty plastic champagne glass on the floor of the plane and began stomping it in traditional Russian fashion. Countess Crespi cheered.

It was almost too much, even for the BPs. Rarely had they been treated to three full days of such sumptuous free-dom. (They were even able to wangle deals within the deal. Count and Countess Crespi, who came with the European contingent, again flying gratis to New York to attend to some business.) The whole surrealistic impact of the weekend hit a peak Sunday night in the lobby of the Paradise Island Hotel when the BPs were checking out. Countess Crespi, resplendent in a brown linen Valentino dress, brown Valentino stockings, and scuffed brown Valentino shoes (who else but a very secure BP could get away with wearing scuffed Valentinos) spied a pal across the crowded room. "Oh, darling, don't forget," she sang out. "Dinner Tuesday. Black tie. Our place—Rome!"

(Naturally, any gathering of the BPs will also have its share of PPs—the Popular Press. The Paradise Island bash was no different, but it was selective. There was WWD. Plus the reporter-photographer duo from both *Time* and *Life*. Ditto from *Look* and *Vogue*. Plus the *London Daily Mail*. Not to mention—Suzy and Earl Wilson. Small and select. None of this tacky business of getting in every wire service and small-town paper, right? It was quite easy to separate the BPs from the PPs, however. The PPs stuck together over countless Bloody Marys and were readily identifiable by their notebooks and cameras.)

The list of junkets is endless. Jules Stein winging hundreds out to Hollywood to open his Century City hotel complex. Mary Wells (head of Wells, Rich, Greene advertising agency and married to the president of Braniff) organizing a trip to Peru for fashion designers—on Braniff, of course. Another Mary Wells trip to promote the Love cosmetic line, made by Menley and James (the company that also makes Contac "for twenty-four-hour cold relief"). What better place to stage the promotion than in Paris, City of Love. So Mary's crowd got Le Drug Store, the Parisian version of an American drug store, and rounded up a bunch of BPs. Then they convinced Liza Minnelli to act as hostess. In trooped Marchese Emilio Pucci, Gloria Swanson, Baronne Guy de Rothschild, the DuBonnets, the Vicomtesse de Ribes, Serge Obolensky, Earl Blackwell. Suzy was on hand to cover it for the PP. And the high spot of the evening—the arrival of the Duke and Duchess of Windsor. "Hi there, Duke. Hi there, Duchess," trilled Liza. Donovan and Mary Hopkins provided the entertainment. And, of course, the food. (Face it, even the BPs need food, especially if it's free.) Omelettes, steak, and chocolate sundaes. The Duke ate every bit of his, then wound up the evening with a big smelly cigar.

Then there are Charity Parties, which are different from Press Parties. They might be exactly the same people—after a while you do notice the same names repeating themselves— but there is a big, basic difference. A Charity Ball must be paid for by those attending, with tickets running around $75 per couple, whereas a Press Party is free, aimed solely at garnering publicity from the invited Press corps. There are countless dozens of Press Parties held in town. A party to open Buffalo Bill's, a Wild West bar inappropriately located on the East Side. A party to inaugurate an expansion to the third floor by Jackie Rogers, lady male hairdresser. Any excuse will do. Then there are those mixed bags. A charity and a restaurant, say, will combine. The restaurant will pick up the tab, the charity will sell tickets—both will get publicity and hopefully the charity will get some dough. Like the party held at Adonis last year with proceeds going to the Sloan-Kettering Cancer Clinic. The point is to round up the people who will act as an automatic draw. Buffalo Bill's wisely got designer Giorgio di Sant'Angelo, who probably has never been near a western saddle or an American Indian but who gives a damn. Giorgio is a Big Name and heavy into the American Indian look, all of which worked well with Buffalo Bill's purposes. He agreed to act as host, helped work out the guest list. Some five hundred people came clamoring to get in just to see the place and eat some chili and drink some beer. All free, of course.

To occupy themselves in the winter—between junkets, Charity Balls, and Press Parties—the BPs generally head for the city of Palm Beach. Palm Beach was actually one of the first planned communities in the United States. Today the resort is abristle with money, mansions, and matrons. It is estimated that the average age in the city is dangerously close to fifty. When the ladies describe their homes as "tiny houses," forget it. A tiny house to Palm Beach is very much like what Mrs. Reed Albee lives in. (She's the mother of playwright Edward Albee.) It is a mansion with a living room that measures twenty-five by forty feet. It doesn't take much to figure out how much more house must be tacked on to a twenty-five-by-forty-foot living room to go around. There is a swell swimming pool stretching on and on (note: both the Atlantic Ocean and Lake Worth are within a good spit of Palm Beach). The whole villa is pink, replete with pink furniture, pink geraniums, pink fabrics, pink potted orchids. There is a pavilioned terrace and the pool is, of course, heated.

In the murky mornings of Palm Beach, an overhead flight makes it look like a scene out of *Twilight Zone.* All that steam rising silently up off all those heated swimming pools. Bela Lugosi could come manifesting himself out of the mists, swirling his cape and curling his lip, and it would seem absolutely appropriate. Sadly, most Palm Beachers never hit their beautiful beaches. It is estimated that 95 percent of all bathing is done in pools. Which means there is a lot a *plage* with no one *sur* it.

Shopping? Worth Avenue and Mizener Alley, if you please. In fact, shopping is so *cher* along this stretch of the imagination that last year Au Bon Gout, a little shop selling china and rich kitchen utensils and a few spindly antique pieces, slapped on a $50 admission charge in the form of a membership fee. This was done to keep the tourists out.

And where to stay? Well, first of all, if you don't own you own, try to houseguest. There is such an exchange of beds going on—sometimes with the hostess there to supervise, sometimes she is off houseguesting herself—it would take a computer to keep track of it.

(If houseguesting is not practical, the *only* place to stay is the Colony Hotel for about $50 per night.)

Palm Beach during The Season (winter) is parties, parties, parties, luncheons, coffees, dinners, balls. And those balls! Even in a recession year, the Palm Beach crowd could come up with $700,000 for St. Mary's Hospital.

Another spa for wintering is Acapulco, but it is a whole different batch of folks. Palm Beach is, for the most part, old money. Like Phipps (steel, investment bankers, real estate—there are so *many* of them), Kellogg (International Mining Corporation), Bolton (bankers and industrialists), Munn (founder of the Everglades Club and married to Dorothy Spreckles of the San Francisco sugar Spreckleses). Acapulco is a little newer and with a crowd running to those who have made it in the last few decades (dare we say "nouveau riche"?) and wealthy Hollywood show biz types. Merle Oberon (born Estelle Merle O'Brien Thompson in Tasmania some fifty-odd years ago) is the queen bee of the social set down there, especially after having married Bruno Pagliai, filthy rich steel man, industrialist, and publisher, who once managed the Acapulco race track. And that house. It took two years to build and it is estimated the land alone is worth $250,000. Nobody is even hazarding a guess as to the cost of the house. "Bruno won't tell me how much it cost," Merle sighs, but one knows, deep down in the heart of hearts, she is not losing a bit of beauty sleep over her ignorance. Called El Ghalal (from an ancient Mexican-Indian phrase meaning "To love"), it is a sumptuous wonder to behold. The main house, Moorish and mysterious in character, is contained within a series of domed arches made of concrete covered with powdered marble. The interior is constructed on two levels and on top is a thirty-five-foot-square living room, two master bedrooms with Roman-size baths and room-sized closets (Merle is on the Best Dressed List after all).

Neighbors to Merle and Bruno are Warren Avis (formerly of the Avis Rental Car business, before he sold it) and Eleanor Lambert, fashion publicist. Loel and Gloria Guinness bought a weekend place there a few years back.

For island buffs—Barbados. Princess Margaret and Lord Snowdon water ski there. Ari and Jackie park the Christina there.

Now, if Palm Beach (and Acapulco for a few) is home-away-from-home in the winter, what do the poor souls do in the summer? Hot-town-summer-in-the-city time, suffering through blackouts and brownouts and dimouts and heat and humidity and an Air Pollution Index that would test the mettle of even a John Wayne. Fortunately, the BPs have a summertime home-away-from-home. What else? The most popular place these days is the Hamptons—East Hampton and Southampton. Gloria and Wyatt have a little pad out there, the old Sanford White house.

Henry Ford has an enormous place in Bridgehampton, surrounded by potato fields. Most of the mansions and homes are set back from the beach area (since most are equipped with pools, and since much of the beach gets polluted from offshore oil spills), hunched on lawns that are so sweeping and so green, they sting the eyes of the city visitor. (It is rumored there are more tree surgeons in the Hamptons than general practitioners.) Parties consist of tents pitched in the backyards or entertainments at the Southampton Beach Club.

Tennis is a big pastime in the summer, as are bridge and charity luncheons. There are mixed feelings about how loose and casual the Hamptons really are during the summer. Some feel there is still a stiff, uptight undercurrent cutting under all those sandals and slacks. A certain discomfiture when a West-hampton resident wanders over into East or South, for example. Absolute apoplexy at the mere thought that the Hamptons might be "going Miami" with all its implications. "You can mix your dinner parties in New York," one hostess said, "but you damned well better straighten things out in the Hamptons."

For those who desire to flee the country in the summer, there is always the Riviera. Monte Carlo, Cap-Martin, St.-Jean-Cap-Ferrat. Little palaces along the Côte d'Azur. Yachts, as far as the eye can see. Exquisite refuge from the RealWorld that lurks Out There. Just tuck yourself in around your pool with the palm trees bending in the breeze, the blue sky hovering hot and high above your head. "It's one little informal party for fifty guests after another," Margaret, Duchess of Argyll once said of the whole Riviera scene (she never goes out in the sun—bad for her skin). Regulars who drift in and out along the Riviera over a summer are apt to be Lady Sassoon of Nassau, Mrs. Ernest Kanzler (Henry Ford's aunt), Cristina and Henry Ford. Lady Bird and Lynda Bird vacationed here a few seasons back, with Lynda Bird enthusiastically hitting the gaming tables at the Casino in Monte Carlo.

The social life along the Riviera is mad and woolly and continuous. The most famous blast of recent years—chron-icled for posterity by Charlotte Curtis—occurred when a gaggle of BPs, led by Henry Ford, met at a restaurant in Cap-Martin. Somewhere between dessert and dancing, someone let fly an unshelled almond. Before anyone could cry *Zut alors!*, the whole place had exploded into wild abandoned fun and adult games. Guests were lobbing champagne glasses into the fire, pelting the musicians with rose petals (they, meanwhile, were valiantly sawing away trying to keep up with the ever-maddening pace of the fun-loving guests). And zinging nuts at each other. The apogee of the High Spirits that evening occurred when one Count Giovanni Volpi armed himself with a plate of gooey vanilla ice cream and raspberries and climbed a tree strategically located right above the rollicking festivities. He spent some delicious carefree moments up there, dropping globs of the goo down on the guests. It was left to Henry Ford, the all-American boy, to come to the rescue. Menacingly shaking a bottle of Perrier water, Henry advanced on the tree and let loose a blast of Perrier water at the Count. "You got him!" Anne Ford Uzielli announced proudly of Papa's prowess with the Perrier water.

Oh, fun and games. Group therapy for the big kids.

11

Being Rich and/or Social does have its problems. For one thing, people in this country today are so eager to classify people.

Being Rich is also very time-consuming. One is constantly having to go out and spend money on clothes, furnishings, houses. Up to Veneziano's. Over to Valentino's. Off to the snow. Off to Adolfo's. Off to the ball. It takes a lot of time to have a lot of money.

So why do they do it? Why do these poor rich people drive themselves to distraction, dressing up and going forth and putting out. Wouldn't it just be a lot more fun to sit home with a good Annual Report. Or doing a needlepoint pillow depicting Wall Street on a bullish day.

"This so-called Society we are surrounded with today is so involved with acquiring and aspiring and showing off," says

Charlotte Curtis. "They are terribly mobile people and their values are often dictated by what's fashionable at the moment. The Aristocracy, on the other hand, just doesn't go with fashion." As for status seeking, "Many of them actually *care* that they have met the Duchess of Windsor. The next thing is to have the Duchess for dinner. These are the goals in some people's lives." These are the last of a dying breed. Super-consumers. Practicing the last ritualistic rites of conspicuous consumption.

It took the son of immigrant Norwegian parents to blow the whistle on the lot of them, and damned if he didn't do it in 1899. "The consumption of goods is an evidence of wealth," wrote Thorsten Veblen in *The Theory of the Leisure Class*, "and conversely, the failure to consume in due quantity and quality becomes a mark of inferiority and demerit." So be it. And God knows, the last thing any Super-consumer wants to do is to be marked with inferiority and given demerits. It becomes, then, a deadly game wherein the only winners are, of course, the shopkeepers. There they are, ripping off the Super-consumers, all in the name of good taste and some nebulous thing called Status, convincing them that their $30 jeans are far superior to those selling for $5.95 at the Army-Navy store or Sears, Roebuck or J. C. Penney's. That a pair of $15 sneakers are somehow inherently superior to a pair of $1.50 Japanese models from a Fourteenth Street discount store or even a pair of $5.95 Keds from Thom McAn.

"This is like a mother who takes her child to a pediatrician. If one drop of medicine is good, ten drops will be ten times better," figures psychiatrist Dr. Robert Campbell, at St. Vincent's Hospital in New York. "So the poor mother poisons her child. These women who rush out and buy all those Midi skirts and HotPants—it's the same thing. They are operating on the mistaken theory that anything that works in small doses will work that much better in larger doses. It doesn't matter whether it's clothes or parties or houses or vacations."

"The motive is emulation," Veblen wrote. "The stimulus of an invidious comparison which prompts us to outdo those with whom we are in the habit of classing ourselves." As Veblen saw it, and there is no reason why it is not just as pertinent and to the point today, "with the exception of the instinct of self-preservation, the propensity for emulation is probably the strongest." Midi skirts. Southampton cottages. HotPants. Diamonds as big as the Ritz. The Ritz itself! We'll keep up, or die trying.

Psychiatrist Edmund Bergler figured that "this type lives in constant fear that people might not believe he is well-off. He is a flashy dresser, buys only the very latest, overpays, overtips. He is a social climber and a snob. He admires money and has to prove constantly to himself and others that he possesses it and can afford to spend it." (Actually, Bergler went further and surmised that this sort of status-seeking might be "a free spender for display purposes in public, but at home he is a miserable miser.")

Interestingly enough, Dr. Joyce Brothers—our gal from the $64,000 *Question*—points out that the only animals who share man's ability to recognize himself are close relatives like the chimpanzee and the monkey. "Like a man, a chimp is fascinated by his own image," says the doctor. "He will spend hours admiring himself in a variety of poses."

Which, naturally enough, leads right into the market place. "Simple conspicuous waste of goods," Veblen asserts, "is good *prima facie* evidence of pecuniary success and consequently *prima facie* evidence of social worth." But underneath all this buying and buying and buying—all this rushing through the market place conspicuously consuming everything in sight— are murkier meanings.

Sigmund Freud, that scourge of Women's Lib and Gay Lib, pondered these very same questions. Herd instinct he called it. Freud figured there were four areas of primary instincts: self-preservation, nutrition, sex, and the herd. Quite simply, Freud saw the herd as a sad state manifested by a "lack of independence and initiative in their members, the similarity in the reactions of all of them." Among the features of this "herd"—"the weakness of intellectual ability, the lack of emotional restraint, the incapacity for moderation and delay." Good heavens. Here comes the thundering herd, HotFooting it up Mad Avenue, through Fifth Avenue duplexes and Park Avenue triplexes. Out through Southampton. Down to Palm Beach. Over to the Riviera. Hell-bent on keeping up Thorsten's ideas of conspicuous consumption. The thundering herd instinct. All wrapped up in ego and anxiety. Fearing public opinion. Afraid to take a chance. Pursuing all those safe Park Avenues of activity. "The essence of conscience is 'social anxiety,' the fear of public opinion," said Dr. Franz Alexander, Emeritus Clinical Professor of Psychiatry at the University of Southern California and the University of Illinois College of Medicine. "In following the herd, social anxiety necessarily disappears in the members of the group."

"The herd instinct is a different form of status-seeking," says Dr. Campbell. "They are trying to buy a disguise to hide behind. In many cases, it is an attempt to hide inadequacies—or what people believe are their inadequacies. And John Fairchild rules whether or not the disguise has been successful."

To Freud, the heard "is impulsive, changeable, and irritable. Though it may desire things passionately, this is never so for long, for it is incapable of perseverance. It cannot tolerate any delay between its desire and the fulfillment of what it desires."

"Inclined as it itself is to all extremes, a group can only be excited by an excessive stimulus. What [the group] demands of its heroes is strength, or even violence. It wants to be ruled and oppressed and to fear its masters." My God! That frightened woman who called and asked not to be quoted about *Women's Wear Daily*. Those anonymous designers, speaking spookily to the mass media. Those don't-quote-me confessions. The fear instinct. The herd instinct. Beat me, daddy. Kick me. But don't quote me. And don't cancel my subscription.

According to Freud's interpretation of the herd instinct—the group ego—a person "is no longer himself, but has become an automaton who has ceased to be guided by his will." Staggering along in Midi skirts and boots. Then casting off all that fabric and shrugging into HotPants and textured pantyhose, all the while keeping a watchful eye cocked for what might come over the fashion horizon next. The sun sets on the Midi—it's sunrise on HotPants. Where will High Noon find us?

(Bergler called them "fashion apes"—women who "automatically accept every new decree." Oh, yes. Fashion apes, swinging vaingloriously through Fairchild's Fashion Forest.)

"You know, a lot of people are hoping to gain from group identification," says Dr. Campbell. "They feel somehow inadequate and feel that if they can relate on a concrete level of wearing what they are wearing, they can get closer to people in general. There is a lot of loneliness involved in this. A lot of people feeling like outsiders wanting to be in." He ponders. There is more. "Maybe they feel inadequate about other things. Money *doesn't* buy everything and it very frequently is some hidden feeling within themselves. They are trying to overcome something else so they go out and spend a lot of money. They are looking for something, often they don't know what. Just looking. They are unable to verbalize their feelings."

The recession of 1970 not only limited the verbalizing of the herd, it damn near rendered them speechless. Home—especially theirs—is also a good place to entertain, and 1970 will go down in the annals of the BP as the year the BP sat down and got it all together in their parlors. There they were, jamming around like mad in their ball gowns all during the 1960s, flashing their jewels and flaunting their social positions. Lo and behold, somewhere along the way the BP cast off their diamonds and by the 1970s were known to wander about in more simple mien, say, slacks and pullovers and trenchcoats.

In 1970, for a myriad of complex reasons, the BPs pulled into their duplexes and triplexes and townhouses and turned off most of their motors. Not that the horsepower wasn't there for a fast getaway just in case a situation arose that warranted it. There were quiet little vroom-vrooms of activity even within the quietude that had descended over Upper Manhattan. Was it the economic recession that caused it? The Vietnam War? The whole topsy-turvy nature of our country that saw us, for the first time in a long time, questioning our very technology? Probably not. Nobody deserves that much credit. But something happened. Something calmed things down. Most likely the BPs just got tired.

After all, they'd been at it for years. Years of dressing up night after night and eating that same Ball food and dancing to Meyer Davis or Lester Lanin and then battling for their party favors. It can become a crashing bore, can't it? Even WWD, it would seem, got a bit tired of it all. Instead of hovering in corners at dinner parties, WWD reporters were out covering political campaigns. Instead of covering a ball right down to the last diamond, WWD was interviewing Republican Senators *vis-à-vis* their party leader. WWD was up in Harlem talking about black economics.

So, things settled down in Dreamland. "Last year [1970] was just one big thing after another," summed up Mrs. T. Suffern Tailer, wife of an independently wealthy golfer. And this season? "People just don't want great big snarling parties." The whole town began talking about how quiet it was. There were a few big parties, but mostly it was small intimate dinner parties. Six or eight at Chessy's for a sit-down dinner. "New York went through a phase of charity parties of all types," Chessy Rayner said one morning, after a hard night of working crossword puzzles. Ginger, the Rayners' golden Labrador had snuggled in on their flat-weave ethnic carpet in their Park Avenue apartment, snoozing and shedding and looking terribly peaceful. "Maybe because some of us had never done it before, and we were all terribly amused by it. But it paled very quickly." She ticked off the reasons. "For one thing, husbands absolutely loathe those evenings. Hauling themselves into black tie. It's a real drag for them, especially if you come home from the office after a hard day's work. They want to sit and talk to a pretty girl—they don't want to go to an icky big black-tie party. And the food—the food is never very good. You can't get a drink. And the noise. Nobody ever talked, or at least about anything important. You couldn't hear." She sighed. "It was amusing at the time. But I don't know—I hope we all just sort of grew up and out of it. How long can you live going to the hairdresser every day and out every night and buying clothes and worrying about how you're going to look."

How long can a girl take all that shampooing and bad food. Why, 1971 may well be known as the year of the small dinner party. Six or eight people, sixteen in a pinch, sitting down around tables. That's it. "I believe in feeding people," Chessy said.

Gosh, it all got so earthy, so homey. "I've been having chili parties in my new kitchen," confessed Mrs. Anne Slater, who used to model in fashion shows and wear designer clothes out in public with everything but the label showing just so her latest find could get a little publicity. "We all gather around the stove and take things to the table—you know, very casual." Just like RealFolks. Mr. and Mrs. Richard Feigen, of the Feigen Art Gallery Feigens, have been known to grab corned-beef sandwiches and take off for a West Side movie or two. Or packing up all four kids and heading down to Chinatown for a load of spare ribs and egg rolls. Even Estée Lauder, whose dinner parties used to hit forty and fifty, began tucking eight or so in around her dining room table. Oh, not that it is tacky and tawdry. Today's BPs are casual, but not that casual. "I mean, you know they went home and had a bath before they came to dinner," explained interior decorator Billy Baldwin.

But they didn't gussy it up in sequins and satins like the year before.

"It became smart and chic to carry on about the state of your finances. To throw little spaghetti dinners," mused Charlotte Curtis from her vantage point at the *Times*. "It was also very coincidental with the fashion changes we were going through. All that black." Ugh. She wrinkles up her little nose, lights another Newport menthol. "Women walked around New York looking like a bunch of Victorian widows. Black *everything*. And you talked about the terrible economic times and ate spaghetti," she says. "It became a game here—I am poor and we must all eat spaghetti, as a contrast to the incredible voluptuousness of the 1960s. It's very Marie Antoinette, you know. Coming down out of the castle and sitting in the barnyard with the rest of the folk."

Some of the folks even discovered doing well by doing good. Judy Peabody and her husband Sam (an ex-banker who dropped out a few years back to teach school) are both heavily involved in Reality House, a drug addiction center. Judy spends three mornings a week as co-leader of a group of former heroin addicts. Sam is on the board of directors.

Another of the Ladies doing good with a vengeance is Sandra Feigen, wife of gallery owner Richard Feigen. Back in 1967, Sandy Feigen became involved in something called the National Welfare Rights Organization. They needed money and she was a society lady who could help throw a bash to throw a little cash their way. Done. Her initial involvement came through a friend, Mike McDonald, who was doing a piece on the organization for *The Village Voice*. Well, the *Voice* pal, "hauled me down to the Hilton for a convention of social workers and I met Dr. George Wylie who runs the National Welfare Rights Organization in Washington. He educated me about the movement and I asked how I could be of help."

Sandy Feigen sits in the front parlor of her Seventy-ninth Street triplex, just off Park Avenue. "I have to help spread the word that welfare is not some kind of immoral backwater of funds where money is being squandered," Sandy cries out, banging her little fist into her beigey-gray plush sofa. "It's got to be worked out because, dammit, these women want to get the hell off welfare." One cold winter morning last year, Sandy bundled herself into a chartered bus with her ladies and made a futile trek to Albany to try convincing recalcitrant legislators to reinstate the cuts in the school clothing allotment. It was breakfast in a church basement, then a long day of trotting around buttonholing legislators. "We didn't get what we wanted, but we opened a lot of eyes. Do you know, some of those men up there had never even met a welfare recipient before? They were damned surprised these women could talk, much less think."

Thanks to her friend Betty Friedan, Ethel Scull even got involved in the Women's Lib Movement. "Not that I have to be liberated," Ethel says. She threw open the garden of her East Hampton home for a fund-raising do for the Women's Strike for Equality. Betty Friedan was there. Gloria Cooper came. Gloria Steinem. And lots and lots of press. (One guy was furious because he wanted to goggle at Ethel's house. "The damned doors are locked," he fumed.) Ethel figures the whole thing was a success—even when Jill Johnston, *Village Voice* dance columnist and self-professed Lesbian, liberated herself even more and went topless into the Scull pool.

During the ladies' march for equality, Ethel marched in the front ranks down Fifth Avenue. Ethel admits it took some pretty strong proselytizing on the part of Betty Friedan to get her even interested in the movement. "She's been talking about this for years to me," Ethel recalls. "I kept telling her the whole thing was just a lot of dykes and kooks. Get out of it. But the more she talked and the more I listened, the more I learned," Ethel says. "Little by little, it made a lot of sense. Why shouldn't women be paid the same as men if they do the same job in the same way? Why should women be held back in hiring, promotions, salaries, just because they are women? This is racism!" Ethel is all wound up. She slaps a little foot—clad in gold lamé house slippers—down on her polished parquet floor. "And the march. Oh, the march was marvelous. You know, no matter how much kicking and screaming the men do, it's *got* to happen."

Not that Ethel did not have severe misgivings about her whole role in the Women's Lib Movement. "When Betty asked me if she could use our house for a party—oh, my God. I told her I had to ask Bob." Well, Ethel asked and Bob agreed and Ethel was stuck with it. "The press, the press," Ethel agonized. "They'll make mincemeat out of me." Well, as usual, the press couldn't figure out who its enemy was. But Ethel recovered.

"Social relevance?" says Charlotte Curtis. "Social relevance in this country goes back to the Revolution. Parties were held in Boston to talk about the Revolution. Today, it's a cocktail party." What dismays Charlotte Curtis is the lack of follow-through. The cocktail party or the dinner party or the lawn party, and then what? Then where's the action? Caesar Chavez on the lawn in East Hampton. The Panthers in a Park Avenue duplex. Women's Lib in the Hamptons swimming pool. "Society picked up on these and raised money, sure. But what is unfortunate is the lack of follow-up. Of follow-through. As for the people who went to these big lawn parties and garden parties and cocktail parties, they were shilled. Maybe it was just a kind of summertime entertainment for them."

And WWD was right in there, thumping away at Society's walls. Relevant stories on blacks and politicians and sexual discrimination rather than glittery pieces on banquets and parties. John Fairchild got jolted by America's own brand of Future Shock, realizing that the inhabitants of the Fashion Forest were living in the same world as the rest of us.

So there they sit, Meissen figurines in a Fabergé world. But it is a fragile world. For if it is indeed true, as those mournful lamentations would lead us to believe, that there really is no Society today—Society with a capital "S"—then we must further admit that those very things that broke down the barriers to begin with are still with us. Money broke down the barriers. New money that came rolling in with each war, with each expansion of technology. Education broke down the barriers. Education that now sees most of the revered Ivy League schools not only co-ed but operating full-tilt on scholarship programs that have opened the doors of even the tightest Ivory Tower to a mad, gamey influx of Negroes, Indians, middle-class whites, sons of blue-collar men, and sons of tycoons who looked at Dad and figured God—there must be a better way. Media broke down the barriers by bringing the war and the protests and the problems right smack dab into our very own living rooms, whether they be Salvation Army modern or signed Louis XVI antiques. Sooner or later—one imagines sooner, judging by any day's dose of *The New York Times*—even the BPs will have to acknowledge the RealWorld, for it will be right there in front of them, menacingly seated on a Louis XVI chair in their gilt living rooms.

But face it—there is a great force for good among the BPs. Look at all that champagne they drink: the bottles are bio-degradable, after all. If someone would just haul them off to the recycling center. All those Porthault napkins and towels that are briefly used and then handed over to the live-in laundress. Much better than paper products. Insist on phosphate-free detergents, ladies! Oh—get involved BPs of the world!

12

In 1961, shortly after John Fairchild returned from Paris, he paid a visit to the Washington bureau of the Fairchild News Service.

According to one Fairchild dropout (formerly a reporter in that bureau, and now an investment banker cooling his ego and his journalistic ulcers on Wall Street), Fairchild arrived at the bureau and gathered the troops together for an announcement. Once the staff was assembled, Fairchild leapt nimbly to the top of a desk, smartly striking his head on the office's low-slung ceiling. Since standing with his head bent was hardly appropriate, not to mention uncomfortable, Fairchild slid to the floor and announced to the assemblage, "I do not think Walter Lippmann is the greatest writer in America." (The investment banker swears Fairchild made a pregnant pause—left unfilled by the group—as if waiting for a low chorus of "Who is?" before continuing. When that gambit miscarried, Fairchild was forced to proceed on his own hook.) "No—I believe that one of the greatest writers in America is—Eugenia Sheppard." Another pregnant pause. The investment banker then attests to a lot of internal rumblings which burst forth in a chorus of groaning disbelief once Fairchild had left the premises. "Eugenia Sheppard!" Eugenia Sheppard? Yes, Little Miss Fashion Right (that's WWD's sobriquet). Right up there with the Big One, Walter Lippmann, confidant and adviser to presidents and potentates. Only instead of being surrounded by presidents and potentates, Eugenia Sheppard is surrounded with what passes for the power elite of the fashion world. Instead of discussions of a nuclear balance of power and/or a re-ordering of priorities in order to shape a more perfect society—for Eugenia it's still another discussion of hemlines or waistlines or necklines or bustlines. Iron Curtain *vs* silk stockings.

Eugenia's late husband, Walter Millis, was the household heavyweight. The two were married in 1944. Millis, then of the *Herald-Tribune,* was the author of such respected books as *Arms and Men,* a study of American military history. At the time of his death in 1968, Mr. Millis was writing articles that were deeply critical of mounting United States involvement in Vietnam. As a couple, they were rarely seen together since Millis made no bones about his aversion to mingling with his wife's fashion-society friends. Hence, Eugenia usually went on her nightly rounds accompanied by designers, fashion publicist Eleanor Lambert, or in groups large enough to accommodate an unattached female.

In his own particular way, John Fairchild was absolutely right. For Eugenia Sheppard, in her own funny little way, is a member of a small, very select, and terribly influential group of women in town. Fashion editors! The shrieks echo off the walls like balls in a handball court. They are powerful, sought-after, and exercise absolute authority and control in a tight little society that, eventually, reaches out and touches every single human being in the world. We might live in anything from tents to the White House, snooze in everything from a thermal sleeping bag to a water bed and have sex every which way, even on Sunday. Clothing is the one bond that ties us all together.

As usual, most of the power is centered in New York City. The Big Three of the fashion press are Eugenia Sheppard, Suzy Knickerbocker (Aileen Mehle in civilian life), and Charlotte Curtis of the *Times*. In no particular order. Eugenia writes a daily column for the New York *Post*, which is syndicated to 283 newspapers around the world. Suzy does a column for the *Daily News*, which is syndicated around the country to some sixty newspapers. Charlotte Curtis is women's editor at *The New York Times*, and if she isn't syndicated on a daily national basis, it doesn't matter—she's ripped off sufficiently by the national magazines to accomplish the same thing without all the fuss and feathers.

This troika of newshens is not similar in any way, shape, or form. Eugenia writes a fashion-oriented column, and though she sometimes strays off the point a bit, she always has some tenuous tie to fashion. Suzy, on the other hand, is a frothy gossip columnist who will keep all the proper blanks filled in on Italian *principesse*, Polish counts, tin industrialists, motor tycoons, and movie stars. Who goes where and does what to whom. Charlotte, on the other hand, is the doyenne of the women's pages at the *Times* and, as such, controls such diverse elements as the cookery features, the fashion coverage. Additionally, she is forever marching out features on alcoholic women, radical minority groups, unwed mothers, black/white dating, pre-marital affairs. The one thing that ties the three together is their direct aim at women.

Eugenia Sheppard is a peppy little blonde who looks more like the guest of honor at a surprise birthday party. She is teeny-tiny, barely five feet tall. One could easily miss Eugenia in a crowd, not only because of her size but because there is a certain lack of flamboyance to her. She is, as Marylin Bender described her in *The Beautiful People,* "a blond dumpling." She does *not* look like the typical fashion editor. She is not dramatic, svelte, up-to-the-minute. When ladies were wearing structurally engineered hairdos, Eugenia was still around in her little blond bob. She attempts to get it all fashionably together—a see-through blouse in Rome, her Midi unbuttoned to her dimpled knees—but it's like a puzzle and often all the pieces are not there.

Eugenia was born in Columbus, Ohio, educated at Bryn Mawr, and worked as society and fashion editor of the Columbus *Dispatch* from 1932 to 1938. She was a former Junior Leaguer and a divorcee when she chucked it all in 1938 and headed for New York. Her first job was *Women's Wear Daily.* One day, word came into the office that a fashion show was being held in Brooklyn. Eugenia begged to go, while editors goggled at the idea of covering a fashion show in Brooklyn. Ah, but fortune was there. It was in Brooklyn, Eugenia met Katherine Vincent, then women's editor of the *Herald-Tribune.* Katherine Vincent hired Eugenia Sheppard away from the Fairchild family in 1940. Eugenia had been in town a scant eighteen months. When Katherine Vincent retired in 1947, Eugenia slipped right in as fashion editor and in 1949 was promoted to women's feature editor. When the *Trib* folded in 1966, Eugenia did a brief stint with the patchwork polyglot that came out of those murderous newspaper strikes of that time (which saw the demise not only of the *Herald-Tribune* but also of the *Journal-American* and the *World-Telegram*). Called the *World-Journal-Tribune* it lasted only briefly before sending Eugenia and everyone else once again scuttling for new territory. For a while she was right back where she started—writing for *Women's Wear Daily,* only this time she had a column. It did not work, but the parting a few months later was amicable. From there, Eugenia settled in at the New York *Post,* writing her Monday–Friday column, "Inside Fashion." From this position she has carved out a domain over which she is, in her own way, undisputed queen. Suzy might throw in a little fashion news here and there—what somebody was wearing—and Charlotte might put her own brand of fashion covering onto the pages of the *Times*. But it is Eugenia who is the absolute monarch in the fashion world. Marylin Bender calls her the Boswell of Pop-fashion society. If *Women's Wear* was responsible for the eventual marriage of fashion and society, back in the late 1960s, Eugenia Sheppard arranged the introduction. She lifted fashion out of press releases and pretty descriptions of clothes at collections and humanized the whole process. She started the whole trend of taking the labels out of clothes and introducing them as the designers. Designers became names and then they became adored.

Today, Eugenia is adored. She cruises on the Revson's yacht, the Ultima II. She and the C.V. Whitneys go around together. Gloria Vanderbilt Cooper is a pal. And although she is beyond retirement age, she is something of a swinger. Indefatigable. Budd Calisch, an account executive for Dorell Associates, figures Eugenia could dance the night away while others are panting on the sidelines. A big do in Palm Beach for the World Wildlife Fund had Eugenia ferried down and back in a private jet. After the main function, which was an auction of a matched pair of Royal Worcester pheasants with Winston Guest acting as honorary auctioneer, Eugenia and Budd ended up at 4 A.M. frugging at Trude Heller's Palm Beach discotheque. Once, while out on the town with the Whitneys, the gang ended up at the now-defunct Cerebrum, a head nightclub which had ramps and softly throbbing lights and where it was suggested you doff your clothes and don filmy togas to best enjoy the surroundings. It was designed to be the ultimate experience, where you could sit, stand, lie down, listen, talk, movie, dance, meditate. Pits and ramps and areas. No booze. Marshmallows and Cokes and lemonade and raisins. Well, there was Eugenia in her toga and without her shoes, digging it all. Good vibrations were zooming out of the walls. In fact, Eugenia got so zapped on good vibes and lights and music she fell off one of the ramps and ended up in a conversation pit with a broken leg.

When Salvation II opened on Central Park South, one woman showed up wearing strange brown hair. She had a ticket and was on the arm of a very respectable gentle-man—and she seemed to know everyone in sight by his first name. And there was something disconcertingly familiar about the woman, too. Everyone tried to figure out who she was. After all, there are very few swingers and/or BPs who are barely five feet tall. Who would show up wearing a brown fright wig that stood up like Little Orphan Annie's cork-screws? Eugenia, that's who! It was her big gag and nobody laughed harder than Eugenia.

But if Eugenia started out as the iconoclast—one who could nip at the heels of the fashion world—she did what so many of the radicals and rebels of the world have done throughout history: she settled down. But, why not? If a Black Panther could go from radical activities to a $650-a-month apartment, why couldn't Eugenia, with equal dignity and logic, settle down and get comfortable within the world she helped create. After all, there are those who argue the world needs shaking up in areas far more vital than fur coats and designer labels.

To those whose business was fashion, there was a refreshing gutsy quality to Eugenia's early columns. Partly because no one else was doing such things. She would periodically take gentle little pot shots at one thing and another. But mostly, she was a Master Builder. The Ladies loved it. She dropped names into her stories like pieces of gold in a rushing mountain stream. She went into dressing rooms and boudoirs and ladies' rooms and kept up a running chronicle of events and personalities, everything from who wore false eyelashes (practically everybody) to Margaret Truman's trousseau.

Believe it or not, this was new and exciting and adventure-some. To the fashion world, Eugenia's early columns were like a breath of excitement, the gangland killings and rape-murders of the *haute couture* scene. The fashion scene really thought it had something there—and, indeed, in their own screwy way they did, for no one had thought of covering it in just this way before.

It is difficult to judge Eugenia's column today. Marilyn Bender of *The New York Times* says it has slipped more than somewhat, due to the pressures of putting out a daily column and of having everybody you are writing about considered close personal friends. Those two items alone would put a cramp in any original style. If you are invited to the Coopers' Christmas buffet, you don't look at the patchwork quilt and then write a piece ripping Gloria and Wyatt to shreds. And if you have to live with those designers—sometimes using their elbows for night-time forays to soirées—you don't stick pins and needles in them during the day.

Still, readers thrive on it. To have read Eugenia is to have become informed for one more day at least. To those who are not craving a daily and steady diet of fashion tidbits, two-thirds of a page devoted to the Best Dressed List (a project overseen by her good friend Eleanor Lambert) is more than trivial—it is frivolous. So be it. She is not *The New Republic* or *Foreign Affairs Quarterly*. Neither is she *Screw* or *Rat*. To some Eugenia is exciting and fun. To others she is a crashing bore. Take your pick.

When the *World-Journal-Tribune* died in 1967, it also added Aileen Mehle to the list of journalistically unemployed about town. All over town, people were paralyzed into inactivity, for as "Suzy" Aileen Mehle had become the super-fix to thousands of New Yorkers as she raced pell-Mehle through a heady world of champagne bubbles, parties, intrigues, marriages, divorces, rumors of same, and ditto denials. Her column was as sprightly as a senior citizen after a B-12 shot, peppered with names of international celebrities, multimillionaires, and titled royalty. They constituted a never-never land of make-believe that, somehow, made the world around all those addicted morning readers a little more palatable. Suzy's stars would be there, dripping with money, jewels, furs, and peace of mind! Suzy populated her megalopolis with a people who never caught the flu, had upset stomachs or diarrhea, worried about dental bills or keeping their window sills clean. Suzy cooked up an Oz and served it fresh every day. Fortunately. Suzy was unemployed only about two months before she was picked up by the New York *Daily News* and given daily column space.

Suzy was born in Texas, no less. A dropout English major from the University of California at Santa Barbara, she married (1) a young Navy ensign, Roger W. Mehle (now an admiral) and (2) an East Coast real estate promoter, Kennith Frank. As a gay divorcee, her name has been linked (in other columns—it's only fair) with the late Walter Wanger, Aristotle Onassis, Frank Sinatra.

"Suzy" was born in 1952 in Miami when the publisher of the Miami *News* decided he needed still another gossip columnist. Suzy wrote three "absurd little columns" about Palm Beach, signed them all "Suzy," and that's how it all began. And "Suzy" was a hit. She was kept completely anonymous, not even listed on the payroll. All sorts of cloak and dagger methods were employed to keep her from being found out—nipping off to the ladies' room to jot her notes down, delivering her copy in the dead of night to the publisher's secretary. This went on for two years until Suzy remarried and moved to Washington, living quietly free of her typewriter for five years. By the time the second marriage broke up, the New York *Mirror* was calling to see if "Suzy" could be revived. She could, and she was. She lasted at the *Mirror* as long as it did. When it folded, she traveled to the *Journal-American*. When it closed down, she trekked with the bunch to the *World-Journal-Tribune*. And, thence, to the *Daily News* when the *WIJIT* folded. Newspapers come and newspapers go, but Suzy goes on forever. Or so it seems.

What Suzy does, she does well. She has created a fantasy world full of palazzos, chateaux, manor houses, titles, and treasures. It shimmers like a piece of gaudy gauze, at once as firm and secure as money can make it yet as ephemeral as the make-believe mirage it most surely must be. For how long can it last—certainly not as long as money lasts, that's for sure. A whole brave new wave of antimaterialism is sweeping the country—the world. Twilight of the Goods.

But until doomsday comes—that final death knell tolling in society's situation room while a social seismograph charts the final downward plunge of Oz—Suzy is there. Bubbling, ebullient, breezy.

"Mr. and Mrs. George Plimpton are expecting in approximately six months," she wrote in November, 1970. "Mr. Plimpton writes those best sellers and appears on television. I'd like to say he's a household word—so I might as well."

"Summer has reached Rome with a big bang and everyone has started entertaining *al fresco* on their terraces. The most titillating subject of conversazione, *al fresco* or locked in a closet, is the marriage tomorrow of Princess Maria Gabriella, second of the three daughters of former King Humbert of Italy, to Robert de Balkany at Eze-Sur-Mer in the south of France."

"Barbara Hutton, now shedding via the Mexican courts, her seventh husband, Raymond Doan Vinh Champassak (a Vietnamese or Laotian, depending on where you're standing), is resting from the ennui of it all in the south of France. I mean, she has shed so many times she must have it memorized."

"Pity the poor international set!" she lamented, tongue-in-chic, one season. "Whatever are they going to do with themselves this September? They need a pacifier, that's what they need. This will be the first year the glittering nomads have not had a reason to all meet and show off at the end of the summer. Remember last September? Then it was Portugal, with the Patino and Schlumberger extravaganzas. And the year before it was the lavish costume ball at the Palazzo Rezzonico in Venice."

"Southampton just slogged through one of its wettest weekends. The rains came and stayed," she dutifully reported once. Ah, but never fear. "But if the weather was a drag, the beautiful people who summer in Southampton managed to rise above it. There's nothing like a sunny smile and two or three sunny Bloody Marys to cut through the fog. Mrs. T. Suffern Tailer put on her black Cire raincoat and her black Cire pants and went to lunch at Mrs. William McKnight's. She didn't have to wring herself dry when she got home because, did you know, water rolls right off Cire. Let's think about that for awhile."

She once referred to Zsa Zsa Gabor as "Miss Chicken Paprika of 1910" and calls the Dakota apartments (where, by the by, Eugenia lives) "a swinging Wuthering Heights."

After the quickie marriage, strange honeymoon (complete with the ex-wife) and equally quickie baby and divorce, Suzy wrote of Charlotte Ford Niarchos: "Charlotte Ford Niarchos has been schlepping around the Greek islands with her ex-husband Tanker King Stavros Niarchos on his yacht Creole. This has been the most romantic divorce," she opined. "Remember how sticky it was when they were married? Charlotte hardly ever saw Stavros and the only thing she had to remember him by was her sixty-one carat diamond ring—and the baby, of course."

Before she met Frank Sinatra, she wrote in a column: "All I know is if I were on a desert island alone with Frank Sinatra and he said to me, 'Hey, you over there, shinny up that tree and don't come back till you come back with coconuts'—I'd shinny. Oh, how I'd shinny. And I don't even like coconuts."

Well, she finally met Sinatra, and now they are the greatest of pals. When he was set for a benefit in London, Suzy winged over in Frank's private jet. Like that. Before doing some houseguesting in Acapulco with Merle Oberon.

Sinatra returned the compliment in Wyatt Cooper's now-defunct *Status* magazine by stating, "I adore Aileen Mehle. Aside from being articulate, witty, charming, groovy and incredibly bright, she brings an ingredient to her reporting rarely found in a gossip column—Humor." He also pointed out that, "it's important to remember that a lady writer in her position has a great deal of power. Aileen wields that power with a feather duster."

No denying it—the lady is powerful. She is syndicated in those sixty newspapers across the country, with an estimated readership hovering in the hundreds of thousands. Publicists know if they want to have a person or an event noticed—get a squib in Suzy's column. "I used to go to two or three parties a night," she says. "But that's too much. Now it's down to one." Friends keep her posted on who was at what dinner party and what they wore along with what was served. She is a stickler for accuracy and if a pal ever so much as gets a fish course wrong—not to mention a guest's name or her designer—onto the scrap heap for him. Hence, informers know the cardinal sin is inaccuracy.

Like Eugenia, she is also of and part of the whole scene. She houseguests with Merle Oberon in Acapulco, gets invited to cruise the seas with Jackie and Ari on the Christina. She shows up at Raffles, New York's exclusive pop club. She is an invited guest to the *très chic* Nine O'Clocks functions. No standing on the outside, pencil and notepad in hand, looking in. Her nose is never pressed to the windowpane in a desperate attempt to catch a glimpse. Her nose is right there at ringside, next to the Duke's, while he puffs smelly cigars, and eats ice cream and scrambled eggs. When Suzy showed up at Raffles in HotPants after the Muhammed Ali–Joe Frazier fight she rated a picture in Eye. Although WWD does not commit itself one way or the other about Suzy—she is neither a "Fashion Right" nor a "Tiger" to them—they do not ignore her.

She is everywhere. She even endorsed a vaginal spray in a

two-page spread for Pristeen. It was very genteel, and Suzy never mentioned the word vagina in the ad. There was a row of mug shots of Suzy across the top of the ad; at the end of the copy the adman's pitch for cleaner vaginas.

If a person could miss Eugenia in a crowd, there is no ignoring Suzy. She might be short—but she certainly isn't small. *Ladies' Home Journal,* in its own polite, mid-American, housewifey way once described Suzy as "looking positively smashing" in her black taffeta Oscar de la Renta, "with its bodice slit down to there for a dazzling display of that fantastic bosom." The key words: "fantastic bosom." She is, quite noticeably, endowed. In fact, whenever people cannot think of anything nasty—or nastier—to say about Suzy, they zero in on her endowments.

Beyond her "fantastic bosom," Suzy is truly a standout knockout. She is tiny (does it run in the profession?) with a rosy corona of reddish hair frothing out from her head. Her teeth are perfect little whiteners set in her big, laughing mouth. Her eyes are Paul Newman blue, usually weighted down with heavy eyelashes. She looks to be in a constant state of merriment. Her friends call her such things as "life of the party" and "barrels of fun." Joshua Logan swears that if he goes to a party and finds Suzy there, he knows the gang is in for a good time. "It's those merry eyes and that gay smile. She bubbles."

And by God—she does. At Serge's Paradise Island party—Suzy's table was rollicking. At Le Drug Store in Paris—Suzy and the Duke chattered away a mile a minute. When Truman Capote threw a benefit bash at the Electric Circus, there was Suzy—in foam green and frothing hair—her exuberant laugh bouncing off those undulating walls like sunbeams in a solar power plant.

Oh, not that she takes any exulted view of her exalted position. She is her own biggest put-down. "I'm just the champion of the overprivileged," she sighs. "I do my job and I have no illusions about it. People tell me I'm a powerful influence. Look, I know what I do. I write a gossip column. If it's amusing that's all I intended. To entertain. To fulfill a few fantasies."

Then there is Charlotte "Tiger" Curtis, as *Women's Wear Daily* calls her. As women's news editor for the *Times* there is no denying she is one of the single most influential women journalists in America today. Her influence extends beyond a local by-line in the *Times* metropolitan area. Charlotte Curtis does a story and it reverberates down the various and sundry corridors of power in the Ivory Towers of New York.

Charlotte goes to Leonard Bernstein's for a fund-raising benefit for the Black Panthers, and smartly raps Lennie's knuckles for having Panthers into his Park Avenue drawing room to discuss radical politics and starving black children. Radical chic is born. Tom Wolfe picks it up and runs with it in *New York* magazine. And there it is, all over the country faster than a speeding bullet.

Charlotte was born rich in Chicago, moved to Columbus, Ohio, (shades of Eugenia!) at age ten. She roomed down the hall from Jacqueline Bouvier when both were students at Vassar. She graduated from Vassar in 1950, with a major in American cultural history, and she started working full time for the Columbus *Citizen*. In 1950 she married a Columbus lawyer, Dwight Fullerton, Jr., but by 1954 she had shed her husband and had moved up as women's editor of the *Citizen*. On March 18, 1961, Charlotte resigned her job on the *Citizen*, packed her bags, and headed for *The New York Times*. She began as a general assignment women's reporter, covering Macy's and Gimbel's, and in 1965 she became women's news editor.

Charlotte Curtis is concerned, involved, *sincere*. She weeps for baby seals. Quivers with outrage over the plight of the American Indian. Lifts her nose over the idea of waltzing in a $5,000 ball gown so you can donate $75 for a child crippled with muscular dystrophy. All of this is absolutely evident in the women's pages of the *Times*. Singlehandedly, Charlotte Curtis has raised the idea of a women's page out of household hints and cookie recipes. She has lifted the women's page into relevance! Even when her troops—Enid Nemy and Bernardine Morris, and Judy Klemesrud—are covering fashion shows and celebrities and what have you, there always seems to be a point to their coverage.

While the rest of the fashion world was in an absolute tizzy over the Nine O'Clocks Winter Ball honoring Serge Obolensky, Charlotte took one look at it and called it an "extravaganza, a private $10,000–$20,000 party for members and their friends." Further, she said it was "patterned after galas at the Winter Palace in St. Petersburg in 1910—troubled days when autocratic Czar Nicholas II's Russia was torn with peasant revolts, industrial strikes, political assassinations, liberal opposition to the regime, and the bloody beginnings of the Revolution."

It was a précis of revolutionary conditions in Czarist Russia, worthy of inclusion in a college cram exam book. And all that *before* you got to the heart of the matter: the Ball. It was a gentle blow aimed right at the midsection—and it struck its mark.

After watching the new Mrs. Henry Ford get involved in a particularly strenuous session of dancing on the Riviera, Charlotte sat down and pecked out the description that she was "writhing around like a sea anemone."

When she covered the Riviera, she also zeroed in on the kind of people it attracts including "men and women of noble origins, aristocratic birth or celebrated accomplishment mingle freely with those of uncertain provenance or wavering gender." *Wavering gender!*

In an attempt to analyze why it was suddenly becoming very chic to stay home, Charlotte wrote: "For a while, it looked as if what New York's chic upper echelons call 'this new mood' might have been nothing more than a variation of the old Marie Antoinette game: the rich tiring of their diamonds and—strictly for the fun of it—casting them aside and dressing like the poor." Ah, but it goes further than that, Charlotte figured. "Whether because of the recession, inflation, Vietnam, campus unrest, the desire to get closer to nature, a new introspection or simply boredom with the old extravagances, a new life style is emerging, and emerging quickly."

Two of her most famous pieces involve Wendy Vanderbilt, the young lady of *the* Vanderbilts who was part of the 1960s Jet Set and who painted professionally in her East Side duplex furnished with her family's castoff furniture. In one instance, Charlotte was covering a benefit fashion show with celebrity models. It was here she characterized Wendy as looking "remarkably like the plastic store mannequins for which she modeled." That is just about as rough as Charlotte gets. Another time she covered a benefit auction where Wendy, the Artist, auctioned off de Kooning's *Torso*—holding it upside down. Nothing escapes her eye. Nothing escapes her references to relevance. Pounds of diamonds equal food for the starving poor.

She is the hard-nosed reporter who just happens to be stuck on the women's page. One wonders how much better she could be utilized out on page one? She crashed George Plimpton's wedding; she published the guest list of Truman Capote's Masked Ball in the *Times's* 8 P.M. edition—while the ladies were still powdering their noses and adjusting their masks for the 10 P.M. starting gun.

While covering the opening of the Royal Poinciana Playhouse in Palm Beach a few seasons back, Charlotte and a critic of hers were heard exchanging words. Seems Charlotte had referred to the man as a "gambler" in one of her stories. The man protested. "But you are a gambler," Charlotte persisted. "Doesn't owning a gambling casino make you a gambler? Isn't this investment company set up to run casinos? Didn't you just buy into a casino in Vegas? Have you ever gambled?" Well, um, yes. "I'm very much afraid you are a gambler then, aren't you?" It was the classic confrontation between the recalcitrant child and the school teacher. As usual, the school teacher won. "He's a goddamn gambler," Charlotte insisted to herself after the gambler/guy had slunk off into the sunset. "But I do rather like him."

Shortly after Charlotte Curtis became women's editor at the *Times*, she was treated to lunch by John Fairchild. *Times* staffer Marylin Bender says Fairchild was indicating he was "ready for new alliances" but Charlotte didn't pick up on his friendly overtures. WWD now refers to her as Charlotte "Tiger" Curtis and wonders in print how many women will continue to consent to sit down and be interviewed by Charlotte. (They must be still wondering, because just about *everybody* not only sits down but pulls Charlotte's chair up for her.)

She is a tiny woman, barely five feet tall. One former Columbus *Citizen* compatriot described her as having "the disposition of a thoroughbred: overtrained, overbred, and tense." Observers contend she is shy, often dragging people over to talk her through parties and dinners. But she is tough. Back in Columbus she was on the Newspaper Guild's negotiating committee, standing up and not only demanding an equal shake for her women—but fighting for it. While most women's editors are content to rest on their laurels—usually at some fashionable French restaurant—Charlotte is out there with all the rest of the poor working stiffs, standing in the wind and the rain and the snow and the dark of night covering banquets and parties and balls and bashes.

She is always working, talking, and taking copious notes. A lot of the material never makes it directly to the story at hand. But sooner or later it is used. Charlotte is very history-minded; for a story on Boston, she read the W.P.A. books prepared on the city and she also reread Henry Adams. To get started on a particular story, she reads everything the *Times* has ever written on the subject. She has a special liaison with the sports department "because so many of the people I am concerned with are horsey in one way or another. They own them, breed them, race them." She checks Standard & Poor's because "finance is such an important part of this job."

When she started at the *Times* she freely admits she didn't know her Vanderbilts from her Astors. "The history of America—and of the important early families—is to be found in railroads," she says. The New York Central, the New Haven—"these were the starting points for the mainstreams of American society." Indeed, the Philadelphia Main Line is a railroad reference and a Society reference, too.

Charlotte Curtis has deliberately separated herself from the world she covers. She has never broken her leg while out on the town with the likes of the C.V. Whitneys. In fact, she seems the consummate professional journalist. Her office is a cluttered hodgepodge in the *Times* building off Times Square. A shopping bag in Charlotte's office proclaims, "The people will carry the Panthers out of jail." HELP! cries a sign on her bulletin board. "I have developed a new philosophy," says a card. "I only dread one day at a time." A photo of a little old lady from Dubuque in a silent vigil for peace. "This is America," Charlotte says, gesturing to her little old lady. She has no truck with people "who have been to London fifty-five times but don't know Chicago." To Charlotte, America is a big, beautiful land full of possibilities and opportunities. Provided, of course, its people are educated.

So much for the Superhighways—Eugenia, Suzy, Charlotte. What about secondary roads? Are there no footpaths being hacked out through John Fairchild's Fashion Forest?

Well, for starters, there's *Rags*, the undergrounds' very own fashion magazine. It happened very simply. Daphne Davis was talking to her pal Mary Peacock shortly before Thanksgiving, 1969. Both had reacted strongly and favorably to Blair Sabol's columns in *The Village Voice* (which Blair quit writing in 1971) and wondered if a hip anti-Establishment fashion magazine would go. They called Barry Wolman, who was one of the founders of *Rolling Stone*, the popular and successful rock magazine. Wolman set about raising the money—$54,000 —and the gang incorporated themselves as Rosy Cheeks Publishers, Inc. They called themselves *Rags*, the derogatory Seventh Avenue name for the garment business. Wolman became publisher. Mary Peacock, a former associate literary editor for *Harper's Bazaar*, became editor. Daphne Davis, once Carmel Snow's assistant at *Harper's*, was named contributor, and Blair Sabol became an editorial consultant. They were off. Aimed directly at the seventeen to twenty-five-year-olds "who are aware and imaginative." Within six months they were selling at the rate of 50,000 copies on the newsstands. Since it only costs $16,000 to get an issue out—it's printed on newsprint and comes out in a folded tabloid size—they are not socking all their money into slick paper and four-color press runs.

They must be doing something right. It is a professional-looking magazine, with the most ungodly collection of stories, features, hints, and columns ever assembled. Articles on body tattooing; how-to-do-it features on decorating boots and jeans and T-shirts by painting, dying, scorching, patching, appliquéing, and studding them. Articles on transvestites and hard hats and hair-spray manufacturers. A big feature on Frederick's of Hollywood. You know the ones—with cutout bras and padded girdles. The one with the ads that make every chick look as if she's launching a Saturn 12 rocket from her right-on C-cup. A food column by Dr. Eatgood. Astrology from Barbara Birdfeather. Suggestions ranging from rinsing the hair in Jell-O (to give it body) to a home sewing feature on where to get a pattern for a masculine codpiece. Where to buy surplus Navy nurses' uniforms, French navy underwear, Australian army shorts, and imitation police truncheons "in gentle pastel shades." An article on casket couture—all about what the well-dressed body is wearing to his own funeral.

Rags tried relentlessly to interview John Fairchild and was rebuffed each time round. "John Fairchild, Mr. Big at *Women's Wear Daily*, has refused to do an interview with *Rags*," they wrote, "offering the explanation that: 'I have nothing to say.' Just as we suspected." A large photograph accompanying the story, taken at Orsini's restaurant, shows John Fairchild sitting with his hands covering his face. The photo is credited to "Brenda Starr."

"The slick fashion magazines bear about as much relationship to reality as toothpaste does to sex appeal," Wolman wrote in his first letter. "For us, fashion is not an isolated moment on some exotic island with a porcelain model, but simply an everyday sense of how people are dressing themselves."

Mary Peacock is as unlikely as the rest of the crowd. The daughter of a midwestern businessman (he sold bottled garlic and onion juice by mail), Mary lived a nomadic life up and down the East Coast on a boat, on a farm in the Midwest, and finally on to Ft. Lauderdale. She ended up graduating from Vassar in 1964 with an A.B. in English. Once her main ambition was to be literary editor of *Esquire*. My, how things do change. "*Rags* is aimed at the alternate culture," she explained once. "People who believe something a little different from what most people believe in. That girl in our first issue—she really walked around with her head shaved. Now Diana Vreeland probably would have done it for her. Like, *Vogue* is Vreeland's own fantasy trip. But *Rags* just takes people who are already into it." Imposing from without *vs* already there. Something for Everyone.

"Fashion designing is not art," insists John Weitz, who should know since he has designed everything in his life from shirtwaist dresses to prison uniforms and now men's clothing, socks, airline jumpsuits, "but it's a very professional craft." And "The life of a fashion designer is such a tenuous life," adds Dr. Robert Campbell, psychiatrist. "Trigère probably doesn't give a damn—she's got it made. But most designers are not all that secure in reality and to have to work under such terrific insecurities—wondering whether women will love them or hate them a couple of months from now, will buy what they design or not, whether WWD praises them or damns them—no wonder they get a little hysterical." Fashion designers are bought and sold on the open market. Honesty and integrity rarely exist in the fashion world for a fashion designer. He will design what will sell. HotPants. Or what he is told will sell. The Midi. Not one major American fashion designer left HotPants out of his spring and summer collections of 1971. This was when the HotPants promotion was reaching its peak down at WWD.

And if fashion is indeed a big business then it, like all other big businesses operating in America today, needs promotion people. Publicists. These are people who sell other people—or things or ideas—to the public. The most well-known and influential publicist is Eleanor Lambert. WWD calls her "Herself."

Eleanor Lambert started in Crawfordsville, Indiana, the daughter of a circus advance-man. Crawfordsville, a small city in the west central part of Indiana, is known for its manufacture of farm implements, bricks, and caskets. Eleanor overcame all those tractors and caskets and today she is the *doyenne* of fashion flacks.

But, Eleanor, how did you escape Indiana? How did you crawl out of those caskets and all the way to the top? Easy. "I took the train." She arrived in New York on a cold, blowy day in 1928 and the buy-now-pay-later installment-plan coat she was wearing "promptly fell into pieces." Eleanor, unlike most of the rest of the people in the business, loves her humble beginnings. She is a girl of the soil in the most enviable sense: she got out. Where most of the fashion people downgrade their origins—Eleanor loves hers. They show her mettle.

After arriving in New York, she held a variety of jobs, but all of them pointed toward publicity. Her first job was an afternoon job with a retail consulting firm, scurrying from one store to another observing customer buying habits, then sitting down and pecking out a report on what she saw. Net result: $17 a week. Mornings she did publicity for an ad agency specializing in publishing. Annette Simpson, a Lord & Taylor designer, found her feeding publicity stories to the old *World*, figured Lambert could do likewise for dress designers, herself in particular. "That was the start of it all," Eleanor says simply. Forty years later she owns her own company, Eleanor Lambert, Inc., a publicity firm specializing in fashion.

Lift fashion's skirts and chances are you'll find Eleanor Lambert securely hanging onto the petticoats. In 1943 she inaugurated the Coty American Fashion Critics Awards, the "Oscar" of the fashion world, given to designers judged to be best in the business. She snatched the International Best Dressed List from the French during World War II. In 1959 she organized and presented a fashion show at the American Exhibit in Moscow. She headed up the New York Couture Business Council, formed during the war to bring American manufacturers together. Late in 1962 she rounded up a dissident faction and broke away to form the New York Council of Fashion Designers, a supposedly more prestigious group of couture designers as opposed to the manufacturers left in the NYCBC. In 1963 she produced the Pageant of Fashion for the benefit of the Kennedy Center in Washington. That association with Roger Stevens did not hinder her chances for appointment to the National Council on the Arts in 1965 as a representative from the area of fashion design—the first time fashion had ever been listed among the creative arts anywhere in the world. She also writes a syndicated column simply called "She" which Eleanor characterizes as a "down-to-earth advice column. It's not at all sophisticated, but it's useful. I've learned that women aren't so much concerned with where the hemline is—as they are with what to wear to a wedding and how to dress for a graduation."

In 1936 she married the late Seymour Berkson, president of

International News Service and later publisher of the *Journal American*. Berkson died in 1959. They had one child, Bill, who used to head up the publication division of the Museum of Modern Art in addition to teaching poetry and literature at the New School for Social Research.

Home is a fabulous apartment on Fifth Avenue. She has a house in Acapulco, and can houseguest elsewhere with the likes of Gloria Guinness in Paris.

Naturally, controversy swirls around Eleanor Lambert. First of all, the Best Dressed List. Many say it's a bunch of hokum. Many dismiss it altogether. "If they really want it . . ." concedes Charlotte Curtis. But still it endures. It was one of Eleanor's first flings with public service. Up until World War II, the Best Dressed List had been the sole responsibility of the French fashion industry. The war interrupted the list but, "I just couldn't let it die out," she said. So, in a fit of altruism, she hauled the gasping Best Dressed List out of the ashes that were Paris. A little hand-to-mouth resuscitation and it was alive and kicking.

Today Eleanor supervises and coordinates the list by sending ballots out over the country, to "more than 2,000 observers of the international scene." It is a complicated and complex procedure, this naming of names to this legendary and, some would have it, mythical list. (The correct title, mind you, is the *International* Best Dressed List.) These "observers" include restaurant owners, designers, columnists, socialites (!). Anyway, the ballots go out along with the names of former winners plus a list of 100 or so ladies Eleanor and her committee think should be considered for the list. The committee is composed of Eleanor herself plus some anonymous fashion editors. "The committee never anoints any of the countless women of taste and means who live in Chicago, San Francisco, Detroit, and Montreal," wrote Marylin Bender in criticism of the BDL. To her the reason is obvious: "Those women don't associate with the New York fashion editors and publicists."

"How does she do it?" another lady publicist asks, stalking around her East Side offices, waving the list in her hand. "How does she pull it off? Do you suppose she pays people? My God—this woman's influence is incredible." It is indeed. From a list of ladies most of the editors have never met at all, much less seen in the clothes they wear every day, a List does indeed materialize.

The Best Dressed List is touted by Suzy. Eugenia usually devotes an entire column to it. "We treat it as a news story," explains Charlotte Curtis at the *Times*. "We just list the winners. If we have space for it." And WWD openly ignores it. "Who's best dressed?" asks John Fairchild. "That girl in the subway? That girl out on the street? No one has the right to determine who is best dressed," Fairchild once said. "The best dressed list is a gimmick and a bunch of rot. All it is good for is the fashion business. I'm sure a lot of ladies without a carload of cash look better than those ladies on the list. Those who are dying to make it love being spotlighted—and when they receive this dubious accolade they can tell their husbands it's worth all the money they've spent." (Gwen Gibson, fashion reporter of the New York *Daily News*, figures it takes a minimum of $35,000 a year on clothes to even contemplate making the Best Dressed List. "Money is the *sine qua non* of the best-dressed people," she says.)

There are other skeptics and cynics who point to the personal friendships between Eleanor and some of the Best Dressed winners. She stays with Hall of Famer Gloria Guinness when she tootles over to Paris. (In fact, when Gloria Guinness—of all people—won a journalism competition sponsored jointly by the Singer Sewing Machine Company and the University of Missouri School of Journalism—Eleanor graciously handled the publicity. (Gloria Guinness! Think of the lady journalists in their combat boots and fatigues slogging around Vietnam. Think of Gloria Guinness writing little pieces for *Harper's Bazaar* on Mini skirts and Midi skirts.)

One of Eleanor's best friends is *Post* columnist Eugenia

Sheppard, whose own friends include Best Dressed Gloria Cooper, Best Dressed Lyn Revson, Best Dressed Merle Oberon, Best Dressed Gloria Guinness. In 1963 Eugenia wrote a piece for the *Saturday Evening Post* in which she said the judges admittedly tampered with the BDL returns to eliminate any fringe weirdos and kooks that might turn up.

But as the Duchess of Windsor once sighed, "How could such lists be anything but phony when most of the judges seldom see me or the other people they're voting for." Even Eugenia got a little discouraged last year. "Certainly this time Françoise de la Renta should have been listed among the women fashion pros." On the whole, though, Eugenia conceded, "the List serves a purpose of reporting what the fashion scene is like and who are its most effective players."

The same charges that are leveled against the Best Dressed List are leveled against another of Eleanor's pet projects, the Coty Awards which she inaugurated in 1943. Again, it is an award fraught with meaning and murky with innuendo. Supposedly, winning the Coty is like winning the Oscar.

Until last year, a jury of fashion editors voted on the winners. The jurors were divided between magazines and newspapers, but with the decline of newspapers, magazines started forming the largest lump on the jury. In fact, as many as a half-dozen voters or more from one magazine would form a bloc on the jury and would thus wield an unwieldy sort of power over the whole show. Finally, they were requested to keep it down to four. Then, in early 1971, Coty itself announced that it had ordered up a complete overhaul of the awards. Their name is on the show and they were picking up the tab, ranging upwards of $25,000+ each year. According to Thomas Cooney, vice president of consumer producer operations for Pfizer (of which Coty is a division), "We felt we should have a board of trustees to set up a formal set of by-laws and operating procedures, formalize categories and set the rules on a year-by-year basis." What Cooney came up with was a suggestion to compose a board of the publishers of

Vogue, Harper's Bazaar, Mademoiselle, Seventeen, Esquire, Gentlemen's Quarterly, Ladies' Home Journal, Glamour, the presidents of NBC, CBS, and ABC-TV, and the publishers of the Newspaper Enterprise Association, which represents some 800 syndicated members. According to Cooney, the plan is to have each trustee form the nominating committee by appointing two members of his organization to submit nominations. These would then be sent to a panel of judges for voting, including sketches representative of each designer. The judges who would actually vote on the designer would, of course, be "all the ranking fashion people on the magazines, in the New York newspapers, leading newspaper syndicates, and the presidents of leading stores." The whole idea, according to Cooney, was to make the Coty Awards stronger by "getting those ballots out across the country and making the judging more national by including the retailers." Eleanor would, of course, be kept on as a paid coordinator and publicist for the whole affair.

When Norman Norell won his third Coty Award in 1963 under the old system, he was hailed and regaled to the Fashion Hall of Fame. He promptly rapped the whole shebang, wrapped his Coty statuette up and returned it forthwith from whence it came, the office of fashion publicist Eleanor Lambert. He insisted that the Coty voting was not fair and would never be fair until every judge (fashion editors around the country) saw every designer's collection that they were called upon to vote on. "It no longer means a thing to me," Norman kept insisting as he wrapped up his statuette. "I can't bear to look at it anymore. I was jumping with glee when I got it, and when I got to the Hall of Fame—well, you can imagine. But now I am definitely returning my award to Lambert." And with that, the Coty went whizzing back across town to Lambert's East Side offices. The next morning Lambert returned it to Norell. It took him five minutes flat to utter an invective and whip it back across town.

That dustup between Lambert and Norell—something

which rocked the fashion world—was eventually solved. In fact, in 1967, Eleanor, operating under the aegis of the Council of Fashion Designers of America (her own brainchild, spawned and born in 1963), threw a huge bash at the Metropolitan Museum of Art and the Plaza Hotel dubbed "A Party for Norman." Norman was none other than Norman Norell. The two had somehow made peace with one another.

Twice a year Eleanor produces what is to the fashion world, the Greatest Show on Earth. Members of the Council of Fashion Designers of America pool their talents for a supershow of their designs. Bill Blass, Oscar de la Renta, Donald Brooks, Rudi Gernreich, Anne Fogarty, John Weitz, Giorgio di Sant'Angelo, Kenny Lane's jewelry, Halston, Tiffeau, Leo Narducci, Pauline Trigère. For five days, hundreds of fashion editors from around the country wing in and are entertained in the SA Circus Maximus. (Remember Eleanor's father, folks.) Showings, cocktail parties, dinners, "Meet the Designer" hours. Every day the editors are given a scant hour to sit down and write up their impressions. Needless to say, there is heavy reliance on Eleanor's artfully constructed press packages which contain glossy photos, descriptions of collections, designer bios.

Part of the power of someone like Eleanor Lambert is simply a reflection of the state of the fashion press as a whole. Women's pages, for the most part, have not been liberated. Most editors, while acknowledging that women's news will sell appliances and dresses and some other assorted soft goods, will not knock themselves out to put out a decent product. It's still engagements, marriages, births, and deaths with an occasional party in between. Hints from Heloise and Dear Abby. How to get rid of acne. So, along comes someone like Eleanor Lambert who, in addition to everything else she does, organizes something called "Press Week" twice a year wherein fashion editors come to New York for a week in November and in July to see a prepackaged promotion of the summer and fall collections. Eleanor provides a well-pulled-together synopsis of the season's collections—by her handpicked designers—complete with those capsulized biographies and publicity photos of the designers. Considering the shape of women's pages across the country, it is truly a public service. There are some, however, who are not quite so charitable to Eleanor's Press Week activities.

"It was an outrage," Eleanor Nangle, former fashion editor of the Chicago *Tribune*, recalled of those grim days of Press Week. "Herding all those editors into some hotel and parading clothes and designers and press releases in front of them." Awful. Terrible. Boring. Degrading. So, Eleanor Nangle decided to split from the scene and cover SA for herself. What happened? "Lambert wired all her houses and had me blocked. Oh, it was a terrific fight." Only recently have the walls come tumbling down and are the likes of Eleanor Nangle able to do a little free-lance coverage of SA.

Eleanor Lambert is a controversial figure. She polarizes opinion like an argument over what kind of booze to have at the wedding reception. WWD doesn't need her, but they recognize her tireless talents. "She does her job," shrugs Fairchild. After all—somebody has to force-feed it to all those newspapers across the country who do not have such ready access to Seventh Avenue as the New York editors. She, in turn, returns the compliment. While no big fan of WWD's, she recognizes what it has done. "Just as Walter Winchell humanized the theater and let people look behind the scenes, *Women's Wear* has done the same to fashion. The press and society have been titillated by its gossip and its power has snowballed," Eleanor says.

There are those who strongly feel the New York Media Group—a women's liberation group from the Fourth Estate—should not have stopped at disrupting the *Ladies' Home Journal*. Instead, they should have spread out all across the country liberating the ladies' pages from cooking tips and engagement announcements. Should lift the weightless wedding veil of witlessness that enshrouds many of the women's pages in America. The mind boggles. Organic oatmeal cookie recipes, self-defense featurettes. How to protect yourself from goosing and goggling as well as gorging. But ask this question: Is the Woonsocket *Call* ready for it all? One wonders, indeed. Until then, the BDL and Eugenia and Suzy will abound, dividing and multiplying. For better or for worse.

13

~

The mood of the 1970s is of one big coming out party. Here they come—inspired by the Civil Rights movement of the mid-1960s—Puerto Ricans, Indians, Mexican-Americans, Radical Chinese. Freaks, heads, junkies, doves, antipollutionists, welfare mothers, migrant workers. Every conceivable minority group is timorously opening doors and poking tentative heads out into a world that might not have taken to them too well a few seasons back. They are right up front demanding their rights. The streets are jammed with them. Politicians are overwhelmed with the scope of the groups and their demands. Down the street they come thundering. Occupying hallways. Buildings. Whole damn islands. But, more importantly, occupying the public conscience and headlines. They are the *avant-garde* of a rear guard action to raise America's consciousness level.

And nobody came further and faster out of that McGee's closet of misunderstood minorities than the homosexual. Not that he hasn't always been around. Indeed, he has. But if he ever made it to polite living rooms, a temporary closet was usually built over by the potato chip dip and, like all good minority groups, he knew his place. Ah, but the 1970s are something else again. Suddenly the whole militant mood of the rest of America—a militancy demanding nothing more than basic rights and basic services—began catching up with the nation's homosexuals. Starting with the Equal Employment Opportunity act, the homosexuals started publicly—in the street!—protesting descrimination on the part of employers concerning homosexuals. Creative cruising for basic rights. New York City Councilman Carter Burden endorsed their demands, publicly and actively sought their support in his campaign for the New York City Council. U.S. Representative Bella Abzug sympathized, attended rallies, gave her campaign pitch. They loved her. She became their new Judy Garland. She was Big Battling Bella in a tough fedora, waving a big fist and speaking far from softly. Merle Miller wrote an impassioned piece in the Sunday *New York Times Magazine*, publicly admitting his homosexuality and laying bare some of the most intense sexual emotions ever discussed in public print.

The arts have long been sprinkled with homosexual actors, playwrights, musicians, artists, male models, designers. As Marylin Bender pointed out, the big joke along Seventh Avenue when business was failing was "Go out and hire a fairy designer." Some of them are very swish, quite open. Others are less so. Then there are those unknown quantities: the world's most ineligible bachelors. They constitute a sort of do-they-or-don't-they game for outsiders looking in. As for those who are—both obviously and admittedly—they are certainly out in force. And, with the exception of the theater, nowhere are they more comfortable than on Seventh Avenue, which is a homosexual's dreamland. With the emphasis on clothes, homosexuality can be flaunted. As one young designer said, "You've got it—flaunt it." They can and they do.

Back in 1962, Dr. Edmund Bergler did a psychiatric study of more than 100 male homosexuals who were in some way involved in the fashion field. Many of them were fashion designers. His findings were published in a book he wrote on the subject, *Fashion and the Unconscious.* The book is considered today by fellow psychiatrists to be the definitive work on the subject of homosexuality in the fashion world. The study involved intensive analysis utilizing what Bergler called "a clinical psychiatric-psychoanalytic method." When the whole thing was over, Bergler came to one conclusion: "The majority of the really creative persons in the field are male homosexuals."

Bergler wrote: "It has never been publicly acknowledged that the majority of the great male fashion creators and hairstylists, both foreign and domestic, are homosexuals. But it has been whispered for decades." As far as Bergler was concerned, "The homosexual's commanding position in the fashion field is a fact." The end. So be it. Love it or leave it.

(Bergler also put it all together and it spelled "Mom." As he saw it, there is always "the homosexual's enmity against the female customer, a defensive enmity which originated in the unsolved homosexual conflict with the infantile image of the Giantess in his individual nursery." Rockabye, baby.)

What's wrong with that? God knows we've all been living with homosexuals for years, despite efforts of a conservative coalition of cops, courts, and lawmakers to make us do otherwise. When the closet doors burst open a few years back, attitudes concerning homosexuality—freedom to practice private sexual acts between two consenting adults—began to change. But Bergler's theory went even further. Beyond the fact that, in his view, most of the fashion creators not only feared women but hated them as well. "In every case I have encountered," Bergler said, "analysis of the homosexual proved that a fantastic fear of women lay behind the universal facade of 'distrust' or 'indifference.' "

In his book Bergler recounted this encounter between himself and a male homosexual fashion designer:

Mr. X: "But look at my profession—I am a designer. I have a friendly, indifferent attitude towards women. Why, I even beautify the bitches. . . . Fashion-conscious women would accept any extravagant style even if they had to be placed between two steamrollers before they could fit into it."

Bergler: "Why make it so difficult?"

Mr. X: "Let them wear corsets so tight they can't eat at all. Who cares?"

Bergler hinted to a patient that perhaps he was not so much dressing women as caricaturing them. "You became attached to boys," Bergler told his patient. "To bolster this you began to identify with girls, secretly parading up and down in front of the mirror in your sister's—and later your mother's—dresses. You used perfumes, lipstick; you imitated their gestures and so on."

Bergler figured a person could trace what he called "punitive fashions" right back to the homosexual in the clothes closet. "Since it is common knowledge that male homosexuals are involved in fashion creation," Bergler mused as to whether or not "the unconscious hatred of women typical for every homosexual has been responsible for some of the dress absurdities of the last half century." Hobble skirts, corsets, coats without buttons that force women to clutch themselves or freeze to death. Punitive fashions are "difficult to explain," Bergler said, "except in terms of unconscious ill will." Look, he said, "at the opposition so frequently offered by the big-wigs of *la haute couture* to the substitution of styles which are easy and comfortable to wear."

As for the oft-mentioned theory that designers are just a bunch of homosexuals out to destroy American womanhood, John Fairchild himself snorts at the idea. "That's nonsense—they're businessmen aren't they? That old argument—that designers are just queers who want to make women look ugly—is silly. They want to make clothes that sell, that's all. To make money." Well, at least it establishes the fashion designer as a businessman.

No matter which way the wrist flips, the whole ambiance of the Seventh Avenue world—and the attendant world of the Beautiful People—is fertile ground for the flourishing of homosexuals. With all the banquets, parties, balls, someone was needed to escort all those ladies. "My husband was adamant about balls," confessed one lady whose name is never off the published guest lists. "He figured he worked hard all day and the last thing he wanted to do was come home from the office and go out to a ball. So—I would find someone else to take me." The someone else was usually a homosexual— unattached, good company, and very pleased to be making the scene.

"I get awfully sick of faggots, though," confessed one of the younger, less reverent, members of the social scene. "They're all over the goddamn place. But you must admit, if you find a good one they're very good company. But beware—they come in all sorts of styles. Like, stay away from the kind that are just using you to get into some fantastic cruise scene. I mean, that's like buying a dog so you can use it when you're cruising, right? But the good faggot—well, treasure him. He'll really come in handy. He'll tell you you look gorgeous, he'll fuss over you, and he'll never, never, never make any demands on you. He'll be amusing, he'll gossip. He always looks good. And he always smells good. For some reason that's very important."

Well, so be it.

But what about the husbands? Don't they get upset when wifey is forever flitting off and around with a succession of ineligibles? Of course not. "A husband is absolutely enchanted with the idea of his wife having a homosexual escort," says designer John Weitz. "After all, he's a safe outlet. I'm sure those husbands are perfectly happy because this is a very safe playmate for their wives. Someone who will keep her happy and amused—without hopping into the sack with her." The way Weitz sees it, "The perfect friends a wife could have are her girl friends and those men friends who are hopefully a group of funny faggots." John Weitz obviously enjoys his role of amateur psychologist, Pop-psyching through Fairyland. "You know, it's a constant battle of guilts between some men and their wives. And the husband who plays around is delighted to have his wife spend a fortune on clothes."

Weitz, whose best-selling novel, *The Value of Nothing*, on Seventh Avenue, was liberally sprinkled with homosexuals and their escapades, says the homosexual is just a way of life around Seventh Avenue. Homosexuality runs rampant in the fashion design world—bearing in mind, of course, there are literally thousands of male fashion designers on Seventh Avenue, not just the high-class designers everybody hears about. There are designers who design everything from dresses to bathing suits and belts and jewelry and hosiery. Designers and assistant designers and struggling designers and would-be designers. "There are very few heterosexual designers on Seventh Avenue," Weitz says, and he should know. He's been in the business for more than thirty years now, starting way back at age sixteen when he apprenticed to a famous couturier in Europe. "It's not a Mafia. Not an underworld. They don't spend their lives keeping heterosexuals from their craft. It is just part and parcel of the business of designing and decorating."

Weitz even has fashion's homosexual scene neatly broken down into its basic operating components. "Well, first of all there is the Fag Son–Forceful Mother relationship between the fashion editor and the designers." She is the domineering force, the decision-maker, yes to this, no to that. He is the creative force, trying to please. "Then there's the Fag Son–Forceful Mother relationship between the *grande dame* of society and the young designer." Again, she is in control, taking Our Hero out into Society and introducing him to the important social set. The social set that buys clothes and has yachts and throws country weekends. "Then there are the pet fags. That relationship between young designers and young women." These are perhaps the most honest. No overtones of gigolo and Mrs. Stone, out for her Roman Spring. With youth, at least, there is probably outspoken honesty. The question of homosexuality probably doesn't even come up in the first two relationships. It is there but unspoken. An undercurrent, taken for granted. In the latter, they probably talk about it.

There she is, poor old Mom. She's been slamming around—and has been slammed around—for years. Super-Mother in a housedress. The Giantess in the Nursery, breathing fire from 100mm cigarettes and cutting the old man off on everything from sex to his own son. The stereotype whipping girl, a handy home fetish for all those who want to explain away the homosexual "problem" in the world. A gigantic Thurber Woman busting over the horizon, all the while keeping her boy firmly tucked under her deodorized wing. Standing staunch against a world who would rob her of her little boy, this all-American female, by now assuming Amazonian proportions, cut him off from his pals and smothered him in rosy Mother's kisses, assuring him that with just the two of them this is indeed the best of all possible worlds.

Psychiatrist Irving Bieber, in a study done for the New York State Psychiatric Association, published his findings in his classic book, called, simply, *Homosexuality*. Bieber and those assisting him in the study poked a well-documented hand in the air calling attention to the fact that if one is to be a mother, somewhere, there is a father. And sure enough, to Bieber, father emerges from the shadows and becomes just as blameworthy as his well-known counterpart. Conceived in Prime Time and dedicated to the proposition that all men are good for a few canned laughs, Father is gladly willing to let Mother run the house and him. In most cases, Bieber discovered, this father is physically present but "detached" emotionally. Or, as the good doctors white-coat the definition, he is indifferent and distant from his son. Thus, homosexuals find themselves equipped with overprotective moms and fathers who just are not warmly available to them. Hence, according to both Bergler and Bieber, they develop a pathological need for male companionship and male contact.

Weitz figures all this happens early on in life. "At age twelve a boy who is not fascinated with football will find himself shoved into the so-called 'creative' channels." This does two things: (1) Keeps the kid off the football field where he would probably be killed and out of the locker room where he would die of teasing; (2) Keeps him occupied. "By and large, designers are terribly untalented in a creative way. Designers are only talented in a superficial way, so they end up in the decorative crafts like fashion designing. Because look—don't kid yourself—fashion designing is not an art. It's a craft. A funny and amusing craft. It's like furniture making. If you're very good, you're Chippendale. If you're not, you just, well—make furniture. That's craft. With arty overtones."

WWD, for all its finger-pointing and nose-thumbing at other phenomenon of the fashion world, steers relatively clear of a direct confrontation with the homosexual question in its pages. It will, from time to time, throw out some pretty strong hints and periodically it will show the same sex dancing together, with a caption announcing "X and Friend."

Perhaps the kindest cut of all came from Marylin Bender in *The Beautiful People,* when she wrote that "the word 'fag' is being flung about the jealous jungle of Seventh Avenue as irresponsibly as 'pink' was in the McCarthy era. To be celibate and even moderately successful in a fashion career means being tagged as a homosexual. The possibility of selfish bachelorhood or spinsterhood from lack of opportunity is cruelly disallowed."

Still, the homosexual rumors abound. Seventh Avenue, in its own way, is Show Biz replete with openings and closings. Great successes and great bombs. Every year the doomsayers predict the death of Broadway. Every week or so, *Women's*

Wear Daily gets Charlie Zimmerman and the ILGWU all in a tizzy by slamming SA in favor of Paris. The theater is dead, long live Paris. And if Show Biz has homosexuals, it certainly doesn't have a corner on the market. For every heterosexual designer there are a handful of homosexuals. "Of course, not every designer is a homosexual," protested one of Seventh Avenue's most successful and hardest-working models. "Why there's—" She stopped counting at two.

"I can't imagine a Seventh Avenue homosexual being any different from a Broadway homosexual," says one young theatrical producer, himself a homosexual. "In addition to all our nice qualities, we have a history of being bitchy, fickle, vindictive, and always on the make. If heterosexuals use sex as a tool, to wield power over another person—my God, so do homosexuals. And then some. You can't tell me there isn't power—or the threat of power—being wielded by the faggots on Seventh Avenue. You can't tell me a designer doesn't try to work his way up by sleeping with the right guys. It happens all the time. It has to, sex being what it is. Homosexuals being what they are." For one thing, according to this producer, homosexual sex is now and always has been much freer than heterosexual sex. Maybe not as public and open as it is now, but freer nonetheless. "It has always been much easier for a gay person to pick up somebody for the night at a party, than say, a straight person. Homosexuals go in for one-night stands much more than straights. If it ends up going on and working itself into something more permanent—as permanent as any relationship can be between two homosexuals—so much the better. But that is often not the original intent. Homosexuals are much more casual about sex than straights." All those thousands of designers over on Seventh Avenue—"they sleep around. Hoping to sleep their way up. It's just plain old upward mobility, like Standard Oil or IBM. Only the guys are faggots instead of young executives with a house and a wife in the suburbs."

"Certain professions seem to attract homosexuals," says Dr.

Campbell, psychiatrist at St. Vincent's Hospital in New York. "Fashion design is certainly one of them." He should know. He has treated some of them. "For some of the homosexual fashion designers, what they are doing is dressing themselves as women. They see themselves when they design and produce those dresses. That's why so many of them like tall, flat-chested, thin models: they are built more like them. Some of the designers love women—some of them hate women. As children they were involved in a too-intimate relationship with their mothers. Often they were a sort of mother's dresser, helping her select clothes, put them together, put them on."

As fur designer Jacques Kaplan figured it out, homosexual designers are just hot into making everybody look like their mothers. "A mother has her greatest influence over her boy at the age of five or six," he says. "Now, look at the average age of the top designers today. It's forty or so. When they were all around five, it was 1935—and all their mothers were wearing mid-calf length skirts."

It is an endless argument, isn't it? And very interesting to ponder, considering the social and ethnic make-up of Seventh Avenue. How do the two mainstreams of Seventh Avenue manage to operate in peaceful coexistence—the traditional Jewish garment manufacturer *versus* the fashion-school homosexual. "This used to be a classic confrontation," says Weitz. "Your classic case is a little boy from a small midwestern town who went to Parsons and got ambition. He is now chic and famous but he worked for some of the harshest Jewish people in the world, who took him to Paris and introduced him around Hotel George V and to a few good restaurants. On the second trip, the boy was invited out by a group that didn't invite his boss, the Jewish garment manufacturer. Now get this—that funny little faggot is suddenly socially above that very sound, rich man from West End Avenue. The result is inevitable: there is enormous friction. A constant battle between the sound Jewish businessman and that flippity faggot. That basically anti-Semitic faggot. The faggot would rather not have been invited for a weekend to a Jewish country club. He would rather have spent the weekend in Southampton. There it is: the sound Jewish businessman who couldn't understand why anyone would prefer this funny little faggot—*whom he paid*—over him, socially."

That particular problem seems to be phasing itself out. For one thing, the ethnic qualities of Seventh Avenue are changing. Those first- and second-generation garment manufacturers—good sound Jewish and Italian businessmen all—are being replaced by WASPs and by their own college-educated sons with WASP veneers. Blacks and Puerto Ricans are moving into the garment industry, further changing the old ethnic structures. Moreover, Weitz points out, many of the designers themselves are now Jewish so the whole conflict between the WASP homosexual and the Jewish businessman is falling. Beyond that, the Jewish ego is no longer as bruised and damaged as it once was, Weitz figures. "The garment manufacturer used to adore Europe because it gave him the security he didn't have in his own country. Men who were greeted with raised eyebrows in certain New York restaurants could go to Europe and find themselves complete heroes. Because, despite disclaimers to the contrary, the Europeans have always loved the dollar." That attitude is also changing. There are so many other minority groups to contend with, the world has gotten used to Jewish. The eyebrows don't get raised in the restaurants anymore.

One Seventh Avenue model, from Mannequin, SA's largest model agency, admits however that every now and again a designer will joke about his "dyke look" or his "butch look" but she doesn't think they consciously attempt to make women look bad. "After all, if they were successful enough and women looked absolutely ugly, don't you think the women would notice it—and not buy his clothes." It is just slightly possible, especially today what with women having served notice that they are not sheep that will follow a dictator's lead.

Besides, if the designers are indeed homosexuals—dressing either themselves or their mothers—it doesn't seem logical they would want to make either party look ugly. Right? Right.

What difference does it make if the designer was scared by his mother in the nursery, runs screaming down the street at the sight of a woman, or escorts her to the charity ball? Who cares? It all boils down to what he's into. If he designs things that women buy, that's the whole point. If every now and again they are "punitive" fashions that make her hobble around or choke her to death, whose fault is that? Certainly not entirely with the designer who designed the clothes. No, the fault would seem to lie more with the dumb lady who forked out her husband's good money to buy them in the first place. The time has come for the consumer—even the Super-consumer—to put her foot down and not only react but rebel against such happenings. If the world gets away with putting down the consumer, it is more the consumer's fault for being put upon. And the solution lies right there in the cash register: don't buy it. And what with the more revolutionary attitudes out there in the market place (see the Midi, see the move toward recycling) it seems that the world—even the world of Seventh Avenue—can look forward to more and more consumer reaction. It's about time.

America's history is writ large in its newspapers and in its headlines. John Peter Zenger's crusade for freedom of the press. The birth of the American Underground that sees our newsstand carrying *The Berkeley Barb* next to the San Francisco *Examiner* and the L.A. *Free Press* next to the Los Angeles *Times*. The *East Village Other* next to the good gray *Times*. The New York *Daily News* can snuggle cheek by jowl with the *National Enquirer*. Hatchet jobs next to ax murders. The wide-open sexual spaces have been filled in by such sheets as *Gay* and *Screw*. Radical minority groups are heavy into publishing, too. The Young Lords with *Palante*. The Panthers, Mexican-Americans, radical Chinese.

And tucked in amongst it all is WWD. Now "Lingerie Surprise: Business Is Great" might not be as provocative as, say, "Child Beater Kids Cops." But somebody reads it. "K. Wade Bennett—Macy's New No. 1" is not quite like a fleshy *Gay* piece but to each his own. And there just might be some significance to the fact that both WWD and *Screw* interviewed Gore Vidal at about the same time. Who knows what lurks in the minds of men.

WWD is not the *Daily Planet*. John Fairchild can in no way be confused with Clark Kent—or even Superman, despite what his critics say—and June Weir is certainly no Lois Lane. It is something quite different. Quite unique. It serves two masters, so far quite successfully. For WWD is not only true to its original intent—trade paper to the garment industry—it is also true to the intent of its Dynamic Duo—trade paper to the Social Elite. It is John Fairchild's own personal sensitivity game, where he can play Groupie Therapy to his heart's content. Slapping at Jackie O, sniping at the FVs. It used to be Jim Brady's Front Page Monopoly game, where he could move reporters into Czechoslovakia and the United Arab Republic and Coco Chanel's funeral. Finessing the *Times* and pulling scoops out from under *The Wall Street Journal*. It is June Weir's Winnie Winkle cartoon game. And if **Winnie** changed her clothes endlessly from one frame to the other, so does June Weir oversee the constant changing of clothes that is the American fashion industry.

"We all wear clothes," says June Weir.

"We just report the news," Jim Brady used to say.

"Fashion is in the streets," says John Fairchild.

All of these. None of these. One of these.

If only one of those three is true, you've got the makings of a successful—if not controversial—newspaper. Yes, we do indeed all wear clothes.